THE RIGHT
to LEARN

Resisting the Right-
Wing Attack
on
Academic Freedom

··

VALERIE C. JOHNSON
JENNIFER RUTH
ELLEN SCHRECKER

BEACON PRESS
BOSTON

BEACON PRESS
Boston, Massachusetts
www.beacon.org

Beacon Press books
are published under the auspices of
the Unitarian Universalist Association of Congregations.

27 26 25 24   8 7 6 5 4 3 2 1

This book is printed on acid-free paper that meets the uncoated paper
ANSI/NISO specifications for permanence as revised in 1992.

Text design and composition by Kim Arney

Library of Congress Cataloguing-in-Publication Data is available for this title.
Paperback ISBN: 978-0-8070-4515-2
E-book ISBN: 978-0-8070-4517-6

CONTENTS

FOREWORD

A NYONE READING THIS PAGE should continue and read the entire book—then read it again, share it with others, and buy copies for at least two friends. The essays included speak plainly and comprehensively to the clear and present dangers we face at this moment in America, to the fragility of higher education as a public good in our democracy, and to the fragility of our democracy itself.

The editors of this volume are exceptionally qualified to tell this story. Each is an expert and a nationally authoritative voice on important aspects of academic freedom. I got to know Jennifer Ruth as a powerful voice on Committee A on Academic Freedom and Tenure of the American Association of University Professors, and I was delighted to offer her a reappointment to what is arguably AAUP's most important committee. Valerie Johnson came to my attention as a result of her work (with Jennifer and Kimberlé Crenshaw) through the African American Policy Forum on the enormously successful faculty senate resolution campaign detailed in chapter 8. It was my honor and privilege to offer Valerie an appointment to Committee A, and it continues to be an honor and a privilege to serve with her. I knew of and admired Ellen Schrecker and her work for years before I finally got to meet her. Her intellect, her scholarship, and her plainspokenness—especially in speaking truth to power—continue to inspire me.

The tireless efforts of this book's editors as well as from everyone else involved in the faculty senate resolution campaign resulted not only in powerful resolutions but also in the dawning realization on the part of some of our discouraged faculty colleagues that the faculty as a body can exercise power through their governance functions, and that this power can be transformative of faculty culture and solidarity on a campus. This volume should be another step in that transformation.

This book is not just for academics. The pieces included here are written with the general public in mind. Anyone who wants to go beyond sound bites and tweet threads and is looking for genuine understanding will find carefully researched, well-documented, readable pieces intended to educate and inform. It is my sincere hope that this book will bring to the broader public the facts of the decades-long, well-funded attempt by the right wing to undermine the legitimacy of education in this country as a strategy to preserve a white supremacist society and maintain power in that structure. As detailed in these chapters, that battle has reached a new level and a new intensity as a result of partisan political interference into public education now coming from state legislatures and governors' mansions. We are at a turning point in our history, and this volume could not be more timely in the battle to retain our democracy. Anyone and everyone who cares about higher education as a public good necessary in a healthy democracy needs to read this book and commit to taking action. Saving and strengthening democracy will require hard work from all of us. Happily, this book provides great ideas for fighting back as well as tools and resources for the resistance.

This book is likely to find a place alongside the other books that you can reach without getting up from your desk. I know my copy will stand alongside my AAUP Redbook. In addition, though, we need copies of this volume off our desks and into the hands of any members of the public who care about the future of higher education. Let's make sure that when we look back in a few years, we do not see this book as a careful documentation of the beginning of the end of our grand experiment in rule by the people but as the call to action that fueled the resistance and built the solidarity and the coalitions that helped us reclaim higher education as a first step in defending and strengthening our democracy. For those reading here who believe in a student's right to learn, a teacher's right to teach, and the importance and subtlety of the principles of academic freedom that underlie those rights, I invite you to turn the page and read on. You will not be disappointed.

—IRENE MULVEY

A Time for Faculty to Act

VALERIE C. JOHNSON, JENNIFER RUTH,
AND ELLEN SCHRECKER

WILL THE TRUTH DISAPPEAR from our colleges and universities? For over forty years a well-funded campaign by conservative pundits and politicians has been trying to undermine the legitimacy and integrity of American higher education. Its current iteration is the wave of outrageous laws and proposals now coursing through dozens of state legislatures to prevent teachers at every level from dealing with politically sensitive topics. As we explore the response of faculty members to this massive violation of academic freedom, *The Right to Learn* hopes to provide educators and concerned citizens with tools to combat this unprecedented assault on the freedom to think and the right to learn.

WHAT IS AT STAKE

Today's attack on the university threatens the very function of education in a free society. As part of the broader wave of right-wing reaction directed against our democratic system, the current political attacks on teaching about race, gender, sexual identity, and other purportedly "divisive concepts"—what the free speech organization PEN America aptly calls "education gag orders"—are a greater threat to academic freedom than anything that has happened since the modern system of higher education developed in the late nineteenth century. Worse than McCarthyism, which only targeted individual dissenters, today's culture wars invade the curriculum and the classroom. Not only would they prevent educators from deploying their disciplinary expertise, but they also would force them to shape their courses

1

in accordance with the whims and biases of a retrograde political movement that seeks to roll back decades of progress toward racial and social justice.

These education gag orders violate the First Amendment's protection of free speech—and are being challenged as such. Less understood and appreciated, however, is the fact that these repressive laws are also a full-frontal attack on academic freedom. Enshrined in our universities and colleges for over a century, academic freedom is a concept intended to protect the ability of scholars and scientists to work in their fields without interference from government or commercial interests and pressures. It allows society to come into possession of knowledge and information that has been vetted by experts and that cannot be easily reduced to opinion or hearsay. As a result, it provides citizens with what law professor and the former dean of Yale Law School Robert Post refers to as "democratic competence"—precisely the resource most needed when a powerful right-wing campaign against the university relies on moral panics, misinformation, and dog-whistle race-baiting to advance corporate or hyper-partisan interests.[1]

The university's antagonists claim to be defending free speech and furthering Martin Luther King Jr.'s alleged pursuit of a "colorblind" racial equity. They are not. On the contrary, the current attack on higher education, like previous ones, is a right-wing campaign fueled by a desire to stall or reverse the gains made by progressive social movements since the 1960s. A quick look at today's education gag rules with their prohibitions against teaching critical race theory and such "divisive concepts" as white supremacy reveals that their advocates don't hide their opposition to the struggle for racial equality. If we are to repel today's attack on higher education, we must do so with the understanding that defending our freedom to teach and to learn in a democracy is inextricably connected to the larger struggle against the racial, gender, and other systems of oppression that deform American life to this day.

Ironically, the academy's right-wing enemies have done better than many academics, even on the left, to practice what scholars call intersectionality—i.e., the linkages among the different arenas of struggle within our all-too-siloed identities. Over the years, the culture warriors have identified the targets of opportunity that form the basis of diversity, equity, and inclusion initiatives in the academy, shifting their campaigns rapidly to attack different and intersecting groups of the populace. These tactics require the defenders of democratic higher education to practice—not just preach—solidarity if we are to progress beyond an always one-step-behind "whack-a-mole" strategy. We must extend our efforts beyond the immediate needs of our own cohorts. We must reach out to potential allies, form coalitions, and engage in massive collective action to preserve the university. This volume brings together scholars and activists working in a range of areas and activities in several different organizations and serves as the primer from which such an intersectional coalition may emerge.

That American higher education, under attack and underfunded for nearly two generations, is now struggling to survive as an independent source of knowledge is largely the result of a contest for hegemony among three separate forces. Two forces, which are increasingly appearing to converge, are the libertarian crusade against the public sector and the social conservatives' culture war against secular liberalism and "political correctness." The third force, the expanding demographics of higher education and the transformation such expansion brings, promises a brighter future for an endangered democracy, but only if ordinary citizens join forces with the academy against a well-funded minority.

For nearly fifty years, ultraconservative billionaires, eager to shrink the state, have poured hundreds of millions of dollars into an all-too-successful campaign to undermine public support for higher education. Beginning in the 1970s, and related to this campaign, the systematic defunding of tenure lines and steadily growing dependence on contingent (part-time and temporary) positions gutted the faculty's collective academic freedom by dividing and terrorizing the ranks. More recently, the COVID-19 pandemic and the academy's resorting to remote instruction further weakened and demoralized the university. As a result, faculty members, who have the most at stake in this struggle for the future of higher education, are more isolated and vulnerable than they have been in decades. Despite its precarious condition, the academic community has the power to defeat the political repression we face. But only if we stick together and manifest the courage of our convictions.

It will not be an easy battle, but higher education and democracy depend on it. Those who seek to stifle the truth fight dirty. Despite its talk of freedom, the Republican Party, the main sponsor of the education gag rules, now harbors a sizable contingent of opportunistic and reactionary politicians who are willing to adopt increasingly authoritarian tactics to retain power through misinformation and disinformation. As a result, in most of the states with laws against teaching critical race theory and other "divisive concepts," residents may no longer possess the same rights as other Americans. Instead, they may be said to live under regimes of the kind that existed during Jim Crow, when whole regions of the country could not teach and discuss concepts that should be protected by academic freedom. During those years of racial apartheid, America did not deserve to call itself a democracy—and it may not for much longer. Unless we can roll back the current authoritarian threat to academic freedom, our professional right to teach and to learn and our (albeit imperfect) democracy may disappear again.

THE RIGHT TO LEARN VS. THE EDUCATION SCARE

Still, hope remains. Over the past few years, as the right-wing assault on higher education moved from the fringes into the mainstream, more and more academics and other concerned citizens began to mobilize against it. We view *The Right to Learn* as part of that growing resistance. It brings together in one volume contributions from faculty activists as well as leaders in organizations such as the American Association of University Professors (AAUP), PEN America, the American Association of Colleges for Teacher Education (AACTE), and Higher Education Labor United (HELU), who are on the front lines of the current culture wars and the struggle to save the academy. We hope that this compendium of scholarly essays, contemporary reportage, personal testimony, and key documents from all sides will serve as a source of information and perhaps inspiration for the students, faculty members, journalists, and other concerned citizens in their efforts to defend higher education and the right to learn.

This volume contains three sections and an appendix. The first section, "The Current Culture War," offers an overview of the campaign against the university—placing it within its historical context, profiling the groups and individuals behind that campaign, and tracking the specific measures that comprise it. We realize that the political situation changes quickly, and some of what we write about in this section has already been superseded by events. The chapters in the second section, "White Rage, Twisted Laws, and Patriarchal Control," explain how the ideological constructions promoted by the culture warriors misrepresent today's anti-racist and LGBTQ movements and create the chill that stifles free discussions within the classroom. The third section, "Collective Action and Visible Resistance," chronicles the faculty's early response to the right-wing assault on teaching the truth—the most promising attempt in recent years by professors and their allies to engage in collective action to combat threats to their own academic freedom. The appendix offers links to a sampling of some of the key documents produced during the current culture war.

THE CURRENT CULTURE WAR

The four chapters in this section offer an overview of the long-term war against the academic community. Ellen Schrecker traces its origins to the massive backlash against the campus turmoil of the 1960s and the social movements connected to it. Over the ensuing decades, a drive for austerity promoted by an aggressive and well-funded campaign to prioritize the free market and undermine the public sector transformed American political culture and seriously damaged American higher education. Demonized by right-wing pundits and politicians and under constant financial pressure, the academic community may well be too internally divided and demoralized to resist the current onslaught against teaching the truth, but the collective efforts described in this book provide hope that faculties can come together.

Isaac Kamola's chapter looks more deeply at how a network of right-wing billionaires and the think tanks, pundits, and operatives they funded created the "machinery for mass producing legislative outcomes" that led to the current educational gag orders as well as a host of other antidemocratic measures. He explores this process through four case studies of the attacks on critical race theory; *The 1776 Report* of President Trump; the delegitimization of the *New York Times'* "1619 Project" and its creator, Nikole Hannah-Jones; and the academic gag orders.

PEN America has been tracking the current assault on the right to teach and learn about controversial issues ever since what they dubbed the Ed Scare began in the fall of 2020. Their lucid, detailed, and thoughtful reports on the progress of that outrageous campaign have provided perhaps the single most useful source of information about the current threat to American education that now exists. In this chapter, PEN staffers Jonathan Friedman, Jeremy Young, and James Tager review the history of the ever-proliferating legislation.

The final chapter in this section examines the role that educational gag orders play in the production of knowledge about American racism. Defined as an epistemology of ignorance, the resulting contraction of knowledge has a tremendous effect on higher education and on democracy. Valerie Johnson describes this current attack on education as the latest iteration of the historical battle to preserve white supremacy. The quest to uphold a white racial order, she argues, undermines citizens' ability to make informed choices about the leaders they elect and the policy measures they pursue, thereby impeding the resolution of continuing racial inequities and tensions.

WHITE RAGE, TWISTED LAWS, AND PATRIARCHAL CONTROL

Defending our freedom to teach and to learn in a democracy, as we say above, is inextricably linked to the larger struggle against the racial, gender, and other systems of oppression that continue to deform American life. The three chapters in this section detail some of the ways a resurgent white patriarchy seeks to halt and reverse progress toward racial and social justice. Kevin McGruder opens the section by putting our current moment within its larger context, exposing the historical pattern in which white backlash follows gains toward racial justice. Today's moment, in which the multiracial protests against the murder of George Floyd suggested broader swaths of the nation than heretofore were ready to confront our history of racism, is no different. After providing historical background, McGruder explores some of the forms the backlash takes and then argues that a coalition of like-minded organizations might subdue the backlash and return the nation's focus to justice.

Dennis Parker's chapter looks at the claim made by conservative judges, attorney generals, and pundits that the Fourteenth Amendment makes concepts such as critical race theory unconstitutional and, therefore, ought to be banned. This is in keeping with earlier efforts to attack affirmative action and other racial justice efforts. Claiming that the Fourteenth Amendment mandates "colorblindness," these groups subvert the original intent of the amendment and redirect its purpose so that it reverses rather than facilitates progress. By doing so, they willfully erase the history of civil rights in order to further the partisan attack on racial justice in higher education and society more generally.

In chapter 7, Sonnet Gabbard, Anne Mitchell, and Heather Montes Ireland explain how the same conservative US politicians invested in banning what they refer to as anti-racist education, besides specifically targeting critical race theory in school curriculums, have created legislation limiting transgender healthcare for minors and restricting the teaching of any materials that do not pathologize queer identity and culture. They explore both the rhetoric these politicians deploy as well as their coercive policy agenda based on Judeo-Christian ideologies of divine creation and the "naturalness" of heteronormative nuclear families.

COLLECTIVE ACTION AND VISIBLE RESISTANCE

As the partisan attacks on allegedly divisive education intensified, many previously uninvolved faculty members and organizations realized that they were facing a genuinely existential threat. They began to reach out, create new coalitions, draft public statements, and throw themselves into the growing resistance to the partisan war on education at every level. The first chapter of this section details the history of the African American Policy Forum (AAPF) senate resolution campaign encouraging faculties across the nation to commit to defying the spate of repressive legislation. Explaining how the legislation would destroy independent knowledge production, neutralizing universities so that they served narrow partisan interests, Jennifer Ruth tells how a higher education working committee organized by AAPF circulated a template entitled "Defending Academic Freedom to Teach About Race and Gender Justice and Critical Race Theory." Both independently and in response to the circulated template, more than eighty institutions passed resolutions critiquing the gag rules and proving that faculty across the nation have the determination and will to mobilize in defense of academic freedom.

Sarah Sklaw builds on the previous chapter by exploring insights gleaned from interviews with seventeen faculty members involved in passing the resolutions. Those interviewed came from across the humanities, social sciences, and STEM, with a notable presence of professors from education colleges or departments. Their schools were located in states where legislatures had proposed or adopted divisive concepts legislation in K–12 education, higher education, and professional training as well as states where such bills had not been introduced (or had little chance of passing). Faculty members reflect on the specific challenges they faced as the legislation, in some cases, was only one of the forms of political interference they were contending with. The chapter ends by drawing lessons from the campaign for future action.

As Joe Berry and Helena Worthen emphasize in their chapter on the relationship between job security and academic freedom, nearly three-quarters of American college teachers enjoy little or none of either. This group holds contingent appointments that are either term-limited or part-time and can often lose these precarious positions without any of the procedural protections available to their tenured and tenure-track colleagues. Even so, there are a few ways in which these vulnerable academics can gain some job security, especially if they belong to collective bargaining units that negotiate strong contracts. HELU, a national movement to organize all university employees from the bottom up, also holds considerable promise.

Sharon Austin's chapter details her public battle to defend academic freedom at the University of Florida. In conjunction with other faculty members, Austin ultimately filed a lawsuit to challenge the university's conflict of interest policy that prohibited her and two other colleagues from serving as expert witnesses in lawsuits that challenged the actions of powerful state political actors. Faced with public pressure, the University of Florida capitulated and subsequently the court ruled in the plaintiffs' favor, thereby restoring the faculty's First Amendment and academic freedom rights. Austin's story shows that tenured faculty members possess the power to fight back against colleges and universities that yield to the pressures of powerful political interests. Austin is currently one of the six plaintiffs in *Pernell et al. v. Florida Board of Governors*, a lawsuit filed in 2022 challenging the Stop W.O.K.E. Act. Her courage and integrity serve as a model for academics throughout the United States who hope to preserve the higher education central to our democratic society.

Katie Rainwater's chapter puts the Sunshine State's outrageous assault on public education into the broader context of a long-range campaign for privatization within Florida—as elsewhere. Unions, in her view, are—or should be—the leading institutions for resisting Ron DeSantis's reactionary agenda but all too often avoid directly confronting the serious issues of structural racism and harassment that students of color and sexually nonconforming students experience. She discusses two incidents at her own institution, Florida International University, that illustrate the obstacles facing faculty activists, even as she advocates a long-term project for unions to organize collective political action.

Finally, the last chapter in the volume, written by Marvin Lynn, Michael Dantley, and Lynn Gangone, argues that the demonization of critical race theory (CRT) is a distraction designed to rally voters to support right-wing politicians in the 2022 and 2024 elections. Nevertheless, they note, that its current impact on colleges of education and teacher preparation programs is real and enormously destructive. The authors, who serve in key leadership roles with the American Association of Colleges for Teacher Education (AACTE), have assessed specific ways in which the hysteria surrounding CRT has impacted schools and colleges of education and have developed a racial and social justice task force to provide leaders in educator preparation with the tools to effectively combat disinformation.

The appendix contains key documents of the culture wars, including statements by free speech and academic organizations opposing state legislative gag orders; the faculty senate template and sample faculty senate resolutions affirming the right to teach and learn, which some eighty faculty groups have passed; and a sample of state legislative gag orders.

WHERE ARE WE NOW AND WHERE DO WE NEED TO BE?

We, the coeditors of *The Right to Learn: Resisting the Right-Wing Attack on Academic Freedom*, began work on this volume during the spring of 2022, assembled the chapters, and completed the project mid-February 2023. The June 16, 2021, Joint Statement on Efforts to Restrict Education About Racism and American History, signed by over seventy organizations, the 2021–22 AAPF faculty senate resolution campaign to defend academic freedom to teach critical race theory, the March 2022 AAUP statement "Legislative Threats to Academic Freedom: Redefinitions of Antisemitism and Racism" and others like it, the indefatigable and groundbreaking reporting of PEN America on the metastasizing gag orders, the intensive public education work of AACTE—these were among the most developed and successful efforts to resist the war on higher education when we began. As we write today, in early February 2023, the assaults on higher education are rapidly accelerating as the 2024 presidential election begins to come into view. Headlines feature a new partisan attack on education almost daily. In the last few weeks alone, Florida governor Ron DeSantis has mounted a hostile takeover of a public college, publicly rejected an Advanced Placement course on African American studies to be proposed by the College Board, and announced his intention to defund all diversity, equity, and inclusion efforts at Florida's public colleges and universities; South Carolina and Oklahoma legislatures have called for public higher education institutions to report funding on curriculum relating to race, gender, and sexuality; North Dakota has made moves to abolish tenure; and the University of North Carolina System Board of Governors voted to ban diversity statements in hiring.

On February 5, 2023, the *Washington Post* reported that the Koch network intends to endorse and help bankroll a single Republican in the 2024 presidential election. They have not announced who that will be, only that it will *not* be Donald Trump. The ruling Koch ideology is, or at least used to be, libertarian, but libertarian and authoritarian interests have been converging over the last couple of years. By funding think tanks, academic centers, and fellowships for individual academics churning out stories decrying left totalitarianism, as Ralph Wilson and Isaac Kamola explain in *Free Speech and Koch Money* (2021), the libertarian network has succeeded in portraying universities and colleges as places where left-wing mobs run rampant and conservative speech must be defended.[2] This well-funded and well-coordinated network has been foundational to the political world in which right-wing pundits and politicians argue that authoritarianism is now necessary and desirable so as to, in their minds, preserve or defend a homogeneous America they allege once existed.

On July 15, 2022, during an event announcing the historic affiliation of AAUP and the American Federation of Teachers, AAUP president Irene Mulvey said, "Make no mistake: Higher ed is under attack because those who want to see the US move to authoritarianism recognize the power of education." In totalitarian, authoritarian, and fascist states, where knowledge is controlled by one political party, largely with the aim of perpetuating that party's rule, academic freedom does not exist. It exists only in two-party or multiparty democratic societies that agree to grant universities and colleges the degree of independence from partisan politics necessary to safeguard the integrity of the knowledge they produce and disseminate. Unlike totalitarian, authoritarian, and fascist states, two-party and multiparty democracies have generally respected—or at least professed to understand—the need for higher education to maintain a significant degree of autonomy from partisan politics. Every state in the United States where legislation has passed seeking to restrict teaching on race and gender has rejected this basic precept. As we write in February 2023, Florida is going furthest and fastest as Ron DeSantis eyes the White House. On January 20, 2023, the AAUP issued a statement in response to an announcement issued by the presidents of the twenty-eight institutions in the Florida College System (FCS) declaring they will not fund curriculum if it, in their minds, indoctrinates students "in critical race theory or related concepts such as intersectionality." The AAUP statement read in part:

> In a democracy, higher education is a common good which requires that instructors have full freedom in their teaching to select materials and determine the approach to the subject. Instead, the FCS presidents, while giving lip service to academic freedom, have announced their intention to censor teaching and learning by expunging ideas they want to suppress. By dictating course content, they are also usurping the primary responsibility for the curriculum traditionally accorded the faculty under principles of shared governance.[3]

The state has no business controlling the curriculum of higher education institutions. Universities that cater to legislatures that try to do so betray their broader nonpartisan mission to serve the common good.

Many of the state-level efforts metastasizing across the country, as of this writing, seem to stem from, or at least take inspiration from, the "Laying Siege to the Institutions" playbook aggressively promoted by America's premiere culture-war grifter, Christopher Rufo. "We have to get out of this idea that somehow a public university system is a totally independent entity that practices academic freedom," he said in a speech at conservative Hillsdale College on April 5, 2022. Calling this idea "a total fraud," Rufo added, "We [conservatives] get in there, we defund things we don't like, we fund things we like." Exaggeration, distortion, caricature, a kind of burn-it-down bravado—this is the modus operandi for "laying siege."[4] Universities are not "totally independent entities," but the relative independence that they *have* secured for themselves with the concept of, and infrastructure for, academic freedom is what distinguishes universities in democratic countries from those in authoritarian ones.

As we mentioned at the start of this introduction, it is important to understand why a state that tries to control curriculum is attacking academic freedom as apart from simply suppressing free speech. Unlike, say, politicians in a political ad, professors cannot lie. Politicians can make demonstrably wrong, irresponsible, and race-baiting claims; responsible professors cannot. Academics have First Amendment rights in other aspects of our lives, but we are held to the standards of our profession in our classes as well as when we make claims in peer-reviewed journals or submit our work to promotion and tenure committees or engage in intramural or extramural speech related to our areas of competency. We must meet collectively determined norms that may be challenged, but those challenges must, in turn, also meet norms of coherence and relevance and gain some degree of collectively agreed-upon legitimacy. Banning "The 1619 Project," critical race theory, resource pedagogies, and other forms of knowledge gained over the last few decades suppresses free speech, but that is not the primary problem—a number of speech acts are reasonably suppressed in educational settings. The problem is that this work has earned the protection of academic freedom by having been vetted by expert peers. What we have here is a fundamental violation of academic freedom in an allegedly democratic country.

We hope that this volume provides ideas, resources, and inspiration as we resist the current partisan war on higher education. Our fondest hope is that the book plays a small role in nurturing the organization of the intersectional coalition of faculty groups, associations, nonprofits, and public constituencies that the current moment demands. Consider the fact that those who stand to lose if authoritarianism wins constitute a majority of this country. The strength and resilience of the reality-based majority are, in fact, why partisan politicians resort to authoritarianism in the first place.

PART I

The Current Culture War

1

Academic Freedom and Political Repression from McCarthyism to Trump

ELLEN SCHRECKER

URING THE HEIGHT OF THE COVID CRISIS when classes at Molloy College were being taught on Zoom, the dean summoned Mark James to his office. Over the internet, a parent had been watching him discuss the concept of white supremacy in his course on American and African American literature, recorded the lecture, and complained to the school's president that James had brought "politics" into the classroom. James readily assuaged the dean's concerns. He was, after all, teaching exactly what he had been hired to teach. In his written report on the incident, the dean stressed the administration's strong support for the Black literary scholar's academic freedom and admitted that the parent had been in the wrong.[1]

James, a member of the American Association of University Professors (AAUP) Committee A on Academic Freedom and Tenure, was not intimidated by the incident. He never considered changing his pedagogy. But he recognized that other professors, faced with a university investigation into the content of their classes, might prune their syllabi or avoid discussions about controversial issues. And this was before states like Texas, Florida, and Idaho explicitly banned teaching about racism, sexism, and other forms of oppression within American society.

Worse than McCarthyism, the current spate of repressive legislation is the most serious threat to academic freedom in the history of American higher education. Even at the height of the Cold War Red Scare, when at least a hundred professors lost their jobs for political reasons, the inquisition never reached directly into the classroom. Joseph McCarthy, J. Edgar Hoover, and their allies focused on the past and present left-wing political activities and associations of individual academics but left their teaching and research alone. No longer. Today's wave of partisan political repression aims directly at what gets studied and taught. And at the intellectual underpinnings of our all too fragile democratic system of government.

If we are to avoid the authoritarian future that today's repressive movement portends, we can no longer stand on the sidelines, mouthing tired platitudes about academic freedom and the value of rational discourse. We must act. But first, we must recognize exactly what is at stake in the current culture wars. The prognosis is not good. For all the rhetoric about the university's commitment to academic freedom, the historical record reveals a different story. When powerful outsiders threatened the independence and integrity of higher education, leading administrators and faculty members all too often capitulated, collaborating with, rather than resisting, the forces of repression.

As this chapter shows, for the past fifty years, American colleges and universities have been so buffeted by external enemies and internal divisions that defending themselves effectively is a serious challenge. But there is hope. Even as the current well-funded right-wing campaign against the academic community's hesitant commitment to social justice threatens to undermine its autonomy, students, faculty members, and even some administrators are resisting. They are circulating petitions, mounting protests, and forming coalitions. They have more power than they know—especially when they actually use it. Before we engage more effectively in the necessary struggle to preserve the integrity of American higher education, we need to understand how it ended up in its present debilitated state.[2]

A BELEAGUERED PROFESSION

Throughout our history, educators have occasionally had fraught relationships with the powers that be. Such was the case during moments of social or political unrest when free-thinking teachers were viewed as a threat to the status quo. Think of the laws against teaching enslaved men and women to read in the South before the Civil War or the crackdown against modern science that led to the conviction of a Tennessee high school teacher for teaching about evolution a hundred years later or the dismissals of a few social scientists at the turn of the twentieth century because the wealthy industrialists who founded the universities where they taught feared they might explore the inequities of the economic system those plutocrats had constructed.[3]

The state also turned against teachers during the twentieth century's main external crises, when demands for unity spread throughout the supposedly endangered polity, targeting unpopular minorities and real and potential dissenters. Thus, for example, once the previously divided nation entered World War I, loyalty became a prerequisite for educators at every level. By the 1930s, dozens of states had singled out teachers for oaths of allegiance to the state and national constitutions.

Loyalty oaths and similarly repressive measures proliferated during the early Cold War in the late 1940s and 1950s when the anti-Communist purges we call McCarthyism swept through American society. Hundreds, if not thousands, of schoolteachers and college professors were affected by the inquisition. But they lost their jobs primarily because of their former left-wing affiliations, not because of what they taught. Nonetheless, a chill descended upon the nation's classrooms. Particularly intense within higher education, the Cold War Red Scare produced a silent generation of students and faculty members.[4]

THE GOLDEN AGE OF THE AMERICAN UNIVERSITY

It is ironic that just as Joseph McCarthy, J. Edgar Hoover, and their allies were eviscerating the First Amendment's freedom of speech, the academic community was experiencing what scholars of higher education now call its "Golden Age."[5]

World War II transformed the university. No longer a sanctuary for upper-class late adolescents with a soupçon of scholarship and scientific research thrown in, higher education embraced a new, more democratic mission. Now, thanks in part to the GI Bill, campuses welcomed a cohort of ambitious middle-class and lower-middle-class students seeking intellectual stimulation and social mobility. New types of faculty members emerged as well—less genteel and, in some cases, imbued with a new competitive academic culture. Enrollments doubled and tripled. Most of the increase occurred at public institutions, which came to educate nearly 80 percent of the nation's college students. They not only grew in size and number but also upgraded. Teachers' colleges became four-year liberal arts colleges and then regional universities, offering an ever-growing array of graduate programs.

That expansion seemed to bring the dream of high-quality, affordable mass higher education within reach. Tuitions were low—if not free, as at the New York City municipal colleges and the University of California—while the academic community enjoyed considerable prestige.[6] State legislators plowed money into their colleges and universities, while the federal government subsidized scientific research. Especially after the Soviet Union launched its Sputnik satellite in 1957, universities came to be viewed as essential for national security and the dollars flowed even more profusely.

Faculties were the main beneficiaries. Research grants were easy to get, and graduate enrollments grew exponentially. Terrified that there might not be enough teachers for the expected tsunami of baby boomers, the federal government and major philanthropies literally threw money at those of us who entered graduate school in the late 1950s and early '60s. And the universities hired every one.

The golden age did, however, have a darker side. Women and people of color faced serious discrimination in a racially segregated system of higher education dominated by white men. Although the political chill of McCarthyism was receding, professors still faced loyalty oaths, politically controversial speakers were still barred from speaking on some campuses, and a few faculty members were still losing their jobs after tangling with the anti-Communist witch hunt.[7] Meanwhile, at many colleges and universities undergraduates, women in particular, had to obey curfews, dress codes, and other kinds of restrictions on their social lives and, often, their political activities.[8]

Yet, even with such defects and limitations, American higher education did experience a golden age. Never again would it enjoy as much influence and prestige as it did during the early 1960s. And never again would the bright promise of a near-universal system of affordable high-quality mass public higher education seem within reach.[9]

BERKELEY AND THE BACKLASH: THE SIXTIES BEGINS

If we are to single out a moment when higher education began to lose its charisma, it would be October 1, 1964, when several thousand Berkeley students sat down around a university police car and for over thirty hours refused to let the officers take a civil rights organizer to jail for disobeying a University of California regulation banning the recruitment of students on campus for outside political activities.

It was the first time students at a major American university had engaged in nonviolent civil disobedience directed against their own institution. Berkeley's protest was not unexpected. Even in the 1950s, pockets of left-wing politics existed at schools like the University of Wisconsin, Brandeis University, and the University of California at Berkeley, where both students and faculty members explored Marxist ideas, protested nuclear weapons, supported the Cuban revolution, and—most important—joined the Black freedom struggle.

As the civil rights movement swept through the Historically Black Colleges and Universities in the segregated South, it sparked political engagement at previously quiescent institutions elsewhere. Black and white veterans of the struggle for racial equality emerged as key activists, first in the Free Speech Movement at Berkeley, then a few months later in the anti-war movement, and finally in the Black Power movement, which developed on both Black and majority-white campuses.

In the spring of 1965, a few months after the extensive media coverage of Berkeley's Free Speech Movement alerted the nation to the prospect of student unrest, President Lyndon Johnson escalated the conflict in Southeast Asia. Opposition arose at once, especially on the campuses where faculty members organized teach-ins to explain to their students, their colleagues, and the general public why the war in Vietnam was wrong. Soon students were demonstrating against the draft and their own institutions' complicity with the war machine. African American students, many among the first to integrate their previously lily-white colleges and universities, began to demand better treatment from those institutions. And across the country, previously apolitical undergraduates demonstrated against their schools' constraints on their social and political activities.

Most student protests of the early 1960s were peaceful, if not always legal. A few years later, demonstrations became less decorous. Frustrated by the failure of the peace movement to end the war, opposed to their institution's cooperation with the military-industrial complex, and chafing at its paternalistic control over their social lives and political activities, some students adopted more militant tactics. Still, although most demonstrations remained under control, violence did occur. Protesters disrupted classes, took over buildings, and destroyed property, and especially when outside police forces were called in, endured beatings and arrests. People lost their lives as well, mainly, it must be noted, at Historically Black Colleges and Universities (HBCUs). And, of course, given its proclivity for dramatic action, the media showed up in force, with name-brand institutions and large urban schools attracting extensive coverage.[10]

For a shocked nation, accustomed to viewing colleges and universities as oases of ivy-covered buildings and Saturday afternoon football games, the political unrest that began at Berkeley was inexplicable. It was also inexcusable. Even faculty radicals, who opposed the war and supported most of the students' demands, disapproved of their disruptive and counterproductive behavior. So, too, did most of the public as well as the local press and political leaders.

Conservative politicians, pundits, and ordinary citizens demanded that the universities crack down on their unruly charges. At troubled institutions, where the authorities confronted a completely unprecedented situation, there were no good options. Desperate to end the turmoil, administrators feared provoking violence by calling the police. At the same time, they were under enormous pressure from trustees, public officials, and other powerful outsiders to take a tough stand. Understandably, most waffled. Faculty members were equally flummoxed. They, too, wanted their campuses to calm down. But they were deeply divided about the students' demands and their administrations' response to them. As a result, since outside observers viewed the universities as too confused to handle their own students, higher education began to lose its prestige and credibility with the broader public.

Meanwhile, criticism from within the academic community also undermined its ability to defend itself against external hard-liners. A group of the country's best-known and most prolific public intellectuals—Nathan

Glazer, Seymour Martin Lipset, and David Riesman among them—not only lived through the Free Speech crisis at Berkeley but were also anxiously and futilely trying to tamp it down. They soon broke into print with explanations for the student unrest that most moderates and even liberals latched onto. They were so horrified by the protesters' defiance of academic norms that they paid little, if any, attention to their essentially reasonable demands.

As they reflected on the events at Berkeley, these eminent intellectuals (many of whom had once considered themselves leftists of a sort) were moving to the right. Viewing the campus unrest as a threat to Western civilization, they insisted that the main problem was not the disrespectful behavior of the students but the spinelessness of the university's liberal leaders and professors that facilitated the disorder.[11]

Although these future neoconservatives' jeremiads about the irrationality and destructiveness of the student movement were wildly exaggerated, they were right about how damaging the public's response to the campus troubles would be. For the next fifty years, these pundits' depiction of formerly respected institutions betrayed by their left-leaning faculty members and weak-kneed administrators was to surface repeatedly in the rhetoric employed by the opportunistic politicians and other right-wingers attacking higher education to further their own agendas. While these public intellectuals did not create the backlash against the universities that began in the late 1960s, they did give it intellectual credibility.

BACKLASH POLITICS

No one was to benefit as much politically from the campus disorders of the late 1960s as the former movie actor already running for governor of California in the fall of 1965. "Wherever I went in the state," Ronald Reagan later explained, "the first question and literally the first half-dozen questions were about what I would do about the University of California at Berkeley." He knew exactly what went wrong. The university's troubles, according to Reagan, "happened because those responsible abdicated their responsibilities." Echoing the scenario developed by Glazer, Lipset, et al., Reagan denounced both the early anti-war protests as well as the growing campus counterculture as "the fruit of appeasement."[12]

Ronald Reagan won the election for governor in a landslide—and began to dismantle his state's institutions of higher learning. At his first meeting with the Board of Regents, he persuaded its members to fire the university's president, Clark Kerr. He imposed tuition on California's theoretically free colleges and universities and was soon contemplating major reductions in funding public higher education. "There are certain intellectual luxuries that perhaps we could do without," he mused. Perhaps taxpayers should not be "subsidizing intellectual curiosity." Then, after warning that he would put down the turmoil at schools like Berkeley and San Francisco State "at the point of a bayonet, if necessary," Reagan dispatched the National Guard to impose law and order on campuses wracked by student strikes.[13]

Such tough language and repressive actions were wildly popular—and not just in California. Public opinion polls showed widespread support for punishing student militants and the institutions that housed them.[14] No surprise then that conservative state legislators, governors, and boards of trustees rushed into action. After all, there was no other area over which state-level politicians exercised as much control as higher education. Eager to express their hostility to the campus unrest, these politicians, both Democrats and Republicans, proposed hundreds of measures designed to punish those responsible for the turmoil. They also mounted investigations, many designed to expose the faculty members who, according to the chair of Florida's Select Committee on Campus Unrest and Drug Abuse, "counseled, guided, and occasionally directed" the student leaders.[15]

Most of those inquiries petered out with little impact, as did much of the proposed legislation, most of which never made it out of committee. Still, by the time the protests ebbed in the 1970s, punitive measures dealing with higher education were on the books in more than thirty states.[16] The scope of these proposals ranged from criminal sanctions to the abortive suggestion that North Carolina students be forced to keep their dorm rooms clean.[17] Whether passed or not, they revealed how popular repressing the student movement and its alleged faculty and administrative enablers had become. Invariably, those measures that were enacted received overwhelming bipartisan support.

Financial sanctions were the most ubiquitous—and had the most deleterious long-term effects. Given their own dismay at the campus unrest and the growing resistance to taxes on the part of their constituents, few politicians had compunctions about pulling back from their previously unstinting support for higher education.

Congress led the way. Tacking an amendment onto the Health, Education, and Welfare budget for 1968, it withdrew federal funding from anyone convicted of "inciting, promoting, or carrying on a riot." But, since campus authorities could rarely identify any troublemakers beyond the top leaders, that sanction had little bite.[18] At the state level, politicians rushed to cancel financial aid to unruly students. They also targeted professors. Although efforts to eliminate tenure in states including California, Florida, Illinois, and Wisconsin proved abortive, financial sanctions did not.[19] In 1970, California's legislature simply refused to grant all the faculty members at the University of California and the California State College system the cost-of-living increases every other state employee received.[20]

Even more damaging were the across-the-board budget cuts that occurred almost everywhere—and were almost always explicitly punitive. President Nixon reduced spending on academic research and eliminated entire programs. He also steered federal aid to higher education away from direct grants to institutions and into student loans. Elsewhere, legislatures that had generously supported their public colleges and universities began to pull back. In 1969, Indiana's lawmakers cut their flagship university's budget by nearly 25 percent.[21]

By the time these repressive measures went into effect, most campuses were quiet. The student unrest peaked in the spring of 1970, when protests against the invasion of Cambodia and killings at Kent State and Jackson State spread from the largest and most prestigious universities to small religious schools and community colleges, ultimately affecting one-third of the nation's campuses. Then, surprisingly, the turmoil ceased. The war seemingly wound down, a new generation of students arrived on campus, and institutions began to slough off their most radical faculty members, usually for ostensibly professional, not political, reasons. As a result, by the early 1970s, as academic authorities hunkered down for a wave of unrest that did not come, peace returned to the academy. But it would never regain its former aura.

A NEW ECONOMIC ENVIRONMENT

For the next fifty years, American higher education was buffeted by internal divisions and external attacks that not only cost it further public support but also transformed its mission, structure, and culture. Confronted by the liberatory and egalitarian social movements of the 1960s as well as a major economic crisis, the American political establishment jettisoned the liberalism of the New Deal and the Great Society and moved to the right. No longer devoted to the notion that state action would contribute to the general welfare of American society, the powers that be turned to the free market, adopting a neoliberal mindset that identified individual success as more important than the common good for bettering someone's life chances.

Thanks to the neoliberalism of the era that downplayed the common good, higher education came to be viewed as a personal asset, a meritocratic institution that became the main source of upward mobility for the deserving and talented individuals who could take advantage of it. Few tried to justify its broader value to the community. And as its demographic makeup changed, the university lost the backing of a public that did not want to devote resources to help those who should be helping themselves—especially if they were no longer white, male, or middle-class.

The measure most institutions took to make up for the reductions in state funding and other sources of revenue—imposing or raising tuitions—further increased their unpopularity.[22] Initially, however, paying for college was still manageable for most students; tuitions were still low, the federal government had begun to guarantee loans to cover them, and few could have predicted how deleterious $1.8 trillion of student debt would become. Nonetheless, for an institution whose reputation was already damaged by earlier campus unrest, its growing cost was to make the academic community increasingly vulnerable to populist hostility—manufactured and real.

At the same time, because of the reduced state support and managerial restructuring that accompanied the academy's new financial constraints, the quality of American higher education declined. The increasingly stratified system lacked the resources to provide a first-rate affordable education to most of the people who wanted it. Although elite colleges and universities still managed to supply their students with excellent facilities and an education that was the envy of the world, the less-selective public institutions, serving 80 percent of the nation's students, were operating in what a leading historian of higher education termed a "condition of chronic scarcity."[23]

Faculties took the main hit. As tenured professors retired, they were not replaced. Instead, administrators filled the slots with poorly paid part-time and temporary instructors who were often hired at the last minute and who could be let go without any notice for any reason or for no reason at all. Today, such exploited teachers offer nearly three-quarters of the instruction at American colleges and universities.

THE NEOLIBERAL TURN AND THE CAMPAIGN AGAINST THE MAINSTREAM ACADEMY

Was such a transformation inevitable? Maybe American higher education could have bounced back from its troubles once the economy did. But a powerful coterie of wealthy businessmen and free-market ideologues hostile to government intervention and determined to shrink the public sector mounted an all-too-successful campaign against American higher education. Now, thanks to the work of scholars like Nancy MacLean, we have irrefutable evidence that the free marketeers' decades-long conspiracy (I use that word reluctantly) is largely responsible for the current threat to higher education that is now attacking our democratic polity as well.[24]

These right-wing ideologues and their business supporters had been pushing their free-market agenda for years, but it was not until the economic crunch of the late 1960s and early 1970s that their campaign to delegitimize the state began to gain mainstream credibility. That campaign's best-known early manifesto, the so-called Powell Memo, spelled out its implications for higher education. Produced in the summer of 1971 by prominent Richmond, Virginia, lawyer and soon-to-become Supreme Court justice Lewis F. Powell Jr., at the behest of a local businessman who had just been appointed chair of the US Chamber of Commerce's committee on education, Powell's thirty-four-page proposal called for the corporate sector to mount a massive effort to reshape America's political culture.[25]

Viewing the opposition to capitalism professed by the then-current generation of elite students as an existential threat to the "survival of what we call the free enterprise system," Powell urged the business community to abandon its "appeasement" of the Left within the key institutions of

American life. Corporate leaders would have to embark on a "long-range and difficult project" to transform the media, the legal system, and above all, the university whose "imbalance of faculties" was the "most fundamental problem" the country faced.

By the time Powell dictated his memo, the campaign he espoused was already underway. Supported by a network of ultraconservative foundations and billionaires like Charles and David Koch, right-wing activists, and intellectuals were constructing what one of its main leaders, William Simon, a former secretary of the treasury and head of the Olin Foundation, called a "counter-intelligentsia" to supply policymakers and the media with the expertise that had previously been the province of traditional academics. This network poured hundreds of millions of dollars into think tanks like the American Enterprise Institute, the Heritage Foundation, and the Manhattan Institute, as well as academic programs, endowed professorships, and publications that disseminated the libertarians' anti-statist ideology and also delegitimized the mainstream liberalism that had dominated US political culture since the New Deal.

At the same time they were developing their ostensibly academic ventures, the right-wingers were grooming their own cadres. Funders sought out promising young conservatives on the nation's campuses, subsidizing their publications and political organizations and then bringing them into their think tanks and other operations. It took a while, but, as Isaac Kamola shows in the following chapter, the open purses of the libertarian philanthropists created a critical mass of seemingly respectable conservative operatives who disseminated a devastating narrative about the defects of the traditional university.

THE CULTURE WARS AND THE MYTH OF POLITICAL CORRECTNESS

With Reagan in the White House, the right-wing campaign against higher education came into its own. "There is a sense now," Michael Joyce, the former head of the Lynde and Harry Bradley Foundation crowed, that he and his associates' efforts "have reached a kind of fruition. . . . The ideas we've been supporting have filtered down into public opinion."[26] And so they had. The books the conservative foundations had been subsidizing—Roger

Kimball's *Tenured Radicals*, Charles Sykes's *Profscam*, Dinesh D'Souza's best-selling *Illiberal Education*, and Allan Bloom's even better-selling *The Closing of the American Mind*—made it into the mainstream, where, along with an avalanche of other books, articles, and op-eds produced under the same auspices, they set off the so-called culture wars of the 1980s and '90s.

Many of the same public intellectuals who had complained about academic leaders capitulating to barbarian radicals in the 1960s resumed their charges, joined by such high-level officials as Secretary of Education William Bennett and National Endowment for the Humanities chair Lynne Cheney. As these folks saw it, academic culture had been hijacked by advocates of "political correctness," a left-wing ideology that played upon the liberal guilt of spineless professors and administrators to force them to expunge racism and sexism from their campuses.

In retrospect, we can see that a backlash against the academic community's plans to implement affirmative action also fueled the culture wars. Unfortunately, the attempt to grant individual members of previously excluded groups the benefits that had long been available to straight white males created a no-win situation. Not only did the universities' mélange of special, often underfunded programs for supposedly disadvantaged students of color along with new regulations for handling politically incorrect behavior on campus fail to address the deeper problems of systemic racism within American society, but those measures also unleashed a well-funded flood of anti-egalitarian litigation and conservative outrage against the very idea of giving special treatment to Blacks and members of other minority groups.[27]

The anti-affirmative action backlash hyped stories of supposed PC atrocities designed to convince ordinary Americans that universities were bastions of debased standards and hostility to free speech. Recycling charges from the 1960s, when institutions sought to admit more Black and other underrepresented students and hire more faculty members of color, the culture warriors claimed that those measures would dilute an institution's "excellence."[28] Right-wing funders sought to give credibility to allegations about the intellectual inferiority of minority groups by subsidizing the largely discredited work of such authors as the American Enterprise Institute's Charles Murray, who claimed that intelligence was genetically determined, not the product of socioeconomic factors.[29]

New charges, centering on academia's supposed intolerance for free speech, arose when students tried to disrupt appearances by Murray and other reactionary speakers. The attempts of academic authorities to respond to such altercations in an evenhanded manner—as if both sides were intellectually or morally equivalent—provided opportunities for conservative provocateurs to claim that universities were violating their First Amendment rights. Their trash talk was, they insisted, a legitimate discourse contributing to the marketplace of ideas. Blindsided by the ruthless tactics of the culture warriors, the academic authorities sometimes blundered by developing needlessly restrictive speech codes or failing to provide due process protections for conservative students and professional provocateurs. But they had not violated the academic freedom of the provocateurs—since they had none.

Although the First Amendment protected Murray and similar speakers from punishment for what they said, universities had no obligation to supply platforms for their outrageous presentations. Academic freedom was a professional prerequisite that protected the university's autonomy and intellectual credibility from illegitimate outside pressures by ensuring that its faculty's work would be in accord with peer-reviewed scholarship. Unfortunately, the technical nature of academic freedom and its sometimes sloppy invocation was no defense against the Right's misinformation and malice. To make matters worse, academic freedom's traditional connection to tenure smacked of special privilege and alienated ordinary Americans mired in an increasingly insecure gig economy.

As a result, although there is little evidence that mainstream institutions stifle conservatives' freedom of speech, the cleverly conceptualized and heavily publicized depiction of a repressive academic culture that shamed anyone who dissented from its ultraliberal ideology became a persuasive staple of the Far Right's long-term campaign against the university.

THE MALNOURISHED UNIVERSITY CONFRONTS THE REPUBLICAN RIGHT

By the time President Bush the Elder referred to "the notion of political correctness" as "a cause of conflict and even censorship" in his commencement address to the University of Michigan's 1991 graduates, the libertarians' multimillion-dollar crusade against the university had triumphed.[30] Many

Americans, persuaded by the half-truths, exaggerations, and racist innuendos that the culture warriors unleashed, have come to believe that the university is a decadent, over-priced institution dominated by cadres of "woke" elitists with cushy lifetime jobs who oppose free speech, ignore their students, and propound obscure Marxist ideologies. By the time Donald Trump and the Republican Party turned their exploitation of the race card into an attack on teaching about so-called divisive issues, the academic community was already fragmented and demoralized. Austerity had hollowed out the faculty. Today there are more administrators and nonteaching professionals than professors.

So, what is to be done? How can the academic community respond to the most devastating attack ever on its intellectual freedom and integrity as an educational institution? Clearly, we must act collectively. We have more power than we know, but we need to use it. We must speak out. We must explain to our colleagues, our students, and our fellow citizens what is at stake and why higher education matters if we are to preserve our—albeit imperfect—democracy where ordinary people can think for themselves and try to create a better future. This book aims to provide some of the resources and talking points needed to do so.

2

A Koch-Funded Racial Backlash

*Understanding the Critical
Race Theory Moral Panic*

ISAAC KAMOLA

T HE BLACK LIVES MATTER PROTESTS during the summer of 2020 ushered in a palpable change in how many Americans think about the social, political, and economic implications of race and racism in America. New political possibilities opened as large swaths of the American population educated themselves and each other about structural racism, anti-racism, systemic violence, and whiteness. Armed with these concepts and under-standing, many Americans committed themselves to the hard work of making their workplaces, public institutions, and schools more equitable and just. However, in subsequent months, and seemingly out of nowhere, a moral panic over critical race theory (CRT) emerged to counter and neu-tralize these radical demands. But, unlike the racial reckoning sparked by mass demonstrations and democratic engagement, this counter revolt was manufactured almost entirely by think-tank pundits, Fox News anchors, and—reminiscent of Tea Party activists—small groups of well-organized and well-funded citizens yelling at local politicians.

In a matter of months, the anti-CRT message caught hold among a large bloc of the electorate, now convinced that an obscure academic legal theory posed an existential threat to America. If one could have hoped for a cudgel capable of blunting the real gains made by the Black Lives Matter movement, one could hardly have chosen a more perfect weapon than the CRT moral panic. The sheer effectiveness of this attack, however, is not at all surprising given that the attack was, in fact, designed as a political weapon, deployed in a coordinated fashion, by a massive and well-funded political machinery.

This chapter focuses on the wealthy corporate libertarian donors and the highly integrated network of think tanks and partisan organizations they have developed, over decades, to advance their political agenda. This network has proven incredibly effective at spreading climate denial, passing right-to-work legislation, stacking the courts with pro-business jurists, cutting taxes on the wealthy, privatizing education and other public goods, ending affirmative action, and securing minoritarian political power by defeating campaign finance reform, gutting the Voting Rights Act, while restricting ballot access. The CRT moral panic, and academic gag orders that followed, were similarly manufactured within this well-funded partisan infrastructure. Corporate libertarian think tanks have created an echo chamber by publishing reports, blog posts, podcasts, and editorials warning about the supposed dangers of CRT. And then "grassroots" advocacy groups, funded by the same donors, use this moral outrage to push for the passage of legislation regulating what educators can teach in the classroom.

This chapter examines four seemingly discrete moments within in the unfolding CRT moral panic: Christopher Rufo's initial strategy of fashioning CRT as the "perfect villain" (his words); the formation of Trump's 1776 Commission, populated by think-tank partisans; the decision of UNC-Chapel Hill Board of Trustees to deny tenure to Nikole Hannah-Jones; and the passage of academic gag orders such as Florida's "Stop WOKE" Act. While these four episodes may appear distinct, each instance was manufactured within the political machinery funded by the partisan political network funded by corporate libertarian donors. In the case of CRT, this network simply followed the same strategy it has used for decades, manufacturing outrage within an echo chamber and then offering a ready-made legislative solution to the supposed "crisis." Understanding this political infrastructure helps explain why the attack on CRT has been so ferocious and unrelenting.

AN INTEGRATED NETWORK

Prominent scholars and journalists have chronicled the well-organized libertarian donors who have built a robust and integrated political network designed to bend society to fit their image.[1] The radically individualist philosophy embraced by this donor class—what Nancy MacLean calls "property supremacy"[2]—is grounded in radically individualist notions of freedom developed within the American variants of the Austrian school of economics. This ultralibertarian worldview sees all forms of government regulation, taxation, and social welfare provisions as fundamental threats to personal liberty and, therefore, enemies that must be destroyed. An organized group of wealthy donors has long mobilized this pro-corporate libertarian ideology to justify a whole range of antidemocratic and antisocial policies, including undermining social, cultural, and legislative gains made in the areas of civil rights and racial justice.

Charles Koch has played an outsized role in organizing a reactionary group of donors around his arch-libertarian ideology. At a 1976 conference hosted by the Center for Libertarian Studies (which Koch bankrolled), the fossil fuel scion laid out his vision for creating a libertarian movement built around a core leadership "limited to a small group of sound, knowledgeable and dedicated people" that could focus on gaining popular support for libertarian ideas not only within political circles but also within the media, arts, and academia.[3] Following a disappointing foray into electoral politics (David Koch ran on the Libertarian Party ticket in 1980), the Koch brothers recognized that their hard-right libertarian agenda could not win at the ballot box alone but first required a robust political infrastructure capable of bending all aspects of society to fit their ideological vision. To achieve this end, Charles Koch and the donors he assembled through his regular biannual donor seminars adopted a vision of social change modeled on industrial production. This approach required first securing the "raw material," namely the philosophical, political, economic, and legal theories that come through heavy investments in academic centers and individual intellectuals. These ideas then flow into think tanks which refine them into specific policy proposals, which are then handed to well-funded advocacy groups to mobilize these policies on the ground.[4] The result is an integrated network of seemingly discrete academics, think tanks, media outlets, and advocacy groups all positioned to advocate for the same issues, in unison, creating both an "echo chamber" that demands action on a manufactured problem and the donor-preferred legislation to address that so-called crisis. This integrated infrastructure allows wealthy donors to put considerable direct pressure on politicians, while appearing as if such concerns are raised organically by academics, pundits, the media, and the public at large.

This political machinery became even more potent after the 2010 Supreme Court decision *Citizens United v. Federal Election Commission*, which opened a floodgate of political dark money. In fact, the *Citizens United* decision is Exhibit A in how this integrated political infrastructure functions. Robert Mercer, an attendee of the Koch donor summits, funded a production company that distributed its Hillary Clinton movie in violation of campaign finance laws. With this manufactured test case in hand, the lawyers representing Citizens United—as well as the vast majority of organizations submitting amicus briefs—were also funded by the Koch donor network.[5] And, of course, the majority decision was written by five Supreme Court justices hand-selected by the Koch-backed Federalist Society. In effect, the infrastructure funded by the same small group of political donors manufactured every aspect of the ruling, which legally redefined corporate political spending as constitutionally protected free speech.

In his detailed history of Charles Koch's corporate and political organizing, including how Koch-funded Tea Party organizations defeated greenhouse gas regulations, Christopher Leonard writes:

> The political machine that Charles Koch built was immensely successful— not at fixing this broken system, but at ensuring that it remained hobbled and incapable of passing the kind of sweeping business regulation that defined the New Deal. He applied long-term thinking to a system defined by short-term election timetables, and he won many of the most important fights he cared about.[6]

This analysis could just as easily have been written to describe how the same infrastructure hobbled the demands for racial justice gaining popularity during the summer of 2020. As in previous examples, the Koch-funded political infrastructure quickly revved into high gear, providing the critical infrastructure needed to manufacture—out of whole cloth—a moral panic around critical race theory (CRT).

MANUFACTURING A CRT MORAL PANIC (IN FOUR ACTS)

The anti-CRT backlash is often misunderstood as spontaneous grievance welling up from a disassociated Trumpist political base. However, the rapid insertion of CRT into all levels of local and national politics was not an organic grassroots phenomenon but rather the product of a highly orchestrated and well-funded political machine. This infrastructure provided the talking points, the training, the media amplification, the momentum, and the sustaining support. To understand this point, examining four seemingly discrete episodes demonstrate how fingerprints of the Koch-funded political echo chamber exist at all levels of this manufactured moral panic.

Act 1: Manufacturing the "Perfect Villain"

The strategy of weaponizing "critical race theory" to bulldoze public gains being made by the Black Lives Matter protests originated with Christopher Rufo, a political operative whose entire career is underwritten by conservative libertarian think tanks. Rufo has held positions at the Claremont Institute, the Heritage Foundation, the Pacific Research Institute, the Federalist Society, and the Discovery Institute.[7] He started his anti-CRT crusade in July 2020, writing about an anti-racism seminar hosted by the city of Seattle's Office of Civil Rights.[8] During this time, he explicitly redefined the term "critical race theory" to serve as a go-to bogeyman for the right wing, demonstrating no interest in understanding and engaging actual arguments made by scholars. Instead, Rufo approached this topic in a purely partisan and strategic manner. In a *New Yorker* interview with Benjamin Wallace-Wells, Rufo describes his realization that conservatives lacked the language needed to provide a compelling response to Black Lives Matter. Existing terms—"political correctness," "cancel culture," and "woke"—had limited appeal. To address this strategic deficit, Rufo landed on critical race theory as "the perfect villain." After all, the general public dislikes things that are critical, talking about race, and the abstractness of theory. In a subsequent tweet, Rufo bragged: "We have successfully frozen their brand—'critical race theory'—. . . We will eventually turn it toxic, as we put all of the various cultural insanities under that brand category."[9]

Rufo's cynical weaponization of CRT did not happen in a vacuum but rather because of his connections to a well-funded political infrastructure capable of amplifying his attack. The Manhattan Institute's *City Journal*, where Rufo is now a senior fellow, published many of his pieces.[10] The Manhattan Institute was created in 1977 by Antony Fisher, who, at the encouragement of Friedrich Hayek, established a network of libertarian think tanks around the world, including the Institute for Economic Affairs (UK), the Adam Smith Institute (UK), the Fraser Institute (Canada), the Pacific Research Institute (California), and the Atlas Network (Virginia). The Manhattan Institute receives millions of dollars from prominent right-wing and libertarian donors in the Koch network, including the Bradley Foundation ($8.3 million), the Olin Foundation ($6.7 million), the Searle Freedom Trust ($5.8 million), the Sarah Scaife Foundation ($5.7 million), and the Mercer Family Foundation ($1.7 million). The institute receives millions more from the Koch family foundations.[11]

Rufo's weaponization of CRT spread from the world of Koch-funded think tanks into the mass public in September 2020 when Rufo appeared on *Tucker Carlson Tonight*, where he alleged that "cult indoctrination" has "pervaded every institution in the federal government" and called for an executive order banning CRT.[12] President Trump saw the performance and contacted Rufo the following day. Three weeks later Trump issued an executive order outlawing federal funding for implicit bias training and anti-racism workshops. Since July 2020, Rufo has appeared on Fox News fifty-two times; the channel cited CRT more than 3,900 times in 2021.[13]

Trump's director of the Office of Management and Budget, Russ Vought, wrote the executive order. Vought soon left the White House to create the think tank Center for Renewing America (CRA), which has drafted anti-CRT legislation in more than twenty states, drawing upon language from the executive order.[14]

Act 2: The 1776 Commission Report

On November 2, 2020, the Trump White House issued another executive order, this one establishing the President's Advisory 1776 Commission, tasked with writing a report celebrating "the core principles of the American founding and how these principles may be understood to further enjoyment of 'the blessings of liberty' and to promote our striving 'to form a more perfect Union.'"[15] This commission was created as an explicit rebuke of

"The 1619 Project," which, produced by Nikole Hannah-Jones for the *New York Times Magazine*, argues that America's founding values were largely hollow until the Black freedom struggles pushed the country to live up to those values.[16] "The 1619 Project" essays gained considerable cultural prominence in 2019 and 2020, used even in some school curriculums. Trump's 1776 Commission galvanized the backlash. Its report, published in the days before Trump left office, was swiftly condemned by actual historians as highly inaccurate and incoherent, a mere regurgitation of outdated and often false narratives concerning American exceptionalism.[17] It might be tempting, therefore, to read *The 1776 Report* as just one more clumsy piece of revanchist propaganda from the Trump White House. The more revealing aspect of the report, however, is not what it says, but who wrote it: a commission composed almost entirely of partisans from conservative and libertarian think tanks, many with close ties to the Koch donor network. A closer look at the 1776 Commission reveals how intertwined the activities of that network has been.

The 1776 Commission was chaired by Larry Arnn, executive director of the Aequus Foundation, a funder of right-wing think tanks such as the Heritage Foundation and the State Policy Network, which coordinates the network of national and state-level Koch-funded think tanks. Arnn also serves as president of Hillsdale College, itself funded primarily by right-wing libertarian donors, including Betsy DeVos, Allan Kirby, DonorsTrust, Joseph Coors, Foster Friess, and Blackwater founder Erik Prince.[18] Hillsdale College has since created its own 1776 curriculum for adoption in K–12 classrooms and also established dozens of charter schools in thirteen states featuring its revisionist curriculum.[19]

Another member of the 1776 Commission, Thomas K. Lindsay, is a fellow at the Texas Public Policy Foundation (TPPF), which works closely with the American Legislative Exchange Council (ALEC) to pass bills attacking renewable energy, denying climate change, and undermining environmental protections. TPPF has received $4.1 million from Koch family foundations, millions in contributions from the Koch network's donor-directed pass-through funds, Donors Capital Fund and DonorsTrust, as well as six-digit donations from the State Policy Network, the Bradley Foundation,

Exxon Mobil, the Heartland Institute, the Cato Institute, and many other prominent libertarian donors and organizations.[20]

Victor Davis Hanson, a retired classics professor and visiting lecturer at Arnn's Hillsdale College, is a fellow at the free-market Hoover Institution, which receives its funding from right-wing and libertarian donors (including the Sarah Scaife, Olin, Bradley, and Shelby Cullom Davis Foundations). Charles R. Kesler is a senior fellow at the Claremont Institute, which has collaborated with the David Horowitz Freedom Center to host the Dutch anti-Islam leader Geert Wilders and serves as the institutional home of John Eastman, author of the January 6 coup memo.[21] The Claremont Institute receives funding from DonorsTrust and Donors Capital Fund (commonly referred to as the "Dark-Money ATM of the Conservative Movement"[22]) as well as the Bradley Foundation, the Aequus Foundation, and many other institutions within the libertarian donor network.[23]

Another 1776 Commission member, Mike Gonzalez, is a senior fellow at the Heritage Foundation, where he regularly writes about the coercive effects of identity politics and diversity initiatives. The Heritage Foundation is a libertarian think tank created by Paul Weyrich, who also founded ALEC. It receives funding from the Scaife, Olin, and Bradley foundations, Koch family foundations, and others within the libertarian donor network.[24] Gay Hart Gaines, a Republican activist, has been a member of various Koch network think tanks, including the American Enterprise Institute, the Heritage Foundation, and Hudson Institute, and is chair of the National Review Institute.[25] And Ned Ryun is the founder and CEO of American Majority, which works to elect pro-corporate candidates and is funded by the Milwaukee-based Bradley Foundation; DonorsTrust and Donors Capital Fund; and numerous other members of the Koch donor network.[26]

Given that commission members were drawn largely from think tanks and organizations funded by corporate libertarians, it is not surprising that *The 1776 Report* offers a radically individualist vision of American history, while criticizing universities as a "hotbed of anti-Americanism, libel, and censorship that combine to generate in students . . . disdain and . . . outright hatred for this country."[27] Nor is it surprising that the same libertarian donors and activists were also behind many of the efforts to deny Nikole

Hannah-Jones tenure at the University of North Carolina (UNC) school of journalism.

Act 3: Delegitimizing "The 1619 Project"

In April 2021, a faculty committee at the UNC Hussman School of Journalism and Media selected its star graduate, Nikole Hannah-Jones, as its finalist for the Knight Chair in race and investigative journalism. Hannah-Jones was already a groundbreaking journalist, author of several books, and recipient of more than a dozen prestigious awards, including a MacArthur "genius grant" fellowship and the Pulitzer Prize for Commentary. However, UNC's board of trustees refused to take up Hannah-Jones's tenure file at their November or January trustee meetings, leading the journalism school to offer Hannah-Jones an untenured position, not requiring board approval.[28]

In May 2021, *NC Policy Watch* broke the story that Hannah-Jones had been denied tenure, noting that "conservative groups with direct ties to the Republican-dominated UNC Board of Governors have been highly critical of Hannah-Jones's work and the idea of her teaching at UNC-Chapel Hill" and that "the political environment made granting Hannah-Jones tenure difficult, if not impossible."[29] The board's decision not to approve tenure for Hannah-Jones stemmed from direct interference by the journalism school's largest donor, Walter E. Hussman Jr. In leaked emails, Hussman expressed his concern:

> I do not dispute Nicole Heather-Jones [sic] having her convictions. . . . But I believe giving her a platform to argue for this as a tenured professor in the journalism school will not be beneficial, but instead detrimental, to the school. I believe it will be detrimental because it will be so controversial, contentious, and divisive.[30]

Hussman's influence in Hannah-Jones's tenure vote took place within the broader context of wealthy donors, and the think tanks they fund, seeking to fundamentally transform political culture and university governance in North Carolina.

In one instance, on May 10, 2021, the James G. Martin Center for Academic Renewal published a piece critiquing UNC's hiring of Hannah-Jones and encouraging UNC trustees to actively refuse tenure to all faculty appointments they disagree with.[31] One trustee noted that the Martin Center laid out the "playbook that many powerful conservative interests in the state would like to follow."[32]

The Martin Center is just one of a handful of influential political organizations funded by the John William Pope Foundation. Endowed in 1986 by the founder of Variety Wholesalers, John Pope, the foundation is now administered by his son, James "Art" Pope.[33] Today, the Martin Center (known before 2017 as the John William Pope Center for Higher Education) is funded primarily by the Pope Foundation.[34] In total, the Pope Foundation spent $55 million building "a robust network of conservative think tanks and advocacy groups" in North Carolina, "building a state version of what [Art Pope's] friends Charles and David Koch have helped create on a national level."[35] As state budget director under Governor Patrick McCrory in 2013–14, Art Pope paid considerable attention to UNC-Chapel Hill, scrutinizing its budget and calling for greater austerity, while personally spending millions to fund sports programs and "underwrite classes in politics, economics, and Western civilization."[36] And when law school faculty member Gene Nichols criticized Governor McCrory as a Southern segregationist, two Pope-funded think tanks—the Pope Center and Civitas Institute—blasted out articles critical of Nichols, even acquiring his emails via a public records request.[37]

Committed to fundamentally transforming both state politics and the UNC system, Art Pope actively sought a seat on the board of governors as early as 1995 but was repeatedly rebuffed as too partisan. In 2010, however, Pope funded the Redistricting Majority Project (REDMAP for short), pouring money into legislative races and then using the new Republican majorities to heavily gerrymander the North Carolina legislature. In subsequent years, "[t]he Republican legislature engineered by Pope—and its all-white caucuses—have sought to transform . . . UNC Board of Governors and UNC-Chapel Hill Board of Trustees into Republican strongholds and place them under tighter control."[38] In 2020, Art Pope fulfilled his ambition and was appointed to the University of North Carolina Board of Governors.[39] The activities of Art Pope and other wealthy activist donors have led the American Association to University Professors (AAUP) to conclude that "political interference . . . has recently characterized the entire UNC system."[40]

Even prior to the denial of tenure to Hannah-Jones, Pope-funded think tanks, including the Martin Center, John Locke Foundation, and Civitas Institute, already spent considerable resources delegitimizing "The 1619 Project" and critical race theory more generally.[41] These efforts are consistent with other national and state-level Koch-funded think tanks which have focused on whipping up outrage over issues such as critical race theory, "divisive concepts," "gender ideology," and "cultural Marxism" in K–12 and higher education.[42] The Koch-funded echo chamber, however, has not only whipped up outrage over CRT but also refined that manufactured outrage into specific pieces of legislation designed to shape what can be taught in classrooms around the country.

Act 4: Academic Gag Orders

In March 2022, the Florida legislature passed the Stop WOKE bill (HB 7/SB 148). The bill, predicated on a grossly mischaracterized account of the public and academic conversations about white supremacy and structural racism, seeks to legislate the content of Florida's classrooms. HB 7 is not unique, however (see chapter 3). During the first nine months of 2021, legislatures in twenty-four states introduced fifty-four bills seeking to shape what could be taught in K–12 classrooms, higher education, and/or in trainings of public employees.[43] By October 2022, this number reached 194 proposed bills, with nineteen passed in fifteen states and six additional executive orders signed. Since January 2021, twenty-three bills have attempted to restrict the teaching of "The 1619 Project" specifically, including Texas's SB 3 signed into law by Governor Greg Abbott in June 2021.[44] Justified by the anti-CRT outrage ginned up by Christopher Rufo, supported by *The 1776 Report*, and amplified within an echo chamber of libertarian think tanks and media outlets, the barrage of legislation has been developed within Koch-funded think tanks and advocated by astroturfed parent organizations, funded by the same donors.

One of the key proponents of the repressive gag rules was the American Legislative Exchange Council (ALEC), a long-standing advocate of school privatization that has developed its own anti-CRT model legislation. ALEC, founded in 1973 by right-wing activist Paul Weyrich, has long brought together "private sector members" (corporations, lobbyists, and think tanks) to write pro-corporate model legislation for "public sector members" (state legislators) to pass into law. In December 2020, ALEC hosted a workshop, featuring representatives of the Heritage Foundation and the American Enterprise Institute, as well as Christopher Rufo himself. State representative Mark Cisneros of Iowa attended the conference, then returned home to advocate for HF 802 banning CRT in schools. State representative Brian Seitz of Missouri also attended the workshop and subsequently introduced a state ban on critical race theory and the teaching of "The 1619 Project."[45] In July 2021, ALEC released its American Civics and History Act, a model for legislation that requires K–12 educators to make their social science teaching materials "available online for parents to review."[46] And the November 2022 Honesty in Teaching Act model legislation draws upon a distorted and partisan portrayal of actual public discourses about structural racism as an excuse to reshape classroom content.[47] Of the nineteen sponsors of Florida's HB 7, at least eleven have connections to ALEC, many of whom sit on prominent ALEC committees.[48] ALEC is funded by numerous corporate funders, including the Koch Foundation ($2.5 million), the Bradley Foundation ($1.5 million), DonorsTrust ($1.4 million), and other members of the Koch donor network.[49]

The Koch-funded Goldwater Institute has also developed anti-CRT model legislation, which would prohibit the use of diversity statements in hiring and "taxpayer funded indoctrination in critical race theory."[50] A constitutional amendment, HCR 2001, containing much of the language from the Goldwater model legislation, was introduced during the 2022 Arizona legislative session.[51] The Goldwater Institute received $6.4 million from the Charles Koch family foundations, Bradley, and DonorsTrust/Donors Capital Fund between 2001 and 2019.[52] The Heritage Foundation has also created model legislation, signed into law in Mississippi and taken up by legislators in Arizona, South Carolina, Georgia, and elsewhere.[53] The Manhattan Institute has developed its own anti-CRT model legislation too.[54]

In addition to producing model legislation, the Koch donor network has also funded on-the-ground organizing muscle used to manufacture the semblance of public demand for laws regulating the teaching of critical race theory. One group, Parents Defending Education (PDE), was founded by Nicole Neily, who previously worked for several Koch-funded outlets (Independent Women's Forum, the Cato Institute, and Speech First). The leadership of PDE, including Neily, Karol Markowicz, and Asra Nomani, regularly appear on Fox News and other right-wing media outlets criticizing critical race theory, without revealing their relationship to PDE.[55] And lawyer Edward Blum, another PDE director, has received funding from DonorsTrust and other dark money sources to litigate against affirmative action at Harvard and UNC. He also spearheaded the legal strategy in the 2013 Supreme Court case *Shelby County v. Holder*, which disemboweled the Voting Rights Act.[56]

Moms for Liberty, which incorporated itself in January 2021 and partnered with PDE in May 2021, presents itself as a group of local moms who spontaneously organize on Facebook over a shared interest in preserving parents' rights in education, including preventing the teaching of CRT.[57] The group, however, enjoys considerable connections to the Republican political establishment and a close relationship with the Heritage Foundation.[58] The Independent Women's Forum (IWF)[59] is an anti-feminist libertarian advocacy group that advances pro-corporate policies, such as the deregulation of tobacco and fighting against paid family leave, under the banner of representing the political interests of women.[60] IWF's interest in educational policy began with its aggressive opposition to mask mandates, which quickly pivoted to issues of CRT and gender identity.[61] During the Virginia governor's race in 2021, IWF launched a website charging Democratic candidate Terry McAuliffe with allowing pornographic images in schools. It also issued a primer claiming that CRT "is divisive," "disseminates despair," "is unpatriotic," and "is systemic," meaning it is no longer "confined to the ivory tower" but "today infects almost all of our most basic institutions."[62] It should come as no surprise that IWF has also received considerable funding from a handful of incredibly wealthy libertarian white men, including $3.4 million from DonorsTrust and other groups tied to the Koch donor network, including the Bradley, DeVos, Scaife, and Pope foundations, among others.[63]

Building Education for Students Together (BEST) is yet another group that plays an important role astroturfing the semblance of mass public opposition to CRT in schools. BEST is a subsidiary of FreedomWorks, the latest incarnation of the Koch-funded Citizens for a Sound Economy (CSE). Funded by the tobacco, the fossil fuel, and other corporate interests, CSE was created by long-time Koch-funded political operative Richard Fink in 1984 to conduct "grassroots" campaigns that advanced corporate interests.[64] In subsequent years, FreedomWorks has received $11.9 million from Koch family foundations as well as the Scaife foundation ($3.4 million), Donors-Trust ($3.3 million), and the Bradley foundation ($1.4 million), among other organizations.[65] FreedomWorks also provided considerable infrastructural support for the Tea Party and the Stop the Steal election-denial movement.[66] Its education-branded group, BEST, trains parents to run for school boards on platforms that focus on "[c]ritical race theory, The 1619 Project, and Common Core [that] have paved the way for biased, anti-American, subjective curricula" and advocates for typical libertarian school policies—vouchers, charter schools, and home schooling—designed to further the privatization of public education.[67]

In December 2021, Christopher Rufo joined DeSantis on stage to announce that HB 7 "provid[es] a model for every state in the United States of America. Critical Race Theory is wrong; it offers nothing to improve the lives of anyone of any racial background."[68] Four months later, again on a stage with Rufo, DeSantis signed HB 7 into law, pointing to "The 1619 Project" as the kind of material that would be banned from the classroom under the legislation.[69] As demonstrated here, what appears as a widespread concern about so-called critical race theory should actually be understood as a manufactured partisan strategy concocted within an echo chamber created and funded by a network of ultra-wealthy libertarian donors.

But why then would this political network, having notched up so many political victories in recent decades, take up the seemingly minor issue of CRT? One answer might be a belief that this cynical strategy will yield electoral victories, riling up the voters to elect politicians who will ultimately advance conservative and pro-corporate legislation, including the privatization of public schools. However, there is something even more pernicious at work. The Black Lives Matter protests seriously challenged the undergirding libertarian ideology that un-raced and ungendered individuals, acting freely within supposedly radically unregulated capitalist markets, can achieve better outcomes simply through individual hard work. The Black Lives Matter insurrection fundamentally challenged this ideological fantasy and did so through a democratic revolt from below. In the face of this actual mass protest, the only response the corporate libertarian donors had left was to harness their network of well-funded political organizations for the purpose of waging a scorched earth culture war.

Defeating this corporate, racist, and reactionary power—one which understands itself in an existential struggle to continue justifying, and therefore preserving, economic and political hierarchies—requires ongoing mass democratic organization. It also requires understanding the depth of the political infrastructure arrayed against us. For that, we need to follow the money.

3

The Rise of Educational Gag Orders

JONATHAN FRIEDMAN,
JEREMY C. YOUNG, AND JAMES TAGER

*There is a legislative war on
education in America.*

B ETWEEN JANUARY 2021 AND MAY 2023, 45 legislatures across the United
States introduced 306 separate bills intended to restrict teaching and
training in K–12 schools, higher education, and state agencies and institutions.[1] The majority of these bills target discussions of race, racism, gender,
sexual identity, and American history, banning a series of "prohibited" or
"divisive" concepts for teachers and trainers operating in K–12 schools,
public universities, and workplace settings. These bills appear designed to
chill academic and educational discussions and impose government dictates
on teaching and learning. In short, they are *educational gag orders.*

Since 2021, twenty-six of these bills have become law in seventeen states,
while three additional states have enacted similar policies via executive order or other state government action. In all, as of May 2023, 125 million
Americans—nearly one-third of the entire population—live in states with
one or more educational gag orders in force.

While bills that have passed into law pose the greatest threat to classroom free expression, the avalanche of proposed bills that did not pass
are also worthy of concern. Such unsuccessful bills evince a desire among
lawmakers to censor educators in even more settings or using even more
extreme measures than in the gag orders that did become law. Many such
bills contain provisions that stand a good chance of being reintroduced in
future years. And even the mere introduction of these bills has created a

broad chilling effect on teachers and professors, putting them on notice that elected officials are watching with microscopic scrutiny what they teach and aiming to penalize those who teach topics or content with which they disagree. The pervasiveness of these legislative proposals, and the censorious impulses they reflect, are part of a nationwide campaign of classroom censorship that shows no signs of abating.

Collectively, these bills are illiberal in their attempt to legislate that those certain ideas and concepts be out of bounds even, in many cases, in college classrooms among adults. Their adoption demonstrates a disregard for academic freedom, liberal education, and the values of free speech and open inquiry that are enshrined in the First Amendment and that anchor a democratic society. Legislators who support these bills appear determined to use state power to exert ideological control over public educational institutions. Further, in seeking to silence race- or gender-based critiques of US society and history that those behind them deem to be "divisive," these bills are likely to disproportionately affect the free speech rights of students, educators, and trainers who are women, people of color, and LGBTQ people.

The vague and sweeping language of these bills means that they will be applied broadly and arbitrarily, threatening to effectively ban a wide swath of literature, curriculum, historical materials, and other media, with a chilling effect on how educators and educational institutions discharge their primary obligations. It must also be recognized that the movement behind these bills has brought a single-minded focus to bear on suppressing content and narratives by and about people of color specifically—something which cannot be separated from the role that race and racism continue to play in our society and politics. As such, these bills not only pose a risk to the US education system but also threaten to silence vital societal discourse on racism and sexism. Arriving alongside similar waves of legislation to restrict voting and protest rights and to enable the banning of books, these censorious bills reflect a larger and worrying antidemocratic trend in US politics in which lawmakers use the machinery of government in an attempt to limit Americans' ability to express themselves, particularly in order to block the expression of ideas or sentiments that lawmakers oppose.

At PEN America, our concern with educational gag orders stems from our mission as a literary and human rights organization to stand for the free flow of ideas, an abiding commitment to the freedom to write and the freedom to read, and when it comes to educational institutions, the freedom to learn. The teaching of history, civics, and American identity has never been neutral or uncontested, and reasonable people can disagree over how and when educators should teach children about racism, sexism, and other facets of American history and society.[2] But in a democracy, the response to these disagreements can never be to ban discussion of ideas or facts simply because they are contested or cause discomfort. As American society reckons with the persistence of racial discrimination and inequity, and the complexities of historical memory, these attempts to use the power of the state to constrain discussion of these issues must be rejected.

FROM PRESIDENTIAL RHETORIC TO REPUBLICAN POLICY

Battles over education in the US are often a proxy for broader societal debates and anxieties, and it is not a coincidence that this legislative on-slaught followed both the August 2019 release of the *New York Times*'s "1619 Project" and the mass protests that swept the country in 2020 in the wake of the murder of George Floyd. As many Americans and US institutions attempted a true reckoning with the role that race and racism play in American history and society, those opposed to these cultural changes surrounding race, gender, and diversity pushed back ferociously, feeding into a culture war. Certain Republican legislators and conservative activists capitalized on this backlash, borrowing the name of an academic framework—critical race theory (CRT)—to serve as their bogeyman, inaccurately applying it to a range of ideas, practices, and materials related to advancing diversity, equity, or inclusion.

We can clearly trace the origins of this narrative. Beginning in 2020, President Trump seized upon "diversity trainings" and anti-racism teach-ings as a scapegoat to rally supporters. In turn, the Trump administration's efforts directly spurred and shaped today's state-level legislative efforts to impose ideological constraints on educators and trainers. These efforts, in the name of saving Americans from anti-racist "indoctrination," represent a substantial and unwarranted government intrusion into the free speech and academic freedom of Americans.

The majority of the state bills PEN America has reviewed draw extensively on an executive order issued by President Donald Trump shortly before he left office. On September 22, 2020, Trump issued Executive Order (EO) 13950, Combating Race and Sex Stereotyping. It claimed that "many people are pushing a . . . vision of America that is grounded in hierarchies based on collective social and political identities rather than in the inherent and equal dignity of every person as an individual." The EO decried this vision as a "destructive," "malign" ideology that "threatens to infect core institutions of our country." The executive order adopted sweeping rules that defined particular "divisive concepts" dealing with race and sex in America, such as the argument that "the United States is fundamentally a racist country." It went on to prohibit the expression of these concepts from any federal employee training and any training that any institution that contracted with the federal government could offer its own employees. The EO also prohibited the US military from offering training or courses in any such concepts.[3]

Trump's executive order was repealed by President Joe Biden on his first day in office, but it had been instrumental in galvanizing a broad effort that gained momentum in 2021 and 2022 to circumscribe discussions of race, racism, sexuality, and gender by prohibiting the teaching of certain ideas. Over the previous two years, what started as an election-season gambit by President Trump to prohibit "race and sex stereotyping" had metamorphosed into a nationwide movement among Republican legislators, governors, pundits, and activists to crush a sweeping set of ideas and teachings dubbed "critical race theory" and specific curricula they associate with it.

LEGISLATIVE ESCALATION

State-level educational gag orders began to appear during the 2021 legislative session and quickly spread to statehouses throughout the country. By the year's end, fifty-four bills had been filed in twenty-two states, of which twelve became law.

These battles intensified in 2022. Lawmakers in thirty-six different states introduced a total of 140 educational gag order bills, an increase of more than 250 percent over the number of proposed bills in 2021. Only seven new gag order bills became law in 2022, but they included some of the most censorious laws to date. The dramatic increase in the number of bills introduced is itself a cause for alarm, reflecting a heightened inclination toward state censorship. Bills introduced in 2022 tended to be more punitive, target a greater number of educational institutions, and restrict a wider array of speech. The trend for the year can be summarized in a single word: escalation.

The most striking development in 2022 was the sheer volume of bills introduced. In the month of January alone, eighteen different educational gag order bills were filed in Missouri, eight in Indiana, and six in Arizona (including one amendment to the state constitution). By the time most legislative sessions wound down in June, virtually every state where Republicans controlled at least one legislative chamber had considered an educational gag order that year. The only exceptions were Arkansas, which had already passed a gag order the previous year, and states whose legislatures did not meet in 2022.[4]

Just as in 2021, Republican legislators were the driving force behind educational gag order bills in 2022. Only one gag order bill, Arizona's HB 2634, had a Democratic sponsor.[5] The bill proposed to prohibit from school curricula "any textbook or other instructional material . . . that contains any matter reflecting adversely on persons on the basis of race, ethnicity, sex, religion, disability, nationality, sexual orientation or gender identity." No matter the motivation behind it, this legislation would pose a similar threat to curriculum and teaching as the other types of educational gag orders. In practice, it would function as a form of government-imposed censorship. The bill must be seen as an outlier, as it was quickly defeated. Every other gag order bill introduced across the country in the past two years has been sponsored exclusively by Republican legislators.

The gag order bills introduced in 2022, compared to those of 2021, tended to be more expansive and target a wider array of educational speech. In both years, instruction related to race was the most common category of speech to draw lawmakers' attention. But 2022 also saw a sharp increase in the number of bills targeting LGBTQ issues and identities; twenty-three such bills were introduced, and one, Florida's HB 1557, became law. Overall, there was also an increase in the complexity and scale of legislation, as lawmakers sought to assert political control over everything from classroom speech to library content, from the professional training of teachers to field trips and extracurricular activities.

Another notable development in 2022 was the growing number of bills targeting higher education. Of the 140 educational gag order bills introduced, 39 percent targeted colleges and universities, up from 30 percent of those filed in 2021. Likewise, of the bills that became law in 2022, 57 percent targeted higher education, up from just 25 percent of new laws the previous year. There was also a significant increase in the number of bills designed to regulate nonpublic educational institutions, including private universities.

Finally, the bills introduced in 2022 included much more punitive provisions: 55 percent contained some kind of explicit punishment for violations, compared to 44 percent in 2021. Moreover, punishments tended to be more extreme, such as private rights of action that would enable parents and community members to sue school districts, large monetary fines, faculty termination, and the loss of institutional accreditation. Some unsuccessful bills even proposed criminal penalties.

Although not classified as an educational gag order, SB 775, a bill that became law in Missouri, illustrates this shift toward criminal provisions. Before its passage, SB 775, primarily related to the rights of sexual assault survivors, was amended to include a provision establishing it as a Class A misdemeanor if an individual in any official capacity with a public or private school distributes or makes available to students any material deemed "harmful to minors."[6] Violations are punishable by a $2,000 fine or a year in jail. The law construes "visual depictions" of sexual acts and nudity as material harmful to minors, and it was the impetus for the removal of hundreds of books from school libraries in some districts in the fall of 2022. The districts that removed books appeared anxious about taking any risk of the law being enforced against their personnel. The breadth of the interpretation led to the removal of an astonishing array of literature, from comics and graphic novels to art history books, adaptations of classics, and even educational books about the Holocaust, including the Pulitzer Prize–winning *Maus*.

WHY THESE BILLS ARE SO CONCERNING

To varying degrees, all 194 educational gag order bills propose tighter state control over what information or ideas educators and instructors can teach and prohibit or limit the presentation of specific approaches to race, gender, and our nation's history. As such, the bills are attempts to impose viewpoint censorship on educators.

First Amendment jurisprudence is especially hostile to viewpoint and content-based regulation. The Supreme Court has previously ruled that government attempts to regulate "particular views taken by speakers on a subject" is a "blatant" violation of the Constitution: "Viewpoint discrimination is . . . an egregious form of content discrimination."[7] While it is possible that some of these bills may withstand constitutional scrutiny, the foreseeable effect of each and every one of them will be to silence speech based on the speaker's viewpoint. They also foreseeably silence educators from sharing specific facts. As such, these bills are fundamentally incompatible with the First Amendment, the norms and guarantees of academic and intellectual freedom, and the foundational democratic notion of civic debate on a neutral playing field.

Educational gag orders that apply to high schools and colleges could tangibly impact large portions of student curricula. Every social studies course—including history, civics, and English literature—would be overlaid with these ideological prohibitions. It is unclear how a teacher could offer instruction or even guide conversation on some of the most important and contentious moments or topics in American history—slavery, the emancipation of women, the treatment of Native Americans—without triggering such a prohibition. This applies to both historical fact and literary narrative, from examinations of race and gender in *Adventures of Huckleberry Finn* or *The Scarlet Letter* to the unvarnished facts of the Wounded Knee or Tulsa race massacres.

It also applies to the presentation of academic ideas. For example, any description of social privilege, a concept that draws upon a wide-ranging body of social scientific scholarship, would seemingly violate at least half of the prohibited concepts under Trump's Executive Order 13950 and the bills that mirror it. In fact, the overwhelming majority of these bills are prohibiting "race or sex stereotyping" or "race or sex scapegoating" in ways that are transparently aimed at shutting down discussions of societal privilege or racial disparities.

A Fourteenth Amendment claim could be levied against each of these bills as written or as implemented: their prohibitions will be wielded in racially discriminatory ways. The wording of the bills, combined with the telegraphed intent of the legislators introducing them, essentially guarantee that the brunt of their impact will fall disproportionately on teachers, trainers, and students who are people of color or women, those less likely to be given the benefit of the doubt that their critical utterances regarding race or sex in the classroom or training hall were not intended as prohibited or "divisive" critiques.[8]

The full scope of a law or policy's censorship should be understood to include not just what expression is prohibited but the extent to which people will self-censor for fear of punishment. This so-called chilling effect is a well-recognized concept in both American jurisprudence[9] and in anti-censorship research and advocacy.[10] While the Supreme Court has been inconsistent over the years about whether a chilling effect alone is sufficient for finding a First Amendment violation, the court's jurisprudence on the issue helps to illustrate the likelihood that self-censorship will occur as a foreseeable result of these bills, deeply implicating the rights of educators and students to express themselves in academic settings.[11]

The concept of the chilling effect is also linked to the legal doctrines of overbreadth and vagueness. A law regulating speech can be unconstitutionally overbroad if its scope appears to encompass a substantial amount of constitutionally protected expression.[12] Similarly, a law regulating speech is unconstitutionally vague if a reasonable person cannot determine what speech is permissible, as "[u]ncertain meanings inevitably lead citizens to steer far wider of the unlawful zone than if the boundaries of the forbidden areas were clearly marked."[13] Much of the chilling effect of these educational gag orders, then, derives from the fact that the Trump-defined "divisive concepts" are vague and overbroad, meaning that all kinds of subjects, opinions, and even verifiable matters of historical fact might be construed as falling within their wide sweep.

Further, many of these bills are marked by serious conceptual flaws that their own drafters have implicitly acknowledged, tying themselves in knots to disguise their ideological censorship. Several of the bills attempt to depict themselves as protecting, not infringing on, academic inquiry in the classroom, mandating that teachers not "compel" students to believe in any divisive concept. While these laws may at first glance seem protective of speech, the fact that the legislature is singling out specific beliefs or viewpoints and purporting to "protect" students from them sends the obvious message that the state disfavors the expression of these perspectives.

Many bills contain so-called savings clauses, which purportedly limit the scope of the bill to better comport with the Constitution. Such provisions state, for example, that nothing in the law should be construed to conflict with the protections of the First Amendment. These savings clauses should be best understood as attempts to conceal or get around the fact that these proposals will foreseeably silence speech. They are the legislative equivalent of painting a happy face on a sad clown: they do not change the underlying nature of the thing but only help cover it up.

Faced with an impossible demand: how to parse which concepts are illegal to introduce into the classroom and how to educate students on a concept without appearing to "endorse" it, teachers and administrators are likely to self-censor and avoid any potentially controversial topics entirely.

EFFECTS OF EDUCATIONAL GAG ORDERS

These bills are already having tangible consequences for both American education and democracy, both distorting the lens through which the next generation will study American history and society and undermining the hallmarks of liberal education that have set the US system apart from those of authoritarian countries. In a very short time, we have seen the chilling effects of this kind of legislation, used to justify suspending a sociology course on race and ethnicity in Oklahoma[14] and providing professors at Iowa State University written guidance for how to avoid "drawing scrutiny" to their teaching under their state's act.[15]

The Oklahoma Board of Education disciplined two school districts for supposed violations of the state's law, in both cases handing down harsher penalties than called for by the law.[16] "This instance," said a spokesman for the Oklahoma State Department of Education, which had recommended lesser penalties, "underscores how the vague language of HB 1775 invites imprecise judgement calls, which in turn can have a chilling effect on classroom instruction."[17]

Much of the laws' chilling effect has stemmed not from such instances of overt enforcement by state agencies but from administrative censorship by school administrators trying to avoid falling prey to such enforcement. In their January 2022 report, *The Conflict Campaign*, education scholars Mica Pollock and John Rogers documented numerous instances of school district administrators withdrawing commitments to support teacher initiatives as a consequence of new policies restricting classroom speech.[18] According to an August 2022 survey by the RAND Corporation, a quarter of teachers nationwide have been directed by school administrators "to limit discussions about political and social issues in class."[19] In the face of nebulous restrictions, and in a climate of fear, administrators are frequently deputizing themselves censors to avoid uncertain consequences.

In one emblematic example from April 2022, a group of students at Iowa's Johnston High School reported "a different atmosphere at the school" after the state's educational gag order became law. One teacher, explaining the history of redlining, allegedly felt compelled to deny in class that they were trying to make students feel guilty; another teacher allegedly felt unable to explain the motivations behind the three-fifths compromise without violating the state's educational gag order law.[20]

Such strained conditions also seem likely to add to the nation's worsening teacher shortage. As Hannah Natanson wrote in the *Washington Post*, a key contributing factor to the 2022 shortage was "some educators' sense that politicians and parents . . . have little respect for their profession amid an escalating educational culture war that has seen many districts and states pass policies and laws restricting what teachers can say about U.S. history, race, racism, gender and sexual orientation, as well as LGBTQ issues."[21]

FUTURE TRENDS

Given the enthusiasm for educational gag orders among many Republican lawmakers and some of their supporters, it is almost certain that more such bills will continue to be introduced, especially in states where Republicans have thus far failed to pass such a law. In these states and others, a new wave of similar bills seems probable.

It is also likely that future gag order proposals will target instruction related to LGBTQ issues and identities, similar to Florida's HB 1557. Those bills will also likely find creative ways to target private K–12 schools and higher education, particularly by threatening any public funding or accreditation status. In addition, we will likely see the adoption of district-level educational gag orders that are not enshrined in state legislation. Some of these policies have borrowed language from state bills and have proposed prohibitions on teachers related to instruction about race and sex. Other districts have restricted LGBTQ identities in new and troubling ways: barring LGBTQ pride flags or other political flags and symbols in schools, forbidding teachers from including preferred pronouns in their email signatures, or even banning them from wearing rainbow-colored clothing.[22] The CRT Forward Tracking Project at UCLA Law has similarly documented hundreds of district-level educational gag order measures on instruction related to race.[23]

New litigation challenges to these educational gag orders seem inevitable. Numerous lawsuits have been filed challenging them in Florida, Oklahoma, New Hampshire, and Ohio.[24] Meanwhile, supporters of educational gag orders have filed complaints of their own in a bid to persuade courts and regulatory bodies to stake out a maximal interpretation of what these laws prohibit; more such actions are likely. One complaint, filed by the conservative America First Policy Institute on behalf of an Iowa student, claims that a planned elective class on social justice in literature would violate the state's ban on "race or sex stereotyping" in education. Importantly, the complaint does not accuse the teacher of promoting race or sex stereotypes or even of assigning texts containing them. Rather, it argues that since students themselves might, on their own initiative, select books to read that contain race or sex stereotypes, the teacher will violate the law if she fails to stop them.[25] Such a law ranges far beyond a teacher's speech, censoring a student's voluntary choice of literature. Another lawsuit, brought by Parents' Choice Tennessee, cites one of the state's two educational gag order laws and seeks to ban Wit & Wisdom, an English language arts curriculum, from Williamson County schools.[26] A third lawsuit, filed in Florida, has centered on a discussion of LGBTQ pride flags in a middle school computer science class, about which a parent complained.[27]

Finally, the future of educational gag orders will likely unfold as part of a broader legislative campaign of educational censorship. At the K–12 level, this includes "curriculum transparency" bills and tip-line-style reporting mechanisms, which have become more common in legislative proposals, as well as bills that make it easier for parents to file challenges for the removal of books from school libraries. In higher education, educational gag orders are just one of the ways lawmakers are increasingly seeking to undermine academic freedom, shared governance, and faculty tenure. In 2022, such measures were adopted or considered in Mississippi, Florida, Texas, Louisiana, and Wyoming; in 2023, new bills of this type advanced or were enacted in Florida, Texas, and Ohio.[28]

Whatever future legislative sessions bring, it is clear that legislative attacks on the freedom to learn and teach are far from over. As organizations and institutions across the country, including schools, colleges, and state agencies, introduce diversity initiatives and other curricular efforts to bring new perspectives to our understanding of American history, society, and identity, it is imperative to ensure space for open debate and a diversity of viewpoints. The passage of censorious laws does just the opposite, setting an alarming precedent for government intrusions on the freedom to read and to learn, academic freedom, and historical inquiry. These trends should alarm advocates of free expression, public education, and democracy alike.

4

The Epistemology of Ignorance and Its Impact on Democracy and Higher Education

VALERIE C. JOHNSON

THE QUEST TO HIDE THE UGLY TRUTH of American history is not new. From its founding down through to the present, there has been tension between those who would like to shroud the truth and those who understand that an accurate accounting of history is the necessary backdrop to reconciling the past and finally realizing a future that recognizes the humanity of all persons.

The late philosopher Charles Mills refers to this orchestrated forgetting of the past as an epistemology of ignorance—a system of knowledge attainment that impedes the ability to accurately understand social reality and its attendant racial and social inequities, and implications. As Mills argues, shrouding the truth of American history produces "the ironic outcome that whites [the majority of the US population] will, in general, be unable to understand the world they themselves have made."[1]

An epistemology of ignorance is at the heart of legislative gag orders, which have sought to limit what can be taught in American institutions of higher learning. The resulting contraction of knowledge has a tremendous effect not only on higher education but, by extension, on the ability of Americans to make informed decisions about the leaders they elect and the policy measures they pursue. To be sure, America cannot move beyond its past until it reckons with the original sin of slavery and genocide, and its continuing vestiges. "America is false to the past, false to the present, and solemnly binds herself to be false to the future."[2]

If America is to become the nation we profess we already are, Americans must confront the lingering consequences of racism and other inequities. As Supreme Court justice Harry Blackmun wrote in his 1978 *Regents of the*

University of California v. Bakke opinion, "In order to get beyond racism, we must first take account of race."

This chapter seeks to provide a deeper understanding of the rationale behind educational gag orders and their corresponding effect on America's body politic. As argued, the battle over what can be learned is nothing short of a struggle for power, with one side seeking to preserve white supremacy, patriarchy, and capitalism, but at a tremendous cost to a democratic society. Legislative gag orders are, in essence, the ideological right's dogged commitment to cultivating an ignorant populace, and in its wake, destroying all hopes for a stable democracy.

Faculty members at institutions of higher learning bear an important societal responsibility. Unlike most Americans, they daily confront the dangers of restricting knowledge as institutions of higher learning have become a hotbed of political activity. Faculty must, decidedly then, be the vanguard in the fight to teach according to their disciplinary expertise and to preserve and defend unrestricted access to learning for all Americans.

THE IGNOBLE VALUE OF FORGETTING

Erasing history, however ignoble, has practical political purposes that confine Americans to an inglorious past. What we know about the past is a mediated experience given legitimacy through the educational system and enshrined in public monuments and museums. The past is manufactured and contested, designed to exclude an alternative past, reinforce patriotism, or legitimize a particular heritage.[3]

The story that is most often excluded today, as in the past, is that of those who have been subjugated. Similar to the experiences of countless Americans, Nikole Hannah-Jones recounts that in her early education:

> [Black people] were largely absent from the histories I read. The vision of the past I absorbed from school textbooks, television, and the local history museum depicted a world, perhaps a wishful one, where Black people did not really exist. This history rendered Black Americans, Black people on all the earth, inconsequential at best, invisible at worst. We appeared only where unavoidable: slavery was mentioned briefly in the chapter on

this nation's most deadly war, and then Black people disappeared again for a full century, until magically reappearing as Martin Luther King, Jr., gave a speech about a dream. This quantum leap served to wrap the Black experience up in a few paragraphs and a tidy bow, never really explaining why, one hundred years after the abolition of slavery, King had to lead the March on Washington in the first place.[4]

My own education growing up in Buffalo, New York, in the 1960s and 1970s echoes Hannah-Jones's. Most of what my brother and I learned about African American history was gleaned from *Ebony*'s Black America series. There was nothing important about Black people to be learned in school. We were largely invisible. White society has, through its laws and actions, historically stripped African Americans, Latines, and Native Americans of their labor, land, creative contributions, and experiences in America.

This convenient forgetting has a tremendous impact on how Americans view racial disparities on all social and economic indicators, be it in the criminal justice system, educational attainment, employment, or healthcare. The contraction of knowledge about the ways that the American political system has shut out these groups from opportunities reserved for whites creates racial ambivalence and racial dissonance that either disassociates whites from conditions affecting people from marginalized groups or preserves the false yet pristine view of American meritocracy that argues that where you are is dependent upon hard work and enterprise. This very fact makes it difficult to bridge America's deeply rooted divisions and has led to continuing conflict and societal tensions. The January 6, 2021, insurrection at the Capitol is the tip of the iceberg and portends what is to come if active counter engagement does not immediately occur. Faculty members must take the fight to state legislatures and the US Congress. This is the battleground, and faculty are uniquely positioned to understand what is at stake.

The American epistemology—what Americans perceive and memorialize, is all-encompassing and represented in every sphere of human comprehension—music, film, museums and other historical sites, theatre, art, the media, and most of all, the education system. It forms an all-encompassing habitus—a bubble—that constantly replicates and reinforces itself with a false narrative about who we are as a nation. It's a willful ignorance whose most logical interrogation point is higher education, and hence, the central focus of education gag orders.

The struggle between two distinct versions of the Civil War period is illustrative of how our national identity has been and continues to be contestable. Participants in the Charlottesville, Virginia, 2017 Unite the Right rally were, for example, straight out of central casting for a post-Civil War drama. In both instances, Americans simultaneously venerated the heroes (the Union) and the villains (the Confederacy). Whenever white people fear a loss of control, America plunges headlong into competing narratives about who we are as a nation. It is no wonder that a rise in right-wing nationalist ideology and a proliferation of Confederate monuments followed World War I and the civil rights movement, which were both periods of expanding opportunities and rights for those who had been historically marginalized.

Confederate monuments are nothing more than political propaganda that generationally constructs a false heritage and inaccurate historical record of a vanquished past. This current period, replete with conspiracy theories like QAnon and election denialism, is but another contest between those committed to a multicultural society and those who believe that America is for white people. It is a war once waged on the plains of America between Native Americans and white settlers brought down to the present period between conservatives and liberals. It is a contest for the past, the present, and the future, motivated by changing demographics and the purported threat of the non-white other. We do not see the same reality and, therefore, are deprived of opportunities to expand democracy and human rights.

As figure 1 illustrates, there is a considerable difference in the perspective of whites and Blacks and between Democrats and Republicans on whether racism is enshrined in our laws and practices (structural) or an individual bad actor phenomenon. Among whites, 70 percent say that the larger problem is racism by individuals, compared to Blacks, who are more split in their assessment, with 52 percent saying the larger problem is in our laws and 43 percent saying racism by individuals is the greater culprit.

Carol Anderson's award-winning book *White Rage: The Unspoken Truth of Our Racial Divide* notes how the "whittling down of racism to sheet-wearing goons allowed a cloud of racial innocence to cover many whites" and thereby exempt society from overturning structural and systemic inequalities. The

FIGURE 1 *Blacks Americans More Likely Than Other Adults to Say Structural Sources of Racism Are a Bigger Problem Than Individual Ones*

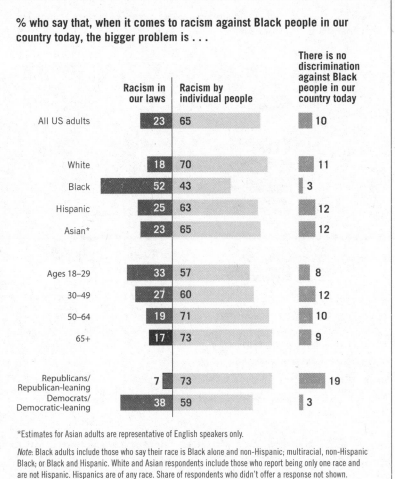

% who say that, when it comes to racism against Black people in our country today, the bigger problem is . . .

	Racism in our laws	Racism by individual people	There is no discrimination against Black people in our country today
All US adults	23	65	10
White	18	70	11
Black	52	43	3
Hispanic	25	63	12
Asian*	23	65	12
Ages 18–29	33	57	8
30–49	27	60	12
50–64	19	71	10
65+	17	73	9
Republicans/ Republican-leaning	7	73	19
Democrats/ Democratic-leaning	38	59	3

*Estimates for Asian adults are representative of English speakers only.

Note: Black adults include those who say their race is Black alone and non-Hispanic; multiracial, non-Hispanic Black; or Black and Hispanic. White and Asian respondents include those who report being only one race and are not Hispanic. Hispanics are of any race. Share of respondents who didn't offer a response not shown.

Source: Survey of US adults conducted October 4–17, 2021

PEW RESEARCH CENTER

focus on individuals over a societal focus on systems absolves whites from doing anything substantive about racial inequities or providing those who have been historically aggrieved greater societal resources.[5]

Further, as figure 2 shows, there are wide racial and partisan gaps about whether more attention to the history of racism is good for American

FIGURE 2 *Wide Racial, Partisan Gaps on Whether More Attention to the History of Racism in the US Is Good for Society*

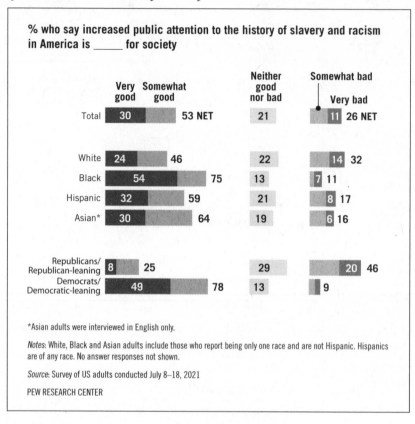

% who say increased public attention to the history of slavery and racism in America is _____ for society

	Very good	Somewhat good	Neither good nor bad	Somewhat bad / Very bad
Total	30	53 NET	21	11 / 26 NET
White	24	46	22	14 / 32
Black	54	75	13	7 / 11
Hispanic	32	59	21	8 / 17
Asian*	30	64	19	6 / 16
Republicans/Republican-leaning	8	25	29	20 / 46
Democrats/Democratic-leaning	49	78	13	9

*Asian adults were interviewed in English only.

Notes: White, Black and Asian adults include those who report being only one race and are not Hispanic. Hispanics are of any race. No answer responses not shown.

Source: Survey of US adults conducted July 8–18, 2021

PEW RESEARCH CENTER

society. Forty-six percent of whites say increased public attention to the history of slavery and racism in America is "very good" or "somewhat good" for society, compared to 75 percent of Blacks and 59 percent of Latines. And consistent with the push for legislative restrictions on what is learned, 25 percent of Republicans and Republican-leaning Americans compared to 78 percent of Democrats and Democrat-leaning Americans indicate that public awareness of the history of slavery and racism is "very good" or "somewhat good" for society.

The lack of consensus about racism and the value of America's racial history, in turn, harms the ability of Americans to work toward common solutions. As figure 3 illustrates, there is significant disagreement between

FIGURE 3 *Majority of Black Americans Say Most US Institutions and Laws Need to Be Completely Rebuilt Because They Are Fundamentally Biased Against Some Groups*

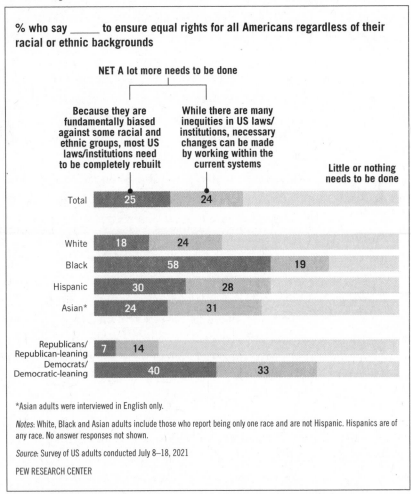

% who say _____ to ensure equal rights for all Americans regardless of their racial or ethnic backgrounds

NET A lot more needs to be done

Because they are fundamentally biased against some racial and ethnic groups, most US laws/institutions need to be completely rebuilt

While there are many inequities in US laws/institutions, necessary changes can be made by working within the current systems

Little or nothing needs to be done

Total	25	24
White	18	24
Black	58	19
Hispanic	30	28
Asian*	24	31
Republicans/Republican-leaning	7	14
Democrats/Democratic-leaning	40	33

*Asian adults were interviewed in English only.

Notes: White, Black and Asian adults include those who report being only one race and are not Hispanic. Hispanics are of any race. No answer responses not shown.

Source: Survey of US adults conducted July 8–18, 2021

PEW RESEARCH CENTER

whites and Blacks and Republicans and Democrats about whether US institutions and laws need to be completely rebuilt or whether necessary changes can be made by working within the current system. Only 18 percent of whites and 7 percent of Republicans agree that most US laws and institutions need to be completely rebuilt because they are fundamentally biased. Conversely, 58 percent of Blacks and 40 percent of Democrats support overhauling US institutions. Because white Americans and Republicans do not view race as a structural problem, they in turn do not see the value of promoting America's racial history or overhauling US laws and institutions. This is the danger of restricting knowledge. Americans are not on the same page, and therefore, cannot agree on our nation's basic values and collective vision for the future.

Taking issue with the sheer hypocrisy of America's constant refrain, "this is not who we are," Soraya Nadia McDonald argues that if we are "honest about the history of the United States, it prominently features white violence, terrorism and revanchism, particularly toward Black people, Indigenous people and women."[6]

Untangling the lie is more complex than ever before. Modes of communication have changed dramatically over the past twenty years, making it unlikely that Americans will acquire similar sources of knowledge and information. Gone are the days when most Americans listened to the legendary Walter Cronkite (whom opinion polls named the most trusted man in America) or accessed one of three channels for their news. Cronkite's signature line, "And that's the way it is," has given way to charges of fake news as algorithms spoon-feed Americans the information that most closely aligns with their political preferences. This very fact makes the battle for higher education all the more urgent. If right-wing nationalists have seemingly won the social media battle, higher education serves as the last stand for truth and the unobstructed pursuit of knowledge.

If faculty are hindered from pursuing knowledge according to their disciplinary expertise, the quest for knowledge will, unfortunately, be the purview of elected officials who lack competence and credentials and are not subject to the routine scrutiny of peer review, an evaluation, and vetting of knowledge by others conducting research in the same field.

Elected officials not only lack the disciplinary expertise of researchers in the field, but they also have divergent motivations. The life of an academic from graduate school to the attainment of full professor is circumscribed by evaluation. Elected officials, on the other hand, are motivated by a desire to be elected, which as recent elections have shown is less about telling the truth than telling the likely voter whatever story they may believe. In the 2022 midterm elections, at least 220 Republicans who cast doubt on or outright denied President Biden's legitimate victory were elected to positions throughout the political system, including the House and Senate, state legislature, governor, secretary of state, and attorney general.[7] Misinformation and disinformation challenge the ability of voters to discern fact from fiction, and thereby, have a deleterious effect on the prospects for American democracy. But it is those who are misinformed and disinformed who have become the targets of the right-wing assault on learning. As Jack Schwartz so eloquently argues, "The Republican Party appeals to a constituency of the aggrieved who fear not so much economic decline as social irrelevance. Consequently, they will do anything to stay in power. If they can save their country by subverting the democratic process, so be it. In their eyes, they are simply 'purifying' democracy by cleansing it of unsavory elements."[8]

A BATTLE FOR WHITE HEGEMONY

Although the battle is often presented as an innocuous disagreement about what should and should not be taught, the battle is, in fact, political and is about undermining legitimate claims on societal resources (the distribution of resources between the rich and poor—the powerful and powerless). As Paulo Freire has argued, education is never neutral but a political act designed to maintain the status quo or bring about social change.[9] Social change—the thing that the architects of the war on learning don't want—is deeply and irretrievably stymied by ignorance. If citizens cannot think critically, they are naturally subject to the whims of those in control. It is only logical that higher education is the principal terrain of this battle for minds.

Legislative restrictions on what can be taught have one common characteristic: an attempt to suppress knowledge and information about American racism and the historical experiences of marginalized people in their quest for equality. This convenient break from the past obscures understanding of the root causes of disproportionate poverty among traditionally underrepresented groups (African Americans, Latines, and Indigenous people) in the present. This allows conservative leaders to promulgate a lie that easily positions disaffected groups as alien and undeserving of the rewards of citizenship in a democratic society.

Legislative restrictions on what can be taught help to preserve the lie about America's original sin and promote racial dissonance among whites who overwhelming view America as a fair and equitable nation, where all people are created equal and endowed with certain unalienable rights—life, liberty, and the pursuit of happiness. But sadly, this has never been the America that we are. For most of its history, America has pursued oppressive policies against African Americans, Mexicans, and Native Americans, which have had cumulative effects on the life chances of these groups into the present period. From the appropriation of African labor and Mexican and Native American land to confinement in barrios, reservations, and urban ghettos, the true story of America has been one where discrimination abounds in all areas of life, from disproportionate treatment in the criminal justice system (profiling and arrest to conviction and incarceration) to underfunded education, inadequate healthcare and nutrition, discrimination in housing and employment, and all other indicators of societal well-being.

This is the story, told in the past and continuing into the present, that red state legislators would like to hide because telling the truth has tremendous implications for the American identity and the debt owed to traditionally underrepresented groups. As Dr. King proclaimed in 1963: "When the architects of our republic wrote the magnificent words of the Constitution and the Declaration of Independence, they were signing a promissory note to which every American was to fall heir. This note was a promise that all men—yes, Black men as well as white men—would be guaranteed the unalienable rights of life, liberty and the pursuit of happiness."

Overwhelmingly, white Republican state legislators would rather uphold the lie rather than pay the debt that would once and for all promote an equitable society. The clear and unvarnished truth would be a strike against the American identity and impose a demand for justice. Unmoored from the historical record, whites acquire a racial ambivalence that makes them unlikely to support policies and practices that seek to rectify past and continuing racial inequities. It is only in times of crisis when oppression is more unbridled and visible that whites are momentarily freed from racial dissonance and racial ambivalence. The media presentation of African Americans attacked by dogs and water-hosed during the civil rights movement or the murder of George Floyd during the COVID-19 pandemic very clearly demonstrated the vestiges of America's past, but unfortunately, a focus on enduring inequality is always short-lived due to the prominence and effectiveness of the ideological right's propaganda campaign.

White Americans are generally insulated from the experiences and perspectives of traditionally oppressed groups and therefore do not see the same reality even when it is in plain sight and is a part of the public record. In 2008 and 2009, for example, the House of Representatives and the Senate passed House Resolution 194 and Senate Concurrent Resolution 26, respectively, apologizing for slavery. Both resolutions painstakingly detail the horrors and resulting consequences of American slavery and, in the process, substantiate the arguments of critical race theory (CRT)—that racism is not merely the product of individual bias or prejudice but also systematically structured in governmental policies and practices that have had enduring social, economic, and political consequences down to the present. The voluminous House Resolution in part reads:

> Whereas after emancipation from 246 years of slavery, African-Americans soon saw the fleeting political, social, and economic gains they made during Reconstruction eviscerated by virulent racism, lynchings, disenfranchisement, Black Codes, and racial segregation laws that imposed a rigid system of officially sanctioned racial segregation in virtually all areas of life. . . . Whereas the system of de jure racial segregation known as Jim Crow, which arose in certain parts of the Nation following the Civil War to create separate and unequal societies for whites and African-Americans, was a direct result of the racism against persons of African descent engendered by slavery. . . . Whereas a century after the official end of slavery in America, Federal action was required during the 1960s to eliminate the dejure and defacto system of Jim Crow throughout parts of the Nation, though its vestiges still linger to this day. . . . Whereas African-Americans continue to suffer from the complex interplay between slavery and Jim Crow—long after both systems were formally abolished—through enormous damage and loss, both tangible and intangible, including the loss of human dignity, the frustration of careers and professional lives, and the long-term loss of income and opportunity.

In absolute contradiction to the current Republican-sponsored legislative bans on learning, the resolution cautions:

> Whereas the story of the enslavement and de jure segregation of African-Americans and the dehumanizing atrocities committed against them *should not be purged from or minimized in the telling of American history*. [Emphasis added]

The Senate Resolution, similar in tone and detail, adds one convenient disclaimer:

> Nothing in this resolution authorizes or supports any claim against the United States; or serves as a settlement of any claim against the United States.

Passage of the long-awaited House and Senate apologies for slavery was announced in newspapers with little fanfare and has since been hidden in plain sight. This is the story, legitimized in the halls of the US Congress, that the legislative bans do not want Americans to learn about. The shrouding of the truth bolsters the epistemology of ignorance, pitting whites against people of color and blinding them to their collective interests and thereby impeding their ability to resolve America's enduring challenges collectively. It is a simple truth that we will not resolve the class problem in America until we have resolved the race problem. As Heather McGhee argues in *The Sum of Us: What Racism Costs Everyone and How We Can Prosper Together*: "To this day, the wealthy and the powerful are still selling the zero-sum story for their own profit, hoping to keep people with much in common from making common cause with one another."[10] Zero-sum thinking encourages whites to view the world through a false prism of "them versus us," impeding societal rewards for the sum of us.

The African American quest for reparations aptly illustrates how an ahistorical perspective undermines attempts to reckon with the past. On April 14, 2021, the House Judiciary Committee voted to pass H.R. 40. This was a historic feat not accomplished since the late Rep. John Conyers (D-Michigan) first introduced H.R. 40 as a reparations bill in 1989. This latest iteration of the bill, introduced by Sheila Jackson Lee, sought to establish the Commission to Study and Develop Reparation Proposals for African Americans, to examine slavery and discrimination in the colonies and the United States from 1619 to the present and recommend appropriate remedies. Although H.R. 40 enjoyed support from 170 Democratic cosponsors and key congressional leaders, it ultimately faced stiff partisan opposition from 74 percent of Republicans, many from states that have passed education gag orders, and never made it to the floor for debate and consideration.

THE EFFECTS OF LEGISLATIVE RESTRICTIONS ON A DEMOCRATIC SOCIETY

A common axiom holds that democracy requires the eternal vigilance of an informed and educated citizenry. America's early leaders recognized the essential connection between education and democracy. As Thomas Jefferson asserted in a letter to Virginia legislator Charles Yancey in 1816, "If a nation expects to be ignorant and free in a state of civilization, it expects what never was and never will be."[11] To be sure, freedom within the confines of ignorance is an impossibility.

An educated mind is essential to the preservation of democracy. Citizens cannot be both free and simultaneously entangled by authoritarian instincts about what to think and how to think. Regarding the centrality of education to democracy, Senator Michael Bennet (D-Colorado) notes that "with education, the common everyday person [is] able to select leaders wisely and fight back against the tyrannical instincts of those in power."[12] This view is in line with John Dewey, widely heralded as the father of modern education. According to Dewey:

> The devotion of democracy to education is a familiar fact. The superficial explanation is that a government resting upon popular suffrage cannot be successful unless those who elect and who obey their governors are educated. Since a democratic society repudiates the principle of external authority, it must find a substitute in voluntary disposition and interest; these can be created only by education. But there is a deeper explanation. A democracy is more than a form of government; it is primarily a mode of associated living, of conjoint communicated experience. The extension in space of the

number of individuals who participate in an interest so that each has to refer [their] own action to that of others, and to consider the action of others to give point and direction to [their] own, is equivalent to the breaking down of those barriers of class, race, and national territory which kept [people] from perceiving the full import of their activity.[13]

For Dewey, education served as a training ground for democratic citizens in America, representing an engagement on equal terms, from student to teacher and citizen and elected official. As Dewey asserted, citizen engagement in the governing process is impracticable without the accountability inferred by each having to "refer [their] own action to that of others, and to consider the action of others to give point and direction to [their] own."

Nearly forty years ago, the *Nation at Risk* report alerted Americans about the dangers of ignorance to a democratic society:

The people of the United States need to know that individuals in our society who do not possess the levels of skill, literacy, and training essential to this new era will be effectively disenfranchised, not simply from the material rewards that accompany competent performance, but also from the chance to participate fully in our national life. A high level of shared education is essential to a free, democratic society and to the fostering of a common culture, especially in a country that prides itself on pluralism and individual freedom.[14]

James J. Harvey, primary author of the report, argued that "the educational foundations of our society are presently being eroded by a rising tide of mediocrity that threatens our very future as a Nation and a people." Further, he said, "If an unfriendly foreign power had attempted to impose on America the mediocre educational performance that exists today, we might well have viewed it as an act of war."[15]

The irony of the *Nation at Risk* report was that although it rightly warned of the risk of mediocre education to American democracy, it was supported by then president Ronald Reagan and the ideological right and subsequently formed the basis of nearly forty years of education reform that has further undermined equitable educational outcomes by insisting that states raise standards without a concomitant investment in resources. Nonetheless, Harvey was correct: a war it is, but one fought internally to control societal resources on behalf of the powerful few at the expense of the whole.

Education is inextricably linked to the promises of democracy and has been the staging site for numerous battles over the right to learn. As Jaroslav Pelikan argues, "The most important legal step forward in civil rights since the Emancipation Proclamation and the Fourteenth Amendment . . . dealt not with jobs or with the ballot box . . . but with the schools.[16] For members of historically marginalized groups, schooling has served as a vehicle of socioeconomic mobility and an expansion of constitutional democracy.

This fact was critical to Thurgood Marshall's dissent in *San Antonio Independent School District v. Rodriguez*, the 1973 ruling that education was not a fundamental right afforded protection in the Constitution and it was up to state legislatures to determine how public schools were funded. Speaking in defense of poor Mexican plaintiffs' right to an equitable education, Marshall argued that the US Constitution affords all Americans the right to education, which made Texas's public education finance system unconstitutional:

> In my judgment, the right of every American to an equal start in life, so far as the provision of a state service as important as education is concerned, is far too vital to permit state discrimination on grounds as tenuous as those presented by this record. Nor can I accept the notion that it is sufficient to remit these appellees to the vagaries of the political process which, contrary to the majority's suggestion, has proved singularly unsuited to the task of providing a remedy for this discrimination. I, for one, am unsatisfied with the hope of an ultimate "political" solution sometime in the indefinite future while, in the meantime, countless children unjustifiably receive inferior educations that "may affect their hearts and minds in a way unlikely ever to be undone." I must therefore respectfully dissent.[17]

The critical goal of democratizing American society places responsibility on schools to advance critical thinking and democratic participation in the political system. Among the early goals of public schooling was to prepare people to vote wisely and protect the freedom of American democracy, to promote cultural unity by uniting a diverse population and transmitting a common language and culture—a sense of what it means to be an American—and to assist people in becoming economically self-sufficient by giving all Americans the basic literacy and arithmetic skills they need to succeed in the workplaces of the nation.[18] These are goals that educational gag orders would like to subvert. Although education is inextricably linked to democracy, it is also inextricably linked to politics and economics and has been parceled out inequitably to maintain the racial status quo, assigning racial minorities to the least rewarding positions. This is the aspect of education that the ideological right wants to preserve.

THE EFFECTS OF LEGISLATIVE RESTRICTIONS ON HIGHER EDUCATION: WHAT IS TO BE DONE

This current moment is a critical inflection point in American higher education. The battle for the mind is being waged across America at a time when faculty at higher education institutions are least prepared to fight. Contingent faculty employment increased from 43 percent of all faculty employment to 63 percent between 1975 and 2005 and to 65 percent of all faculty employment by 2014. As tenured lines have stagnated, contingent lines have risen, particularly at doctoral degree-granting universities.[19]

The exponential growth of contingent faculty (faculty off the tenure track) has led to a weakening of the tenure system and the corresponding protections of academic freedom, the freedom of teachers, students, and academic institutions to pursue knowledge wherever it may lead, without undue or unreasonable interference. Faculty lost or, more accurately, conceded considerable ground that led to the proliferation of contingent faculty. Faculty must draw a line in the sand now, lest they face the end of the academic freedom afforded by the tenure system.

With the rise of contingency, faculty are acutely aware that their term of employment is tenuous and, therefore, are more likely to avoid political conflict inherent in teaching what has been termed "divisive concepts." This is particularly the case in conservative states, the primary sources of legislative gag orders governing what may be taught. Although tenured faculty represent the most logical vanguard to preserve the right to learn, their numbers are thinning at a moment when the faculty voice is most critically needed. This very fact creates an imperative for faculty—both tenure and non-tenure track—to mobilize their ranks and more effectively utilize the resources of educational institutions like the American Association of University Professors (AAUP) and teachers' unions such as the American Federation of Teachers (AFT) and the National Education Association (NEA). There is no other way to fight for the soul of American education. In fact, the recent merger of the AAUP and the AFT could not have occurred at a more propitious time. The ideological right's commitment to ignorance must be met head-on, with a commitment to ensuring that all Americans have a right to learn. But for this to occur, American educational institutions must clearly understand what is at stake. As noted above, education is a political act, designed either to retain the status quo (antidemocratic) or bring about social change (democratic). Educational institutions must comprehend unequivocally that neutrality is a bias in favor of the status quo, and to the extent that it tends to the hobbled craft of teaching by staying above the political fray, it is complicit in furthering ignorance and a retreat from democracy. As Richard Shaull argues in his foreword to Paulo Freire's seminal *Pedagogy of the Oppressed*:

> There is no such thing as a neutral educational process. Education either functions as an instrument that is used to facilitate the integration of the younger generation into the logic of the present system and bring about conformity to it, or it becomes "the practice of freedom," the means by which men and women deal critically and creatively with reality and discover how to participate in the transformation of the world.[20]

The truth of the matter is that predominantly white colleges and universities have never been a crystal stair for academics of color. They have been chilly places where the quest for diversity, equity, and inclusion (DEI) has ebbed and flowed in value and importance to the vast majority of white faculty and administrators. However, this latest assault on education represents a key and important opportunity for interest convergence. It is high time for faculty who profess a value and commitment to DEI and academic freedom to unite.

The battle for the integrity of American educational institutions must be taken to American living rooms to denounce the agenda of the ideological right and to uphold the search for knowledge, wherever that search leads. The fate of American education must be a fixture of campaign debates and the presidential election cycle in 2024. To command that type of attention, faculty, teachers, educational institutions, and nonprofits like PEN America dedicated to free expression must mobilize the participation and resources of entertainers and other influential leaders. Progressive activists like members of Historians for Peace and Democracy (H-PAD) must counter the Right's legislative campaign with a right-to-learn campaign that seeks to pass counter legislation that commits to learning the real and unvarnished truth about American history. Unfortunately, small organizations like H-PAD, in dire need of resources, are ill-equipped to undertake such a critical campaign. Those who are committed to democracy must support such vital organizations.

Today, academic administrators are under tremendous pressure to conform to the dictates of conservative state legislators. No longer are they bound by institutional vision or a grand educational mission. They are compelled by the bottom line—dollars and cents, which state legislatures control. Faculty must counter legislative control by placing pressure on academic administrators to live up to the mission of education in a democracy. This is what the faculty senate resolution campaign is about: a recommitment to academic freedom and the right to learn, thereby disrupting the American epistemology of ignorance.

PART II

White Rage, Twisted Laws, and Patriarchal Control

5

Knowledge and Good Community Organizing Can Counter the "Divisive Concepts" Campaign

KEVIN MCGRUDER

I N 2021, THE MOVEMENT AGAINST the purported teaching of critical race theory in K–12 schools and public colleges dominated public discussions in many communities and resulted in the passage of legislation against the teaching of "divisive concepts" in many states. It is a matter of public record that the controversy is a manufactured one, a masterful disinformation campaign to silence advocates of anti-racism strategies. Still, the divisive concepts controversy, while frustrating in its distortion of the facts, provides educators with teachable moments to share information with students and the larger community that draws on scholarly work to answer the questions about why this is happening now and why the right-wing campaign against teaching the truth about America's past has been so effective. Those interested in ensuring that a comprehensive knowledge of US history and contemporary issues is available to all students can use these insights to develop more effective strategies to counter the divisive concepts campaign. Efforts to limit what students can learn are still ongoing and, if not addressed, will reverse the successful first steps made toward dismantling institutional racism and anti-LGBTQ policies, goals that seemed possible as recently as 2020.[1]

HOW WAS THE DIVISIVE CONCEPTS LEGISLATIVE CAMPAIGN IMPLEMENTED?

The divisive concepts campaign was fueled by the distortion of the meaning of critical race theory. That theory is a framework for considering the legal barriers to the eradication of US racism. It was developed in the 1970s and 1980s by legal scholars such as Derrick Bell, Kimberlé Crenshaw, Richard

79

Delgado, and others in response to what they saw as a loss of momentum following the civil rights legal victories of the 1950s and 1960s. These legal scholars sought to answer the question: Why was racism so enduring despite those victories? They acknowledged the progress represented by *Brown v. Board of Education* and the civil rights legislation that followed, but they also identified the various ways other laws viewed as neutral policies incorporated the vestiges of racism. These critical race theorists concluded that eradication of racism in our society required a recognition of its institutional history and an acknowledgment of the influence of its legacy on contemporary laws, policies, and practices. They noted that while the law can be a vehicle for achieving racial equity, it has often been a vehicle for maintaining racial hierarchy, with people of color at the bottom and white people at the top, a hierarchy that the civil rights movement sought to eradicate. Critical race theorists believed that once scholars and activists understood how structural racism operated, they could develop a plan to dismantle it.[2]

How did a forty-year-old legal theory suddenly become controversial? The divisive concepts campaign was conceived and promoted by the conservative activist Christopher Rufo. From July 2020 through December 2020 in three articles in *City Journal*, the online magazine of the conservative think tank the Manhattan Institute, Rufo disparaged workplace diversity trainings as a "racial justice shakedown" and branded them with a broad brush as teaching critical race theory.[3] He asserted that their purpose was to promote "toxic principles of critical race theory, race essentialism, and neo-segregationism."

Rufo's campaign was amplified by an online workshop, Against Critical Race Theory's Onslaught: Reclaiming Education and the American Dream, presented by the conservative American Legislative Exchange Council (ALEC) in December 2020, that insisted critical race theory was a threat to K–12 education. ALEC then disseminated sample legislation to state lawmakers across the country, prohibiting the teaching of "divisive concepts" at the K–12 and college levels.[4] By the spring of 2021, divisive concepts legislation was introduced in several state legislatures, while local school boards were inundated with complaints from parents concerned about the teaching of critical race theory. In a Twitter post around that time, Rufo confirmed how the demonization of the forty-year-old critical race theory had been accomplished:

> The goal is to have the public read something crazy in the newspaper and immediately think "critical race theory." We have decodified the term and will recodify it to annex the entire range of cultural constructions that are unpopular with Americans.[5]

WHY DID THE DIVISIVE CONCEPTS CAMPAIGN BEGIN IN 2020?

To understand why the divisive concepts controversy occurred in 2020, we must place it within its historical context. The disinformation campaign that Christopher Rufo fueled is part of a long tradition in the United States of organizing backlashes against the possibility of achieving racial equity. On paper, we are a multiracial democracy, but in practice, we are a country in which some white citizens expect to maintain a dominant voice and where the possibility of sharing power with citizens of color is seen as a threat to their power and privilege.

The years following the 2014 police murder of Michael Brown in Ferguson, Missouri, and the killings by police of other unarmed Black people, including Eric Garner, John Crawford III, Breonna Taylor, and George Floyd, led to a revival and expansion of the Black Lives Matter movement for racial equity. That movement began after the 2012 murder of teenager Trayvon Martin by Florida neighborhood watchman George Zimmerman. The revived multiracial and multigenerational movement was national, with demonstrations in big cities and small towns. Its breadth created expectations that perhaps this time real change would occur.[6]

The 2019 publication of Ibram X. Kendi's *How to Be an Antiracist* brought the concept of anti-racism to a wider audience. Rufo conflated anti-racism with critical race theory. Although anti-racism as a framework intersects with critical race theory, it is a broader concept: in an environment in which racism is perpetuated by laws, policies, and institutional practices, not being racist is not enough to end racism. Instead, collective, sustained action is required to identify and dismantle policies and institutional practices that maintain the racial hierarchy.[7]

The 2019 publication of the essays comprising Nikole Hannah-Jones's "The 1619 Project" by the *New York Times* challenged the dominant historical narrative of the United States by framing that story from the perspective of the enslaved and their descendants. The systemic racism highlighted by "The 1619 Project" complemented the 2020 demands of Black Lives Matter protesters for anti-racist strategies to eradicate systemic racism. "The 1619 Project" reached the general public, a much broader audience than that of academic texts highlighting similar perspectives. When plans were announced to publish a version of the project for K–12 classrooms, a vilification campaign against "The 1619 Project," and Nikole Hannah-Jones personally, gained momentum.[8]

Introducing "The 1619 Project" into the K–12 curriculum came as a threat to those who consider the US education system a place where students should receive a uniformly positive view of the nation. Since their establishment in the late 1700s, public schools are where students develop skills but also prepare themselves for American citizenship. Citizenship has included an understanding of our system of government, as well as an implicit mission to promote patriotism, or love of country. This latter goal led to the crafting of a dominant historical narrative of the United States that highlights positive themes and minimizes or, in many cases, ignores atrocities and other less than admirable events. By accurately placing the founding of our Anglo-American nation with the 1607 founding of the Jamestown colony and highlighting the year 1619 as the colony's first step toward the creation of the institution of slavery, Nikole Hannah-Jones disrupted the narrative that most Americans received in elementary school. That older story linked our nation's founding to the 1620 arrival of the Pilgrims on the *Mayflower* in Plymouth, Massachusetts. By inaccurately identifying the founding of our nation with New England, this version could highlight the commendable quest of the Pilgrims for religious freedom, though it failed to explain that this freedom also involved prohibiting practices that strayed from theirs.[9]

It is important to remember that the backlash against critical race theory and "The 1619 Project" is only the most recent manifestation against attempts to improve the lives of Black Americans. Carol Anderson describes this history in *White Rage: The Unspoken Truth of Our Racial Divide*, noting:

The trigger for white rage, inevitably, is black advancement. It is not the mere presence of black people that is the problem; rather it is blackness with ambition, with drive, with purpose, with aspirations, and with demands for full and equal citizenship.[10]

The current backlash represented by the divisive concepts campaign can be placed in historical context by considering other backlashes of the past. During the early years of the United States, most states restricted voting to male property owners. In the 1820s, most states rewrote their constitutions to eliminate property qualifications for voting. They were responding to the growth in the proportion of white men unable to meet the property-based voting requirements and to changes in the social structure of the population toward a less hierarchical society. Under the new constitutions, almost all white men gained the vote. At the same time, many of these same states introduced voting restrictions for Black men in order to ensure their political and social subordination, regardless of their wealth.[11]

During the Reconstruction period that followed the Civil War, Black men again gained the vote, first when the former Confederate states were required to rewrite their constitutions and provide for Black male voting in order to return to the Union. Responding to the erratic implementation of this policy, the Fifteenth Amendment to the Constitution in 1870 gave Black men the vote nationally. The result of these changes was the election of Black men: two to the US Senate (Blanche Bruce and Hiram Revels in Mississippi), sixteen to the US House of Representatives, and hundreds to state and local offices. This Black participation in the democratic process fueled a backlash of violence, motivated by the claim that such electoral successes were the first step toward "Negro domination" and racial "amalgamation." The newly formed Ku Klux Klan and other secret organizations, as well as individuals, unleashed a reign of terror in southern states targeting Black people, their allies, and their churches and schools. By the 1880s, Black voting was virtually nonexistent in the South. Eighty years of racial segregation, accompanied by racial violence to maintain it, followed.[12]

The modern civil rights movement of the 1950s and 1960s strove to achieve the racial equity denied to Black people since the end of Reconstruction. But these victories outlawing discrimination in public accommodations, employment, and voting were followed by the migration of many white Southern Democrats to the Republican Party. Adopting what became known as the "Southern strategy," Richard Nixon framed his 1968 presidential campaign as a quest for "law and order" that would deal with Black civil disturbances and white anti-war protesters. The 1970s War on Drugs, employing long mandatory-minimum prison sentences, targeted Black and Latine people and ushered in the era of mass incarceration. Black and Latine communities and families were disrupted while the overwhelming majority of white people, who used illegal substances at the same rate as Black people, research has shown, were unaffected by the laws.[13] The 1980 election of Ronald Reagan to the presidency, made possible in part by racializing public benefits through his denunciation of a Black "welfare queen" and other rhetoric, solidified the anti-Black perspective and policies of many conservative politicians.[14]

Barack Obama's unexpected 2008 election as president unleashed another wave of backlashes. Donald Trump led a sustained campaign claiming that Obama was born in Kenya and, therefore, not eligible to serve as president. The fact that there was a relatively large, receptive audience for this claim helped move Trump from minor television star to legitimate political candidate. Obama's presidency was also accompanied by a rise in white nationalism, consistent with the historical trend identified above wherein Black achievement is followed by assertions of white supremacy. This rise continued after Barack Obama left office, colliding with anti-racist initiatives to remove a Confederate statue in Charlottesville, Virginia, where a white nationalist killed white counterprotester Heather Heyer at the 2017 Unite the Right rally.[15]

The run-up to the 2020 presidential election was accompanied by legislation that restricted the vote in several states with large Black populations. In spite of voter restrictions, get-out-the-vote efforts for the presidential election resulted in record Black turnout and the election of Joseph Biden. Viewing Biden as an advocate for the issues relevant to people of color, his Republican opponents mounted challenges to the election results that precipitated the invasion of the Capitol on January 6. Other tactics denying the election outcome continue to this day.[16] The current divisive concepts campaign, like the backlashes to successful movements toward racial equity outlined above, isn't about critical race theory or divisive concepts; it is about a much larger issue—an age-old fear of sharing power and privilege with Black and Brown people.

WHAT CAN BE DONE TO COUNTER THE DIVISIVE CONCEPTS CAMPAIGN?

Many organizations are countering divisive concepts legislation by targeting the legislation directly and by attempting to influence the court of public opinion. In 2020, the NAACP Legal Defense Fund, representing the National Urban League and the National Fair Housing Alliance, filed a class action suit in US district court to strike down President Trump's Executive Order 13950 prohibiting discussion of divisive concepts in workplace trainings. In one of his first actions as president, Joe Biden revoked that order. The American Civil Liberties Union (ACLU) is challenging divisive concepts legislation at the state level. In New Hampshire, it filed a case on behalf of the National Education Association in federal district court in December 2021, challenging the state's "Banned Concepts" act. The grounds for the case included claims that the act's provisions are vague and that even education lawyers are unclear as to what it bans. The American Federation of Teachers filed another legal challenge in New Hampshire that same month. In Florida, in November 2022, the ACLU successfully challenged Florida's Stop the Wrongs to Our Kids and Employees (WOKE) Act, which "limited the ways concepts related to systemic racism and sex discrimination can be discussed in teaching or conducting training in workplaces or schools."[17] The ACLU argued that by restricting instructors from teaching and students from learning certain viewpoints, the law violated the First and Fourteenth Amendments. Legal challenges are underway in other states, among them Arizona and Oklahoma, with decisions in several cases pending.[18]

Scholars for a New Deal for Higher Education, formed in 2021 through a collaboration among the American Association of University Professors (AAUP), the American Federation of Teachers, and the Roosevelt Institute, seeks to increase federal funding support for higher education, reduce student education debt, and reclaim higher education as a public good. The organization's work includes advocating for the reauthorization of the Higher Education Act of 1965, writing articles on divisive concepts legislation in order to mobilize challenges among educators and allies, and organizing roundtables advocating increased federal funding of higher education. In 2021, PEN America, the organization of writers and writing professionals, joined with the AAUP and the American Association of Colleges and Universities to issue a statement denouncing "educational gag orders" as threats to free speech. PEN America's ongoing focus issues include disinformation, campus free speech, educational censorship, book bans, and free expression and education, all areas intersecting with the goals of the divisive concepts campaign.[19]

Other organizations are linking progressive educational policy with community-based action. In June 2022, the Zinn Education Project, Black Lives Matter at School, and the African American Policy Forum organized Teach Truth Action rallies in more than twenty-five states as part of a campaign designed to directly counter the divisive concepts campaign.[20] The organizers represent a larger network of groups that are working to meet the divisive concepts campaign with a clear counternarrative directed at students, parents, and families. Named after Howard Zinn, author of the popular textbook *A People's History of the United States*, the Zinn Education Project continues Zinn's work by introducing students "to a more accurate, complex, and engaging understanding of United States history than is found in traditional textbooks and curricula."[21] Its curricular campaigns, such as Teach the Black Freedom Struggle and Teach Reconstruction, provide a counternarrative to the version of US history promoted by divisive concepts advocates. The Zinn Education Project is coordinated by two other nonprofit organizations, Rethinking Schools and Teaching for Change. Rethinking Schools calls itself "a nonprofit publisher and advocacy organization dedicated to sustaining and strengthening public education through social justice teaching and education activism."[22] Teaching for Change encourages teachers and students to draw direct connections to real world issues "to question and re-think the world inside and outside their classrooms; build a more equitable, multicultural society; and become active global citizens."[23] Its programs include professional development, publications, and parent organizing. The other two organizers of the June 2022 Teach Truth rallies advocate for issues particularly relevant to Black people. Black Lives Matter at School is "a national coalition organizing for racial justice in education" that not only participated in the Teach Truth rallies but also holds an annual Week of Action in the first week of February.[24] The African American Policy Forum (AAPF) is a think tank that "connects academics, activists and policy-makers to promote efforts to dismantle structural inequality [by using] new ideas and innovative perspectives to transform public discourse and policy."[25] Its initiatives include the podcast *Intersectionality Matters*, with cofounder and critical race theorist Kimberlé Crenshaw, and the publication of *Black Girls Matter: Pushed Out, Overpoliced, and Underprotected.* The faculty senate resolution campaign, discussed in other chapters in this volume, also originated with the AAPF.

Despite the substantial work being done by many organizations to promote a progressive approach to education and counter the divisive concepts campaign at the grassroots and policy levels, it is clear that messaging about these efforts has not broken through nationally in any way comparable to that of the divisive concepts campaign. A search of the online database Newspapers.com illustrates what the divisive concepts campaign has been able to accomplish in a few short years, and the challenge facing a counter-narrative campaign such as Teach Truth. A keyword search from January 2018 to December 2019 using the phrase "divisive concepts" results in four articles. But searching from January 2021 to December 2022 results in 1,243 articles, illustrating the very effective work of Christopher Rufo and the conservative information network that amplified his message in the press and through state-level legislation. A similar keyword search from January 2018 to December 2019 using the phrase "teach truth" results in 184 articles, suggesting that the Teach Truth concept had a head start on the divisive concepts campaign at that time. But continuing the search for the period of January 2021 to December 2022 results in 397 articles, illustrating that, in spite of good grassroots and policy work, the Teach Truth campaign has substantial work to do to influence public opinion nationally.[26]

The organizations doing such important work to promote progressive education messages can ensure that their work is known and supported by a much wider segment of the population nationally by drawing on well-developed strategies of successful grassroots campaigns of the past. Before entering academia, I worked for over two decades in the field of affordable housing development and in HIV-prevention service provision. Much of this work was aided by collaborations with community organizers who worked with ordinary people to develop campaigns to achieve their goals. An important part of community organizing is developing strategic communication initiatives, ranging from hyperlocal to national campaigns. The work of the AIDS Coalition to Unleash Power (ACT UP) to push the federal government to expedite HIV medication availability in the 1980s and 1990s is an example of effective community organizing linked to national strategic communication efforts. In ACT UP chapters across the country, rallies, "die-ins," and iconic messaging, such as "Silence=Death" to encourage government officials and individuals to speak about HIV and AIDS, generated substantial media coverage that put pressure on officials to take action.[27]

The organizations working to create a counternarrative to the divisive concepts campaign mentioned in this chapter need to consider collaborating to develop a coordinated and coherent strategic media plan that would use all media formats to report on their work, prevent duplication and contradiction of messages, illustrate the broad support that they have, and amplify their messages. A start would be to brand the various policy and grassroots campaigns mentioned above under one phrase, such as "Teach Truth." The phrase "divisive concepts" serves this purpose for their adversaries.

The Teach Truth campaign could broaden its base of support and the visibility of their perspective in the national public discourse by expanding their work to what is sometimes called the "movable middle." These are people who do not have a strong opinion on the topic of divisive concepts and are open to considering the Teach Truth perspective. For example, by sending community organizers to some conservative areas in a sustained way, Teach Truth advocates could identify parents, teachers, administrators, and students who do not agree with the prevailing divisive concepts discourse but feel isolated and therefore are reluctant to speak out. Organizing these likeminded people could lead to Teach Truth events in communities that previously were thought to be uniformly supportive of divisive concepts legislation. Similar tactics could be used, possibly in collaboration with the State Innovation Exchange, a national network supporting progressive state legislators, to organize those who do not support divisive concepts legislation already passed or being considered in various states. The result of this organizing could lead to additional legal challenges to divisive concepts laws as well as to increased financial and legislative support for public education in the states. This work would attract media coverage in ways that Teach Truth's and other organizations' current activities have not.[28]

CONCLUSION

In 1805, President Thomas Jefferson wrote a letter to Virginia congressman Littleton Waller Tazewell regarding the legislature's deliberations over establishing the school that became the University of Virginia. In his letter, Jefferson noted the importance of township schools, also under consideration at the time, that could prepare students for higher education. He envisioned that these schools would be places where "such a degree of learning [would be] given to every member of the society as will enable him to read, to judge and to vote understandingly on what is passing."[29] An important message in countering the divisive concepts campaign is making the case that if that campaign is successful on a national basis, the educational gag orders would usher in generations of uninformed students. The message of Teach Truth and other progressive advocates for teaching accurate historical information is what is needed in a multiracial democracy. But the divisive concepts campaign has overwhelmed the Teach Truth perspective in the court of public opinion, demonstrating that presenting accurate information—knowledge alone—is not enough to overcome it. The initiatives to counter the divisive concepts campaign must be accompanied by the skillful use of community organizing, collaborative work between allied organizations, and the strategic use of media. Those who adopt effective strategies in using knowledge to assemble and wield power will be able to use it to determine the knowledge that our children acquire.

6

Subverting the Intent of the Fourteenth Amendment

DENNIS PARKER

C ONSERVATIVE JUDGES, ATTORNEYS GENERAL, politicians, and think-tank pundits claim that the Fourteenth Amendment makes concepts such as critical race theory unconstitutional, and therefore, they should be banned. This is in keeping with earlier efforts to attack affirmative action and other racial justice efforts. The claim is that the Fourteenth Amendment mandates "colorblindness," but this is a perversion of the amendment and its purpose. The historical context of the amendment is being willfully erased to further the partisan attack on racial justice in higher education.

In an oft-repeated statement about the misuses of history, the philosopher George Santayana warned that "[t]hose who cannot remember the past are condemned to repeat it." The serious consequences of ignoring history have been worsened by the right-wing efforts in the United States to not only ignore history but to suppress and even twist it in the service of racial inequality and inequity. Among the most egregious examples of this perversion of history are state legislative efforts to restrict teaching about race in K–12 schools and the repeated attacks on affirmative action. The arguments behind these attacks repeatedly invoke the Fourteenth Amendment, arguing that teaching about race and the limited use of racial categories in admissions violate the alleged colorblindness of the amendment. This is particularly ironic given the fact that the Fourteenth Amendment was specifically adopted to address the deeply entrenched discrimination against Black people both before and after emancipation under the Thirteenth Amendment.

In *Educational Gag Orders: Legislative Restrictions on the Freedom to Read, Learn, and Teach*, PEN America reports that in 2021 alone, twenty-four state legislatures introduced fifty-four separate bills "intended to restrict teaching and training in K–12 schools, higher education, and state agencies and institutions."[1] The majority of the legislation is directed toward discussions of the roles of race and gender in American history. The report quotes historian and writer Jelani Cobb describing the attacks on critical race theory as "an attempt to discredit the literature millions of people sought out last year to understand how George Floyd wound up dead on a street corner. The goal is to leave the next dead black person inexplicable by history."[2]

Heaping insult on injury, proponents of efforts to repress racial history have suggested that the bans are *required* by the Fourteenth Amendment. In a May 27, 2021, opinion, the Montana attorney general stated, "[M]any of the activities undertaken in the name of CRT . . . are violations of the Equal Protection Clause of the Fourteenth Amendment to the Constitution."[3] The fact that all of these attacks misconstrue the teaching that they condemn is less important than the potential long-term impact of those attacks. The attacks occur against a backdrop of repeated judicial challenges against affirmative action in higher education, despite the Supreme Court's repeated endorsement of the careful consideration of race in efforts to increase diversity. This chapter considers how the invocation of the Fourteenth Amendment in those attacks on teaching the truth erodes the meaning of that amendment and could potentially lead to exacerbating inequality in education from K–12 to higher education.

Generations of Brown and Black parents, themselves denied equal educational opportunity, have urged their children to fight for the best education possible because education is something, as the saying goes, *they can't take away from you*. The US Supreme Court echoed that view of education's paramount importance in *Brown v. Board of Education of Topeka*, its landmark case striking down racial segregation in schools, when it stated that it "is doubtful that any child may reasonably be expected to succeed in life if he is denied the opportunity for an education."[4] *Brown* represents an example of the way that the Fourteenth Amendment to the Constitution has been a tool to address the nation's long and shameful history of racial segregation.

Since its ratification on July 19, 1868, the Fourteenth Amendment has been a powerful tool in fighting inequity and inequality.

Recently, though, the Fourteenth Amendment has been invoked as a way to perpetuate deeply entrenched inequality and white supremacy. This harmful application of the amendment has generally been the result of the subversion of its purpose. The primary way of twisting its purpose has been by subverting its aim of eliminating the oppression of historically subjugated minorities and substituting that goal with a neutral "race blind" alternative that often serves only to cause or perpetuate oppression. This is achieved by erasing historical context while simultaneously denying existing inequality in the country's racial landscape. That erasure and blindness to prevailing inequality informed the Supreme Court's late nineteenth-century *Plessy v. Ferguson* decision upholding the pernicious and hypocritical doctrine of "separate but equal." It continues to drive efforts attacking affirmative action in the present through the misleading and damaging contention that the purpose of the Fourteenth Amendment was to create a system of "colorblindness" in relation to issues of race and ethnicity. This contention seeks to transform a weapon in the fight against injustice into a tool to perpetuate discrimination.

The blindness that courts and conservative activists advocate is, in fact, contrary to the express purpose of the Fourteenth Amendment and is, in reality, blind only to the pervasive role of race in continued subordination in the United States. In fact, the pervading purpose of the Fourteenth Amendment was to eliminate the prevailing oppression of recently emancipated enslaved people and to provide them equality of opportunity.[5] The Fourteenth Amendment was not enacted in a vacuum but was passed to address the uncertainty left after the Thirteenth Amendment freed enslaved people but left open the question of their status as US citizens. This silence on status was all the more problematic, given the Supreme Court's earlier holding in *Dred Scott v. Sanford*, which denied the right of American citizenship to all Black people, free or enslaved.

Consider the legislation being considered and passed at the time of the amendment's ratification. During this period, Congress enacted a series of explicitly race-conscious programs to fight past and ongoing forms of racial discrimination. This legislation, distinctly not "colorblind," was aimed at eliminating the specific injuries that Black people faced. Such legislation included the creation of the Freedmen's Bureau, special assistance for Black veterans, and special relief to Blacks in the District of Columbia. Although some members of Congress were opposed to such clear intent to assist Black people, proponents of the Freedmen's Bureau Act argued successfully for the need for race-conscious programs. With the shared understanding that the bill was race conscious, Congress passed it twice—and overrode a presidential veto by a sizable majority. As pointed out by the most recent addition to the Supreme Court, Ketanji Brown Jackson, in her spirited defense of race consciousness in the enforcement of the Voting Rights Act, the Fourteenth Amendment, in addition to building on the Freedmen and related acts designed to assist the newly emancipated, provided a constitutional foundation for the Civil Rights Act of 1866, which "specifically stated that . . . Black citizens would have the same [civil rights] as the white citizens."[6]

These acts formed the backdrop for the drafting, debate, and eventual adoption of the Fourteenth Amendment. Not only would Congress have been aware of the race-conscious features of acts like the Freedmen's Bureau Act and the Civil Rights Act of 1866, but it is clear that the intent of the Fourteenth Amendment was to provide a constitutional foundation for them. As stated by legal historian Jacobus tenBroek, "The one point upon which historians of the Fourteenth Amendment agree and, indeed, which the evidence places beyond cavil, is that the Fourteenth Amendment was designed to place the constitutionality of the Freedmen's Bureau and civil rights bills . . . beyond doubt."[7]

Despite Congress's good intentions in enacting the Fourteenth Amendment, its purposes began to be undercut in the nineteenth century, not long after the nation abandoned the post–Civil War Reconstruction efforts. In his *Regents of the University of California v. Bakke* opinion, Justice Marshall bemoaned a series of cases that "whittled away a great part of the authority presumably given the government for protection of civil rights."[8] First, the Supreme Court struck down federal law prohibiting racial discrimination in public accommodations in the *Civil Rights Cases* and then, in *Plessy v. Ferguson*, struck a blow that would set back the struggle for civil rights for decades and help solidify the era of Jim Crow segregation that would prevail for much of the twentieth century—and whose broader impacts persist into the twenty-first.

Like modern efforts to twist the Fourteenth Amendment into a tool that would perpetuate white supremacy and thwart attempts to achieve true equality, the court in *Plessy* distorted the racial landscape of its time and tried to impose a benign neutrality on a practice with roots firmly planted in slavery. In its decision upholding racial segregation in railway cars, the court distinguished between social inequalities (segregation) and formal equality, stating that the Fourteenth Amendment was not meant "to enforce social, as distinguished from political equality." The court went on to say that legislatures and courts did not have the authority to eliminate social differences and that "if the two races are to meet upon terms of social equality, it must be the result of natural affinities, a mutual appreciation of each other's merits, and a voluntary consent of individuals."[9] In an extraordinary act of judicial gaslighting that attributed any sense of stigmatization experienced by Black people resulting from segregation laws as being a result of their own biased preconceptions, the court catalogs some of the many ways in which strict separation had long been accepted in the United States including education, public accommodations, and marriage, and then states that if Black people felt that strict racial segregation was a vestige and badge of slavery, that belief was the mistake of *Black* people's inability to appreciate actual circumstances: "[T]he assumption that the enforced separation of the two races stamps the colored race with a badge of inferiority . . . is not by reason of anything found in the act but solely because the colored race chooses to put that construction upon it."[10] Furthering its own disingenuous reasoning, the court insisted that evidence of the neutrality of legally imposed segregation was demonstrated by the fact that those laws restricted white people as well as Black from sitting in cars designated for members of the other race.

Not unlike the current legislation being proposed and passed in order to preempt honest conversations about race in education, the hypocrisy of the *Plessy* court majority's blindness to the actual roots of racial segregation was clear even at the time the decision was rendered. In his dissenting opinion, Justice John Marshall Harlan pointed out the obvious:

Everyone knows that the statute in question had its origin in the purpose
not so much to exclude white persons from railroad cars occupied by

blacks as to exclude colored people from coaches occupied by or assigned to white persons.

Harlan's dissent was informed by the fact that the statutes in question were not neutral ones whose effects were experienced equally by all but were meant to exclude and label as inferior Black people. That fact was evidenced by history and the contemporary impact of that history. In Harlan's view, history and current reality rendered the segregation statutes unconstitutional under the Thirteenth and Fourteenth Amendments.

But since Harlan's position was in dissent, the majority opinion upholding the doctrine of "separate but equal" prevailed and continued to shape racial conditions up until the middle of the twentieth century as, in the wake of *Plessy*, many states expanded their Jim Crow laws. During that nearly sixty-year period, the Fourteenth Amendment's role as a path to equality was a complicated one. Some of the most ignoble policies and practices, such as forced racial segregation in public schools and public spaces as well as the incarceration of Japanese Americans and people of Japanese ancestry during World War II, were found to be consistent with the Constitution. Yet even hampered as it was by the *Plessy* decision approving "separate but equal," the Fourteenth Amendment retained enough vitality to be the basis of cases successfully challenging the segregation of the University of Texas Law School and the University of Oklahoma's Graduate School of Education.[11]

And, despite its clear historical purpose, the Fourteenth Amendment is frequently invoked by conservative judges and commentators now to attack affirmative action and efforts to desegregate schools under the guise of colorblindness. Ironically, those efforts frequently involve coopting Justice Harlan's dissent in *Plessy* and the Supreme Court's decision in *Brown* and suggesting that both espouse the idea that "race consciousness" is the cause of persistent racial discrimination and "colorblindness" is its cure. Neither decision supports these contentions. As noted above, in *Plessy*, Justice Harlan, who is often cited to justify "colorblindness," rejected the view, arguing that "separate but equal" unfairly ignored the disastrous impact that the difference in race made.

Likewise, the suggestion that the *Brown* decision was driven by a vision of "colorblindness" is completely contrary to its purpose and effect. When the Supreme Court in *Brown* overturned *Plessy v. Ferguson*, it was precisely because the doctrine of separate but equal, supposedly a "colorblind" and neutral principle, was in clear violation of the Fourteenth Amendment. Instead of finding that the challenge of segregation in schools was a call for "colorblindness," *Brown* represented a clear-eyed view of the harms caused by segregation, the very thing that the *Plessy* court was willing to overlook in its insistence on a false neutrality. Unlike *Plessy*, which dismissed the stigmatization experienced by Black people as a result of segregation, *Brown* recognized it as the result of persistent discrimination and placed it at the center of its holding. By rejecting *Plessy*, the *Brown* court restored the original purpose and vitality of the Fourteenth Amendment, stating that its "great purpose" is to "raise the colored race from [a] condition of inferiority . . . into the perfect equality of civil rights with all other persons."[12]

The call for "colorblindness" in the context of challenges to affirmative action in higher education admissions represents a real and present threat to equality in education. That threat is particularly disturbing given the extremely stringent constraints that have been placed on the consideration of race in higher education admissions since the Supreme Court's decision in *Regents of the University of California v. Bakke* in 1978.

Bakke created the foundation upon which more than four decades of law regarding race- conscious admission practices is built. Brought as a challenge under Title VI of the Civil Rights Act of 1964, *Bakke* challenged a special admissions program that set aside a specified number of seats for applicants to the medical school at the University of California, Davis, for which white applicants could not compete. The plaintiff, a white applicant, challenged the program as being a violation of state and federal constitutional and statutory law because it considered race in the application process. The court's approach to the challenge has shaped the issue up to the present time. Applying a strict scrutiny standard, the most arduous and exacting standard of judicial scrutiny, the court struck down the university's admission plan as constituting an illegal quota because some students were disqualified from competing for some seats because of their race but upheld the consideration of race under limited circumstances because it fostered a legitimate governmental interest in diversity. Ironically, the fact that the court grounded its decision solely in educational diversity severely limits the scope of the consideration of race.

Rather than finding a compelling governmental interest in addressing past and present discrimination and increasing opportunities for Black students who had suffered a long history of exclusion from higher education, identifying diversity as the compelling interest emphasizes the benefits that the presence of diverse students brings to the student body as a whole.

Since *Bakke* was decided, the Supreme Court has revisited the issue of considerations of race numerous times. The first times were challenges to admissions programs at the University of Michigan and the University of Michigan Law School in 2003 and, more recently, in a case at the University of Texas.[13] Although the fact situations are different, the analysis of whether the use of race was appropriate has remained the same. The way that the admissions process employed race was subjected to a careful examination of whether it was narrowly tailored in a way to achieve the compelling governmental interest of diversity while using race in a manner that minimizes the possibility of harm to an individual because of that individual's race. In each case, diversity was seen as being a compelling governmental interest. As has been the case since *Bakke*, the court examined whether race is considered as part of a holistic review rather than being considered mechanically. As part of that same narrow tailoring process, the court considered whether the educational institution carefully considered race neutral alternatives. In all these cases, the court affirmed, by a slim majority, the importance of diversity in higher education. In all cases, the court held that student body diversity was essential to the creation of diverse leaders prepared to lead in an increasingly diverse society and that "the path to leadership" must be "visibly open to talented and qualified individuals of every race and ethnicity."[14]

Given the number of times that the careful use of race has been affirmed as one of many factors in higher education admissions, it is particularly unsettling that the Supreme Court recently granted certiorari in two cases challenging admissions processes at Harvard University and the University of North Carolina. The petitioners sought to upset more than forty years of precedent supporting the careful and limited consideration of race as one factor among many in accepting applicants to institutions of higher learning. In both cases, the petitioners lost in the lower courts after extensive fact finding and determinations by the lower courts that the two universities had fully satisfied the requirements of strict scrutiny.

One of the most foundational aspects of the American legal system is stare decisis, a principle that imposes order and stability in the law. Under this principle, courts cannot casually overrule precedent but must demonstrate "a special justification," over and above the belief "that the precedent was wrongly decided."[15] It is a principle fundamental to the integrity of the legal system and one designed to preserve confidence in the system because "it permits society to presume that bedrock principles are founded in the law rather than in the proclivities of individuals."[16] The court's review of affirmative action so soon after it has been reaffirmed invites questions of whether anything other than a change in composition of the court has occurred.

But the prospect of overturning recent precedent is only part of the reason that the Supreme Court's grant of certiorari is disturbing. Nothing has changed to justify rehearing and revisiting affirmative action. It has operated for more than forty years in a way that has increased the diversity of schools and created opportunities for a range of students to attend universities. It has benefited everyone in educational institutions by helping to nurture diversity in all of its many forms. Some of the strongest support for affirmative action has come from entities whose needs it serves, like the US Army and the corporate sector, which have submitted amicus briefs supporting its continued operation. Studies have shown that "college diversity experiences are significantly and positively related to cognitive development" and "specifically, interpersonal interactions with racial diversity are the most strongly related to cognitive development."[17]

It is always difficult and dangerous to predict a decision based on oral arguments, but it appears likely that, given the current composition of the court, affirmative action after the decision expected in 2023 will likely be considerably limited or nonexistent.

Perhaps the most disturbing thing diminishing the vitality of affirmative action is that turning back the clock to a time before the *Bakke* decision is effectively turning back the calendar to the time of *Plessy v. Ferguson*. As in the Jim Crow era, race remains a significant driver of inequality in the United States. In education, employment, housing, healthcare, access to a healthy environment, and nutrition, there continue to be significant, opportunity-killing disparities. Denying the existence and relevance of inequality might have a similar impact to that of its decision more than a century ago, when the Supreme Court helped usher in a period in which the continued discrimination against groups denied opportunity is ignored and the members of those groups are denied the means to challenge that inequality. As it did in the 1890s, colorblindness equates to inequality blindness.

And, as in the 1890s, the fact that the Fourteenth Amendment might be the means by which inequality is perpetuated is particularly painful. Subverting a constitutional amendment designed to address the impact of centuries of oppression into one which is required to ignore that history is profoundly ironic. That irony was highlighted by a question that Justice Jackson asked during the oral argument in the Harvard and University of North Carolina cases. In reference to the possible inability of Black applicants to mention their race and its importance in conveying who they are, Justice Jackson stated, "We're entertaining a rule where some people can say what they want about who they are and have that valued in a system and I'm worried that that creates an inequity in the system with respect to being able to express our identity."[18] The prospect of having current racial inequality ignored *and* being denied the ability to say, "This is who I am and it is important to me" is truly tragic. And it is especially tragic that the vehicle for recognizing and remedying the pernicious impact of the stigma of racial segregation in *Brown* was the Fourteenth Amendment and now we face the prospect of stigma resulting from the inability to identify race as being an essential component of who you are. Taken together with efforts to suppress curriculum, the impact of these trends is potentially devastating: not only will Black and Brown students be denied a place in institutions of higher learning, but they will be denied a place in the country's history, left to believe the wide racial disparities that exist in so many areas of American society are their fault.

Whatever the outcome of the two cases and the efforts to limit the teaching of history, the struggle will continue. The nation has survived serious setbacks in the past and gotten through difficult periods; it has still achieved successes in making the promise of equality under the Fourteenth Amendment a possibility. Whatever it takes to recognize our nation's difficult history and its legacy and to eliminate those vestiges that continue to hinder achieving true equity and equality must be done.

7

"Don't Say Gay" and Can't Be Trans

Behind the Anti-LGBTQ+ Schooling Agenda

SONNET GABBARD, ANNE MITCHELL,
AND HEATHER MONTES IRELAND

A MONG THE HUNDREDS of bills introduced across the US seeking to limit LGBTQ rights in 2022, forty-eight bills alone proposed anti-LGBTQ schooling or curriculum restrictions.[1] Another huge swath of proposed legislation has targeted trans children's participation in school sports. By mid-2022, civil rights groups and media outlets were warning of a record-setting year for policy attacks on queer and trans communities. One particularly egregious bill, Florida's "Don't Say Gay" law, caught national attention, and students across the state organized massive walkouts, insisting that they would "say gay," as the Florida law was about hatred and discrimination, not empowering parents. The year prior, the state of Texas proposed more than thirty anti-LGBTQ laws, the most of any state in the country at that point, with thirteen bills directly targeting transgender youth.[2]

Florida and Texas are flash points in larger concerted efforts to promote anti-gay and anti-trans discrimination nationwide, in response to the growing support among Americans for queer and trans rights. These states, with their legacies of racialized and colonial violence, systemic voter disenfranchisement, and overt control of marginalized communities, foster the ideal grounds for anti-gay and transphobic legislation. These conservative policies are attempts to expunge trans and queer people from public life, and are designed to chip away at curricular freedoms, prohibiting K–12 educators from discussing LGBTQ issues. And the cruel barrage of bans on trans children participating in sports and receiving gender-affirming medical care has emboldened homophobic and transphobic activists, further endangering LGBTQ youth.

Many of the same conservative US politicians who have created legislation limiting transgender healthcare for minors and restricting the teaching of any materials that do not pathologize queer identity and culture are similarly invested in banning anti-racist and ethnic studies education in school curriculums. These politicians claim that they are protecting children based on Judeo-Christian ideologies of divine creation and the "naturalness" of heteronormative nuclear families. However, their coercive policy agenda illustrates their need to enforce compulsory heterosexuality and protect the patriarchal nuclear family. Conservatives further insist upon enforcing a debunked binary sex/gender system in which children must maintain strict gender roles and expressions, underscoring that the heteropatriarchal gender system must be maintained with social coercion.[3] Conservative hyper-surveillance of gender identity and transness signals that the binary system is not stable, and therefore, school curriculums must enforce social norms to create compliant subjects. In this chapter, we discuss the singling out of trans and queer youth for regulation, and the ways the figure of the white heterosexual child is leveraged to discriminate against and oppress marginalized youth. Additionally, we trace a brief history of the US anti-gay conservative and Christian nationalist movements. We then explore the vicious legislative attacks on trans youth and the devastating consequences, such as mass violence and suicide, that trans and queer communities endure as a result of being made into targets and identify strategies for resistance and activism.

"DON'T SAY GAY" AND THE FIGURE OF THE CHILD IN ANTI-LGBTQ ACTIVISM

The day Florida governor Ron DeSantis signed what is being called the state's "Don't Say Gay" law (officially, the Parental Rights in Education Act), he sat at a desk surrounded by mostly white people and schoolchildren. The children, clad in uniforms, clapped tepidly as he gleefully held up the new bill designed to undermine children's autonomy. Under the guise of protecting youth, the law outlines new statutes for public education in kindergarten to third grade, yet it has far-reaching and invasive consequences and affects children and adults beyond K–3. The legislation outlaws any teaching about

gender and sexuality not adhering to "state standards." Though these standards have yet to be defined, it appears they maintain outdated notions of
the gender binary and prohibit any interaction with texts or curricula that
affirm queer and transgender people.

All teaching about gender identity, sexuality, or LGBTQ life and history
falls under what DeSantis has termed "woke gender ideology" in a broader
attack on public education and social-emotional learning for social justice.[4] In this way, he promotes a very thinly disguised repugnance for any
marginalized people, especially queer and trans folks, and seeks to further
marginalize LGBTQ folks from the mainstream. This effort by DeSantis and
other conservatives to restrict what teachers can say also includes topics in
race, racism, and US history. The Florida bill restricts teaching about queer
civil rights history in the US or abroad, forces children to abide by the gender
identity assigned at birth, and governs who can use what bathroom. Additionally, it mandates that students use a legal name in the classroom setting
despite having a chosen name that better fits the child, bans the usage of
fictional stories in the classroom that include LGBTQ characters regardless
of whether or not their identity is central to the text, and encourages school
officials to initiate abuse investigations into any student and their family
if they present as a queer-identified person.[5] By isolating education as the
predominant way to surveil and regulate the bodies and lives of LGBTQ
youth and their families, the bill insists on a cruel and detrimental approach
to the "woke problem" of queer and trans youth who, when lacking the few
protections and provisions they may currently have in public schools, can
then be bullied into submission.

The figure of the young white child is key to the intended conservative
message to protect our innocent little ones, and innocence is always presumed
to be the domain of white straight youth. Protecting children and defense
of parental rights, then, is premised upon an imagined child-subject of the
white heteropatriarchal family unit. This is not the first time a major anti-gay
crusade has been galvanized with this narrative. In Florida, entertainer, evangelical Christian, and virulent anti-gay activist Anita Bryant founded the first
national anti-gay group, called Save Our Children, in 1977.[6] This organization
began with an attempt to overturn an anti-discrimination law protecting
gay men and lesbians in Dade County.[7] Today, right-wing media outlets and

politicians use anti-gay and anti-trans rhetoric to stoke fears rooted in similar moral panic. Frequently used terms such as "gay indoctrination," "grooming," "gender ideology," and "gay agenda" imply that there is a concerted effort to overthrow and/or upend "traditional" family values. To leverage the rhetoric of protecting children and ensuring conservative parents' rights, queer and trans children and parents must be rendered outside the boundaries of "the family." Laura Briggs writes, "Throughout the 1970s, a new antigay right-wing movement defined homosexuals as those who had a lot of sex but did not do reproductive labor" and could not possibly be parents themselves.[8]

Queer and trans children and parents are deeply vulnerable to injury from these laws. In a press release issued by the US Department of Education, Secretary of Education Miguel Cardona emphasized how these families are impacted by the Florida policy:

> I've spoken to parents and families in Florida numerous times, and they've consistently told me that this legislation doesn't represent them or what they want for their children, and that it put Florida students in danger of bullying and worse mental health outcomes.[9]

Indeed, suicide remains the second leading cause of death among all young people in the US, and for LGBTQ youth, the threat is four times higher. In a 2021 meta-analysis of studies and data on LGBTQ suicide, the *Journal of the American Medical Association* found that LGBTQ youth have a higher rate of suicide ideation, attempts, and death by suicide.[10] This is in part due to higher rates of bullying, lack of support from school administrators and teachers, isolation, homophobia and/or transphobia in the home, and anti-LGBTQ policies and culture.[11] Studies have shown, however, that "including positive content about LGBTQ people and issues in classroom curriculums" can help to lessen suicide risk for queer and trans youth, by as much as 23 percent.[12] Yet only 28 percent of middle and high school LGBTQ students reported that they had ever learned about LGBTQ people or issues in their classes at school.[13] LGBTQ youth still report feeling unsafe at school and studies have found that students attending schools in states with anti-gay laws, like Florida, are more likely to hear homophobic remarks compared to students in other states.[14]

Perhaps most alarmingly, the Florida law empowers parents—presumably, white conservative heterosexual parents—to sue any school districts they believe have violated the policy, under the guise of advancing "parental rights."[15] In so doing, the law is the "first of its kind in the country."[16] Teachers have voiced concerns about the increased surveillance and the potential loss of employment for any discussion that might arise organically, including the acknowledgment of their partner or queer family for fear of it being construed as "instruction" by any offended parent. Since regulating "don't say gay" does not regulate away the existence of LGBTQ children, families, and teachers, the likelihood that children will, and should, bring their lives to the classroom remains. These inventive forms of legitimized intimidation disguise the fact that anti-LGBTQ groups are pulling out the same playbook over and over, with a shiny new veneer to attempt to skirt the law. As quickly as legal remedies secure protections for marginalized groups, these groups seek to establish new precedents to hate and discriminate legally.

"Don't Say Gay" and other anti-LGBTQ laws open all children to institutional harm, as policies regulating gender identity do not only hurt queer-identified youth. Gender normative policies also harm Indigenous youth whose cultural traditions may not align with white middle-class gender norms. In the same month that the Florida bill was passed, an Oklahoma first-grader, Andreas Garcia of Kickapoo Nation, had his long hair cut by two students in his classroom.[17] The child "was visibly shaken and angry" when explaining how classmates forcibly cut his long hair while his teacher was distracted. Similarly, in a Texas elementary school in 2021, a kindergarten student, J.R., was punished with suspension because of his long hair, according to his family's complaint with ACLU Texas. The school's policy, and that of many others, requires that boys wear short hair. Indigenous youth also deserve the protection that gender-expansive and culturally sensitive curriculums, and policies, would create.

REPUBLICANS, EVANGELICALS, AND THE ANTI-GAY PLATFORM

On June 26, 2015, the Supreme Court legalized same-sex marriage in the *Obergefell v. Hodges* decision. The landmark case had reverberating effects, nationally and internationally, protecting existing gay marriages and allowing thousands of queer people to marry in states with previous bans.[18] It was also a record year for anti-gay, specifically, anti-trans legislation in state legislatures throughout the country.[19] Hundreds of anti-LGBTQ bills have been filed on the state level, despite increasing public support for gay rights. One reason for the increase in homophobic and transphobic legislation is the significant uptick in donations and memberships to anti-gay organizations.[20] With their numbers growing, Christian Right groups like the Family Research Council, Alliance Defending Freedom, Liberty Counsel, and the American College of Pediatricians have become very influential in Republican politics, organizing around a large spate of anti-trans legislation on the local and state levels. The relationship between the anti-gay Christian Right and the Republican lawmakers they influence is not new, but the scope of their power grows as states like Florida and Texas bend to the whim of a small group of anti-gay, anti-trans white Evangelicals.

A 2022 Public Religion Research Institute study found that 80 percent of Americans support protections from discriminatory policies for LGBT+ people. The nonpartisan group's study reported that support for gay rights increased by 11 percent since 2015. The study categorized support by religious denominations and demographics, showing that white Evangelical Christians were the only group whose support *decreased* during that time. And since that time, their systematic and widespread campaign against LGBTQ people has only grown; 2021 outpaced 2015, with seventeen states enacting anti-trans legislation.[21, 22] In recent years, conservative politicians and pundits have ramped up anti-trans rhetoric to galvanize support for their platforms. Conservative politicians have been able to get elected by using different rhetoric for different audiences, gerrymandering districts, and using voter suppression tactics since the removal of the strict protections of the 1964 Civil Rights Act.[23] They actively discourage Black, Indigenous, and People of Color (BIPOC) participation in exercising the right to vote, knowing that they often vote for progressive policy reforms.

The architects of the current anti-gay and anti-trans laws use many of the same strategies and rhetoric as their white supremacist and segregationist predecessors to foment fear and hatred of LGBTQ communities. In fact, the modern religious right's entrance into politics has its roots in segregation in the Deep South. Prior to that, evangelicals remained on the outskirts of politics. Nearly fifty years later, the Evangelical religious right is one of the backbones of the Republican Party, and many of its leaders have been instrumental in crafting, passing, and implementing anti-trans and anti-gay laws.

Today, the Christian nationalist movement engages in a wide range of activities, from writing legislation to banning books, protesting and canceling drag culture events, and arguing anti-LGBTQ cases before the Supreme Court.[24] All signal the Right's anxieties over the broader move toward the protection of queer and trans rights. More than a dozen other states have seen similar bills introduced in their legislatures. Texas lieutenant governor Dan Patrick announced he "will prioritize passing Texas legislation that mimics the recently signed Florida bill" in the 2023 legislative session.[25] Other states are waiting to see if the tactics employed by Florida and Texas will hold up to constitutional scrutiny before enacting their own versions of these laws.

The adoption of sexuality and gender identity comprehensive education—*to* say "gay"—presents a perceived threat to heteronormativity and a false notion of Americanness. Historically, the heteronormative[26] family serves as the foundation of capitalist democracies, like the US, as well as socialist and fascist forms of governance; the family/nation dualism is central to understanding colonial and postcolonial nation-states and population management through regulations of who can create a family and reproduce, and how.[27] White nationalists are concerned with increasing the white population to fulfill their ideals of living in a mythic Christian Aryan nation.[28]

ANTI-TRANS LEGISLATION AND VIOLENCE

In 2022, gun violence was visited upon queer and trans people in Colorado at Club Q, an LGBTQ nightclub. The 2016 massacre at Pulse, a queer nightclub in Orlando, Florida, left forty-nine people dead. Sadly, gun violence is not unique to the LGBTQ community. Other mass shootings in Colorado, such as at the Aurora movie theater in 2012, could also shine a light on the Club Q killings. So could the Columbine High School massacre in Littleton, Colorado, which left thirteen dead. America has a patriarchal violence problem, and the government is disinclined to address it. Couple that with a politically volatile climate, and eventually, anti-queer attacks like Club Q occur. Indeed, the legislation targeting the bodily autonomy of queer and transgender youths and outlawing the teaching of gay history and queer identity works to make trans and queer people the other, the enemy, and the targets of violence. Trans and queer people are endangered everywhere. As Imara Jones, journalist and chair of the Transgender Law Center, writes, "These anti-trans bills signal that trans people are not like everyone else and can be targeted. These bills are designed to create a climate of hostility and they are succeeding."[29]

Just as we consider physical violence against queer folks as an attack, we must consider the content of recent anti-queer legislation across the United States of America. In Texas, Governor Greg Abbott has criminalized gender variation for children. This legislation makes it illegal to identify as transgender in public settings, specifically public schools, and tasks teachers, nurses, school administrators, counselors, and social workers with reporting transgender students and their parents to child protective services for child endangerment.[30, 31] States such as Texas and Alabama are going the distance by criminalizing parents who seek gender-affirming care for their children and attempting to outlaw the use of gender-affirming hormone blockers for minors. The rhetoric surrounding legislation in Alabama, Florida, and Texas is part of a concerted effort to ensure that citizens know that they will be punished and shamed for engaging queerness from a non-pathologizing vantage point. These laws communicate a divide between who is allowed full expression of their bodily autonomy and who is not. One of the earliest examples that gained nationwide coverage was the "Bathroom Bill" in North Carolina.[32] This legislation was shocking in that it aimed to bar trans people generally from full participation in public life and specifically put trans children's bodily autonomy and personal choices up for statewide debate. What caught people's attention was the law legislated that children could not use the bathroom of their gender identity. The law passed, but due to protests and loss of tourist revenue, it was rescinded. After the law's nullification, what remained was a debate that dehumanized transgender children and attempted to force compliance with medical and juridical understandings of binary notions of gender.

ANTI-TRANS IDEOLOGIES AND RACE

Anti-gay and -trans legislation disproportionately affects poor people of color, and within the LGBTQ community, it disproportionately affects transgender people since they are more likely to live in poverty. As noted above, normativity in the West is white, and in the US, people of color, particularly Indigenous and Black people, have been constructed as nonhuman under Western ideology.[33] And as normative gendered ideologies have always excluded Black Americans, anti-trans legislation in the US is anti-Black. During slavery, Black women were rendered outside the discourse on "femininity" because only white women were considered in this category.[34] If Black women were constructed as feminine, it would have precluded slave owners from enforcing labor systems in which Black men and women worked alongside each other, since field labor was viewed as masculine, nor could they enforce birthing standards on Black bodies to continually enrich the slaveholder.[35] The vilification of non-Europeans, and Western society's fixation on the preservation of heteronormativity, come from similar origins ideologically. It is a drive to preserve the White heteronormative family and its wealth through the subjugation of racialized others.

Today, trans people experience discrimination in all realms of US society. Recent statistics show that 71 percent of US transgender people of all races hid their transition to avoid discrimination, 57 percent face familial rejection because of their identity as transgender, 57 percent have delayed getting gender-affirming care to avoid discrimination, and 19 percent experienced refusal of housing because of their identity. Additionally, of the 19 percent that have experienced homelessness, 55 percent experienced harassment in shelters, 22 percent reported being sexually assaulted by the shelter's staff, and 22 percent were turned away from shelters. Trans people of color are among the lowest earners in the LGBTQ community, more likely to experience discrimination and violence because of their gender identity and expression. The poverty experienced by transgender people is intensified if the person is non-white because of the historical circumstances that have marginalized people of color throughout American history.[36]

African Americans, like Indigenous and Latine people in the US, have a larger percentage of people living in poverty today, largely because of systems that have extracted wealth from their community for over 250 years.[37,38]

These groups also have more of their population living in poverty and more in the working classes than the middle and upper classes. Very few BIPOC parents can afford to opt out of the system when public education is under attack by enrolling their children in private school when the curriculum does not meet their needs or moving to another state when their home state adopts discriminatory policies.[39,40]

SEEING BLACK TRANS YOUTH

Queer lives are not guaranteed the same rights as other Americans, owing to discrimination that is both overt and subtle. For all LGBTQ people, but specifically for those in the transgender community, there are no federal legal protections in the realm of housing or sexual harassment.[41] This means that being perceived as a transgender person can lead to ridicule or exclusion from public life in ways that harm the person's ability to lead an agentic life. This is most troubling for youth, considering their attendance is mandatory at public or private schools through age sixteen, although current legislative actions target them specifically. K–12 public education has become a battleground for bodily autonomy for children. Throughout America, we are seeing an increase in legislation that attempts to limit the lives of queer and trans youth.

Blake Brockington, a young Black trans man, became a national sensation in 2014, as the first out transgender Prom King. His story represents one where societal and rhetorical violence against trans youth combine in a deadly way with mental health challenges. In *Black on Both Sides: A Racial History of Trans Identity*, C. Riley Snorton describes how Brockington's visibility brought attention to the struggles of transgender people.[42] Although attention from the case resulted in support, it also attracted hatred toward the youth. Originally from North Carolina, he moved to South Carolina to live with a foster family in high school due to his family's rejection of his trans identity. Embracing both his Blackness and transness was necessary for Brockington; he became an activist, protesting North Carolina's "Bathroom Bill" anti-trans legislation and supporting Black Lives Matter protests. As Snorton reports, Brockington also dealt with mental health challenges that were exacerbated by the heightened attention, and by the spring of 2015, he was dead by suicide. While Blake Brockington represents one story, it is emblematic of why legislation that attempts to push LGBTQ people and history back into the closet is harmful.[43]

CONCLUSION

While the United States has a deep history of bigotry and hate against anyone categorized as the other, it is important to remember that people fighting for social justice have existed all along in our history, too. Through a queer theoretical lens, we must remain open to the idea that LGBTQ history is not limited to people who claim those identities—and that people in those identities show up throughout American history, making waves in other areas of social discourse. Though certain histories are being outlawed, it does not mean that complex lessons on the principles of equality and equity cannot be taught. Educators can still use relevant historical examples to show how other previously stigmatized groups, like immigrants, workers, and women fighting for the right to vote, have overcome similar types of hostility. By engaging new critical perspectives, students can look for complexity and rely on the resiliency of the activist past of this country.

As Imara Jones, the Transgender Law Center chair, notes, "The armed wing and the political wing say that they don't have anything to do with each other, but we know [they] are deeply connected."[44] LGBTQ youth and educators are under attack, and it is the duty of allies and adults to fight back against the armed and political wings of conservative nationalism. Teachers, parents, and community members can resist and protest these curricular decisions in their capacity as citizens. This includes standing on the front lines and in school board meetings, alongside LGBTQ protesters; talking about assaults on LGBTQ youth in everyday activities, such as book clubs, neighborhood gatherings, and workplaces; and "saying gay" at the ballot box and in consumer habits. Queer and trans people are protesting, legally challenging, and socially defying these bigoted ideologies. If we are to fight back, we must follow in our queer and trans forebears' actions and join in coalition to *unleash power*.[45]

PART III

Collective Action and Visible Resistance

8

The Resolutions

Mobilizing Faculty Senates
to Defend Academic Freedom

JENNIFER RUTH

I N THE FALL OF 2020, Michael Bérubé and I were writing *It's Not Free Speech: Race, Democracy, and the Future of Academic Freedom* (2022). We began a chapter that looked back on what was, when we started writing, a mostly forgotten episode: the emergence and relatively short shelf life of critical race theory as a discrete body of work undertaken primarily by Black law professors in the late 1980s and 1990s. We were revisiting the insights of critical race theorists in debates over campus speech that had raged thirty years ago, insights made freshly relevant by the way racist rhetoric circulated under the banner of free speech in the years after Trump's election. We were astonished, then, when critical race theory suddenly appeared to be on everyone's lips, or at least in their Twitter feeds. In a matter of weeks, right-wing pundits had mounted a backlash to the budding national reckoning prompted by George Floyd's murder and made critical race theory their centerpiece.

The Orwellian right-wing campaign to paint anti-racism as itself racist had not stopped when Joe Biden took office in January 2021, rescinding Trump's executive order on diversity training and dismantling the 1776 Commission. Propelled by the media's spread of misinformation about critical race theory, the campaign reorganized itself at the state level. And it metastasized. As Jonathan Friedman, Jeremy Young, and James Tager write in chapter 3, "Between January 2021 and November 2022, 45 legislatures across the United States introduced 306 separate bills intended to restrict teaching and training in K–12 schools, higher education, and state agencies and institutions."[1]

In those early months, people in academia seemed to have trouble taking the proposed bills seriously, based as they were on false characterizations of scholarly work, fear-mongering, and misrepresentations of what educators do in their classrooms. Further fueling the initial incredulity was a widespread belief that these bills could not possibly withstand First Amendment scrutiny. Any attempt to censor educators' speech was bound to fail in a court of law, people said. And while this belief has not yet been fully tested and proven wrong, it missed the point, or rather, a couple of them, the most obvious being that the bills, just by being proposed, would have an immediate effect in chilling speech and (de)forming curriculum. Sure enough, reports that classes on race or gender were being canceled began to circulate by summer. And where bills did pass into law, it would take months, perhaps years, for the challenges to run their course in the courts. (Indeed, the first challenges are only now, almost two years later, beginning to play out in Florida.) Finally, and most unfortunately, it is just simply not true that the First Amendment inevitably protects educators. Academic freedom as a special category of free speech is not a well-understood or well-defined aspect of the law, so what faculty do in their research and teaching is perennially vulnerable to being viewed as the unprotected speech of an employee, not the free speech of a citizen.

In the pages of the *New Republic* around this time (March 2021), critical race theorist and law professor Kimberlé Crenshaw was writing about the January 6 insurrection "to understand how explicitly anti-democratic desires can be framed as defending freedom, as well as how moderate and left responses to this political violence seem to underestimate its continuity from the past and its threat to our future, we have to grapple with the foundational role of white supremacy in our republic."[2] Unlike too many others, Crenshaw had no trouble taking the bills seriously, and accordingly, her organization, the African American Policy Forum (AAPF), was among the first to act. She and her team announced an AAPF Working Meeting on Battlefields: K–12 & College and Universities for the summer of 2021 to "address the proliferating attacks on Critical Race Theory." Sumi Cho, AAPF director of strategic initiatives, called on "LatCrit, Class Crits, SALT,

AALS Min Section, AAUP Committee A, Academic Freedom experts, and scholar-activists to join us to repel these insidious attacks." On June 23, those who attended the meeting broke into two groups—one on K–12 and one on higher education—to brainstorm ideas for fighting the right-wing propaganda and legislative machinery. In the higher education group, we proposed toolkits, teach-ins, and a faculty senate resolution campaign. Afterward, a handful of us, led by Sumi Cho, began to plan a summit for October 14, 2021 (George Floyd's birthday) in which the AAPF would roll out a series of actions, including a faculty senate resolution campaign. As University of Cincinnati professor Emily Houh worked on a toolkit, De-Paul University professor Valerie Johnson and I drafted a senate resolution template that could be circulated nationwide.

In calling upon faculty—and university administration—to defend the academic freedom to work on topics branded "divisive," the template resolution encouraged senators to insert language from the AAUP and from their own faculty handbooks in strategic places as well as to include any previous statements by their university affirming racial justice and/or academic freedom. The template Valerie Johnson and I drafted began with line items that provided context:

WHEREAS state legislative proposals are being introduced across the United States that target academic discussions of racism and related issues in American history in schools, colleges and universities.

WHEREAS these legislative proposals vary but all seek to prohibit or restrict what are often called "divisive concepts" in the teaching and education of students.

WHEREAS many educators do not consider these same concepts "divisive" but rather central to the active and engaged pursuit of truth at the heart of our mission.

WHEREAS the Faculty Handbook and [include here any other governance and/or bargaining language on academic freedom] affirms the importance of academic freedom to the proper functioning of universities, citing the

American Association of University Professors' 1940 Statement of Principles on Academic Freedom and Tenure [if your governance language does
not cite the 1940 statement, consider adding an extra "whereas" line that
specifically notes the 1940 statement].

And it concluded with a series of resolutions:

THEREFORE BE IT RESOLVED that Senate resolutely rejects any attempts by bodies external to the faculty to restrict or dictate university
curriculum on any matter, including matters related to racial and social
justice, and will stand firm against encroachment on faculty authority by
the legislature or the Boards of Trustees.

BE IT FURTHER RESOLVED that Senate calls upon President [ ] and
Provost [ ] to affirm that they reject any attempts by bodies external to the
faculty to restrict or dictate university curriculum on any matter, including
matters related to racial and social justice, and will stand firm against encroachment on faculty authority by the legislature or the Boards of Trustees.

BE IT FURTHER RESOLVED that Senate affirms the "Joint Statement
on Efforts to Restrict Education about Racism," authored by the AAUP,
PEN America, the American Historical Association, and the Association of
American Colleges and Universities, endorsed by over seventy organizations,
and issued on June 16, 2021.

WHY FACULTY SENATES?

The rationale for a campaign organized around faculty senates was simple
and based on the concept of academic freedom. The right-wing legislative
campaign attacks free speech, yes, but it also takes aim at academic freedom
unique to higher education. Banning critical race theory, "The 1619 Project,"
and educational practices proven to increase student success suppresses free
speech, but that is not the central problem. A number of speech acts are,
after all, legitimately suppressed in educational settings. The problem is that
such work has earned the protection of academic freedom by having been

conducted in a sphere open to vetting in one way or another by expert peers. It is work that has achieved some degree of academic legitimation through the procedures of disciplinary bodies (peer-reviewed journals, professional associations, promotion, and tenure) or by other measures (adoption in syllabi and impact on/in the disciplinary conversation).

Academic freedom enables society to come into possession of a body of work that cannot be easily reduced to opinion or hearsay. By enabling the production of independent knowledge that citizens can then use to make informed decisions in a democracy, it provides society with what law professor and former Yale Law dean Robert Post call "democratic competence." In *Democracy, Expertise, and Academic Freedom: A First Amendment Jurisprudence for the Modern State* (2012), Post writes:

> Democratic *legitimation* [emphasis in original] requires that the speech of all persons be treated with toleration and equality. Democratic *competence* [emphasis in original], by contrast, requires that speech be subject to a disciplinary authority that distinguishes good ideas from bad ones.[3]

Free speech is necessary for democratic legitimation; academic freedom corresponds to democratic competence. In authoritarian and totalitarian states where knowledge is controlled by one political regime with the aim of perpetuating its rule, academic freedom does not exist. It exists in two-party or multiparty democratic societies that have tacitly agreed to grant universities and colleges the degree of independence from partisan politics necessary to safeguard the integrity of the knowledge they produce.

Where is academic freedom exercised? It manifests in the peer reviews performed by academic journals, the evaluations conducted by promotion and tenure committees, and on university-wide committees like undergraduate councils and education policy committees that oversee curriculum. The work of these latter committees is conducted at most universities under the auspices of faculty senates or similar bodies composed of faculty representatives or the entire faculty at some very small schools. At senate meetings, faculty members convene to approve or disapprove curricular changes based on the recommendations of such committees. While academic freedom is exercised in and across various bodies and through sometimes complex procedures, it is, in its simplest form, the right of faculty members in their collective capacity to be in charge of scholarship and teaching, and the curriculum that originates in both of these activities. The faculty. Not administrators. Not corporations. *Not partisan politicians.*

Faculty senates are where academic freedom is exercised by a university's largest group of faculty members. That's why they are the bodies to which the AAPF higher education working committee turned when seeking to defend academic freedom from the political interference of state legislators.

The conception of academic freedom and the building of an infrastructure for it (senate committees, systems of due processes conducted by panels of peers, etc.) has been largely the achievement of decades of cumulative work performed by the American Association of University Professors (AAUP). Established in 1915, the AAUP is the organization to whom we owe concepts like "tenure" and "shared governance." Its founding Declaration on Principles of Academic Freedom and Academic Tenure states:

> Trustees . . . have no moral right to bind the reason or the conscience of any professor.
>
> All claim to such right is waived by the appeal to the general public for contributions and for moral support in the maintenance, not of a propaganda, but of a non-partisan institution of learning.

And:

> Once appointed, the scholar has professional functions to perform in which the appointing authorities have neither competency nor moral right to intervene.[4]

The equally important 1940 Statement of Principles on Academic Freedom and Tenure asserts:

> Institutions of higher education are conducted for the common good and not to further the interest of either the individual teacher or the institution

as a whole. The common good depends upon the free search for truth and its free exposition. . . . Academic freedom can serve the public good only if universities as institutions are free from outside pressures in the realm of their academic mission and individual faculty members are free to pursue their research and teaching subject only to the academic judgment of their peers.[5]

By developing policies that came to be widely accepted and that established relative independence for faculty members by placing oversight in the disciplines and in the bodies of peers like faculty senates, the AAUP has managed to protect the integrity of the knowledge produced by the nation's colleges and universities. The template we drafted drew explicitly on the policies designed by the AAUP.

The attempt to censor critical race theory and so-called divisive concepts in higher education is an attempt to undercut—essentially, render null and void—the infrastructure of academic freedom upon which democracy depends. Within the nation's universities and colleges, across the pages of its academic journals and books, "a growing body of progressive white scholars and scholars of color have spent the past several decades fighting for, and largely succeeding in creating, a more honest chronicle of the American past," Jelani Cobb wrote in the *New Yorker* in May 2021. "But these battles and the changes they've achieved have, by and large, gone unnoticed by the lay public."[6] The more honest chronicle of the American past went largely unnoticed, that is, until the national reckoning with racism briefly brought some of this knowledge into the public sphere when a general audience opened up for historical truths that once seemed confined to course syllabi. The swift right-wing backlash coalesced around an attack on this knowledge because, as we saw and as Cobb wrote, "the aversion to unflattering truths can be made into political currency." Some Americans were learning for the first time of, say, the Tulsa Massacre and wondering why they did not know more about it while right-wing legislators strategized to ban curriculum centered on such events by calling it "divisive" and "unpatriotic." This is the context in which faculty senates needed to stand up for the faculty's right to teach the truth and Americans' right to learn.

THE SENATE RESOLUTION CAMPAIGN BEGINS

After Valerie Johnson and I drafted the template, UC-Riverside professor Dylan Rodriguez and Tulane professor Robert Westley contributed comments to the draft. By August, we had a template ready: Defending Academic Freedom to Teach About Race and Gender Justice and Critical Race Theory. (See the appendix for the template and examples of the resolutions passed at a few institutions, in coordination with our efforts or independently.) At that point, Valerie and I tailored the template to our institutions (DePaul and Portland State, respectively) and worked with our faculty senates to revise further and then pass resolutions so that we might have successful examples to share when we contacted faculty across the country. Sumi Cho and the AAPF staff added the resolution template, a cover letter, and the resolutions that passed at DePaul and Portland State to the Truth Be Told Call to Action website. At AAPF's 2021 Critical Race Theory Summer School, over the week of August 10, Emily Houh and I held a session on the resolution campaign. In mid-September, the higher education working committee assembled by AAPF began contacting schools across the country.

As the faculty lead, I began identifying faculty senate leaders across the country, whether presiding officers or chairs of standing senate committees on academic freedom or diversity, equity, and inclusion. I shared our materials and encouraged senate leaders to discuss with their colleagues adapting and proposing this kind of resolution on their own campuses. Initially, we targeted faculty senators at public flagship universities, because if a public flagship adopted a resolution, the campaign might catch fire at other schools within the state. Over the next few weeks, over forty-five schools were contacted. The response rate was higher than anticipated, with about 40 percent of the people we contacted replying within a week or two. The responses were generally respectful, occasionally even enthusiastic, with faculty senate presidents and presiding officers expressing a willingness to discuss the idea within the relevant committees and, in some cases, expressing a firm determination to bring a resolution to the floor. A few responses were noncommittal or otherwise begged off, typically citing the abundance of issues currently facing their senate bodies. Only one was dismissive. This head of an academic freedom committee at a university in the South told me that he was satisfied with the protections his school already possessed and, further, that he had discussed the issue with faculty members who work on race and gender issues, and they, too, were satisfied. (Doubtful of this, I wrote a few faculty at that institution, who were surprised to learn of their colleague's complacency and deeply shaken, in fact, by the right-wing legislation proposed in their states.)

The greatest tension among faculty members about the possibility of a resolution was, of course, at universities in the South. Academics in red states often expressed a desire to pass a resolution but a great deal of understandable trepidation at the same time. They were concerned about possible retribution to the individuals spearheading the campaign for the resolution and, more generally, concerned about a range of possible repercussions for "poking the bear," a phrase we heard repeatedly. Faculty members at a significant number of flagships in southern states expressed a desire to prepare a resolution yet bide their time before proposing it. They wanted to wait to see how the pending legislation unfolded, especially when, at many institutions, administrators counseled them to work behind the scenes and avoid a public gesture.

Senators at schools in states not under imminent threat of such legislation occasionally shared concern that passing a resolution would be a "performative" gesture. We countered that reasserting the norm of academic autonomy from partisan political interference was more than a performative act at a time when authoritarian strategies were in rapid ascendance throughout the country. We argued that such resolutions might prove helpful to faculty in states facing legislation as they would become part of a public record that academics in those states might draw upon when negotiating their own crises. Expressing a commitment to stand with the K–12 educators in their own states was another important reason, given the ground these educators had on which to claim academic freedom was shakier, given greater state control over elementary and secondary education. We also pointed out that individual faculty members in blue and purple states were being targeted by the right-wing machinery funded by the Koch brothers and others and suffering consequences, especially those untenured and easily dismissed. Resolutions would facilitate an awareness and solidarity that might prove critical in such cases, putting administrations on notice that their faculty had spoken with one voice and. Administrators might be more likely to actually defend the academic freedom they claim to support when pressed to dismiss or otherwise punish a faculty member that offended, say, readers of *The College Fix*.

Historian Ellen Schrecker, author of *No Ivory Tower: McCarthyism and the Universities* and *Many Are the Crimes: McCarthyism in America* (and coeditor of this volume), joined the campaign around this time, bringing with her a cohort of activists from the Historians for Peace and Democracy. Schrecker began to publicize it in her various articles and internet presentations, such as one entitled "McCarthyism, New and Old: Today's Culture Wars in Historical Context" on October 12, which compared the present culture wars to the 1950s Red Scare and provided an early version of what became chapter 1 of this volume. Most importantly, on October 14, 2021, the Higher Education Working Group of AAPF held a national critical race theory teach-in where Sumi Cho, Emily Houh, Valerie, and I promoted the campaign to an audience of six hundred after a galvanizing call to action delivered by Kimberlé Crenshaw. Over the next few months, I spoke at AAPF working group meetings and various other places, such as a meeting of the Association of Research Libraries and an AACTE conference, to spread the word. The AAUP sponsored and promoted a webinar Valerie Johnson and I offered entitled "Get Your Laws Off Our Syllabi!"

The campaign began to gain momentum. The faculty senates of more than a dozen institutions—DePaul, Michigan State, Ohio State, Portland State, Washington College, Molloy College, Penn State, Virginia Commonwealth, and the universities of Colorado, Delaware, Minnesota, Oregon, and Wisconsin—passed the resolutions. The chair of the Academic Freedom and Tenure Committee at the University of Minnesota told the *Minnesota Daily*, "Sometimes you have to remind [people] of basic principles."[7] Consulting the AAPF template, faculty senate leaders at the University of Alabama, the flagship in a state with two bills under consideration in the legislature, developed their own unique Defense of Academic Freedom Resolution, which passed on December 14.[8] The resolutions were working. Once the faculty senate of the entire University of Colorado system adopted its resolution, for example, its board of regents dropped its consideration of an anti-CRT measure.[9]

Over the months, we maintained correspondence with those senators who were interested in passing resolutions, sometimes troubleshooting with them when they encountered obstacles. Although we were not always aware of this until much later, senators often faced complex challenges unique to their institutions and states. (See Sarah Sklaw's chapter for more texture about the experiences of individuals on their campuses.) Often, we heard nothing after the first email exchanges and then were surprised by an update with news that a resolution had been proposed and passed. It was incredible to realize what we had experienced as a lull of silence had in fact been busy with activism and organizing. We were especially heartened during this period by the work undertaken at Ohio State, where they organized to pass a resolution quickly and developed one that included very strong language about K–12 education.

Camaraderie began to develop, as senators at various institutions gave advice to senators at other universities. Sara McDaniel in the Department of Special Education at the University of Alabama offered advice, for example, to Andrea Gore, chair of UT Austin's academic freedom committee, as she considered possible objections she might encounter while building support for the resolution. The most gratifying camaraderie to witness as well as hear about secondhand was the solidarity that often materialized among faculty during senate meetings. Faculty who did not teach race or gender justice would counter objections to the resolution by pointing out that their own research in reproductive health might be on the chopping block next if they were banned from studying, say, Planned Parenthood. Scientists whose work touched on climate change voiced the same point. Slowly but surely, it seemed, faculty were recognizing that we all have a dog in this fight. If we did not protect our colleagues' academic freedom, we could find our own research and teaching targeted in the next iteration of political-cultural warfare.

Our greatest concern became getting the word out about the growing number of resolutions so as to encourage action at places we had not yet reached out to. AAPF kept the list of institutions on its website, and the AAUP linked to it and highlighted the campaign on its site. The Modern Language Association (MLA) emailed its members about the campaign. The higher education press, however, had yet to notice. This was frustrating; just one national article could do more to spread the word than could hundreds of emails. This changed when Colleen Flaherty published "A Template for

Academic Freedom" in *Inside Higher Ed* on December 15, 2021.[10] This was followed by "College Faculty Are Fighting Back Against State Bills on CRT" in the *Washington Post* on February 19, 2022,[11] and "Fighting Back Against CRT Panic" in *Salon* on March 7, 2022.[12] "All along, the Truth Be Told campaign has made very clear that we don't think the goal is simply to defend against these negative things, but to proactively stand up for a robust vision of what multiracial democracy means and requires," Sumi Cho said in the *Salon* piece. About the resolutions, she added, "This is a proactive campaign we developed, thinking about the foundations of higher education being grounded in academic freedom and using it to say, that must be respected, whether you agree with or teach CRT or not."

Emboldened by these developments, we began to adopt a more exhortatory tone. "Faculty, You Have Power! Use It!" Ellen Schrecker and I urged on the AAUP *Academe Blog* in February 2022. "We must protect our autonomy over the curriculum," we wrote, pointing out that "a near-universal consensus within every constituency of the academic community agrees that, as the AAUP explains, faculty members 'are distinctly qualified to exercise decision-making in their areas of expertise' and should have 'the chief competence for judging the work of their colleagues.'" We asked what will happen if we don't oppose these measures:

> Will someone like Marjorie Taylor Greene, and not our departmental and disciplinary peers, evaluate our teaching and research? Will state attorney generals, to whom these bills grant incredible power, determine curricula? Will Montana's Attorney General Austin Knutsen, who issued a formal 'Opinion' that using Critical Race Theory and similar materials in the schools is against the law, take action against an instructor if a white student feels bad reading Toni Morrison's *Beloved* or seek to defund a university where sociologists assign Richard Rothstein's *The Color of Law*?[13]

Looking at our prose in retrospect, I can see that we were in that rhetorical bind that fastens around all those who try to satirize something that is fast becoming reality. The Marjorie Taylor Greene line has the rhythm of a joke and yet that is precisely what we were and are facing: partisan right-wing politicians claiming the authority to decide what curriculum is acceptable in the nation's public institutions.

THE CAMPAIGN CONCLUDES

"Showing an unprecedented solidarity," Schrecker reported in *The Nation* in March 2022, "the academic community is mobilizing to confront what its members rightly perceive as an existential assault on their professional work and values."[14] In April, I reported on the *Academe Blog* that "the resolution campaign has decisively turned a corner: faculty senates and AAUP chapters across the country—in red states as well as in blue—have passed resolutions to defend academic freedom to teach race and gender justice and critical race theory."[15] There was no point, many in red states seemed to feel, in waiting to see what happened with the bills. They were not going to go away on their own; they were too useful as political weapons for Republican politicians seeking election or reelection. The question of poking the bear had thus become irrelevant, and the senates at the universities of Georgia, Tennessee, and Mississippi all passed resolutions.

The campaign had proved more successful than we'd anticipated. I had initially commented that I'd be happy with twenty-five institutions passing a resolution. By the end of the 2021–22 school year, at least sixty institutions had passed one.[16] Individual AAUP chapters on campuses had too when their senates did not and, in some cases, in addition to their senates.

We pushed and prodded in the ways discussed above, but of course, where the campaign succeeded was entirely due to the sustained efforts of the faculty members on the campuses. Despite doubts and fears of retribution, these senators did the work of shepherding resolutions through numerous committee meetings—revising and refining the text—all the way to senate floors.

The success of the documents as collective statements over the long term has yet to be known. They are largely untested in the sense that, to our knowledge, faculty have yet to invoke them in a court case or in the context of crises. All of these individual and collective efforts notwithstanding, the senate resolutions are only a beginning to the kind of collective faculty action demanded of this political moment, as a few of the senators whom Sarah Sklaw interviewed for the next chapter point out. The end of the right-wing campaign itself is not yet in sight. The resolutions model one effective step forward and show that in the midst of a country sliding toward authoritarianism, faculty can—and will—mobilize to defend the academic freedom that provides one crucial pillar of our endangered democracy.

9

Silence Gets Us Nowhere

Faculty Responses to Anti-CRT and Divisive Concepts Legislation

SARAH SKLAW

FACULTY SENATE RESOLUTIONS rarely make national headlines, but in February 2022, Texas lieutenant governor Dan Patrick threw the University of Texas at Austin Faculty Council into the political spotlight. Retweeting local news coverage of UT Austin's faculty resolution defending professors' academic freedom to teach about race and gender justice and critical race theory, Patrick commented, "I will not stand by and let looney Marxist UT professors poison the minds of young students with Critical Race Theory. We banned it in publicly funded K–12 and we will ban it in publicly funded higher ed." This scrutiny came as a surprise to Professor Andrea Gore, past chair of the Committee of Council on Academic Freedom and Responsibility in UT Austin's Faculty Council: "We pass resolutions all the time and they never get any political attention."[1] Clearly, this resolution was different. Across the country, professors have joined a national campaign to defend academic freedom and express solidarity with K–12 teachers reeling from censorial legislation's impact on their classrooms. Politicians like Patrick are furious because professors have refused to stay silent.

Over the past two years right-wing activists have transformed the academic and legal framework of critical race theory into a boogeyman for attacks on education. In doing so, they have vilified education designed to provide students with the knowledge and skills needed to reckon with our unequal society. Anti-CRT/divisive concepts legislation is the latest tactic in a long-standing campaign to defund public education and delegitimize

127

schools as spaces to forge multiracial democracy.[2] While early anti-CRT legislation mainly focused on K–12, by 2022, as Jonathan Friedman and his coauthors note in chapter 3, state legislatures were paying increased attention to higher education. And yet, faculty senate resolutions were not mere self-defense. Refusing to abandon their fellow educators to political vicissitudes, faculty members have challenged the division between K–12 and higher education and insisted that their fortunes cannot be separated.

Drawing on interviews with seventeen faculty members, this chapter argues that the power of faculty senate resolutions stems from the coalition building, conversation, and coaxing required to mobilize professors to take collective action against educational censorship. At the same time, a close inspection of the resolution process reveals that passage was not solely a response to anti-CRT legislation. The erosion of academic freedom and shared governance are part and parcel of structural changes in colleges and universities that have left educators increasingly vulnerable to political attacks and professional misfortunes. Faculty involvement in the campaign against anti-CRT/divisive concepts legislation reasserts educators' role in civic life and their importance to the university as an institution.

WHO'S IN CHARGE HERE?

Conflicts around speech, bias, stereotypes, and politics are not novel developments in higher education, but recent battles over critical race theory highlight new and challenging dynamics facing educators in the contemporary university. Political encroachment on academic offerings, higher education's reliance on contingent faculty, a corporatized and commercialized university structure, and discrepant understandings of academic freedom all influenced professors' responses to anti-CRT legislation and their engagement with faculty senate resolutions.

Long-time faculty members have observed significant increases in external interference into higher education. Louis Gross, a Chancellor's Professor Emeritus and Emeritus Distinguished Professor of Ecology and Evolutionary Biology and Mathematics at the University of Tennessee, Knoxville (UTK), served in faculty governance for much of his forty-plus-year career. Gross noted that during his previous term as president of UTK's faculty senate in the early 2000s "there was nothing like these issues." While the state legislature determined a significant portion of the budget, "it was not trying to run the university."[3] Evidently, anti-CRT legislation is part of a broader shift in the relationship between local politicians and higher education.

Many professors cited local legislation censoring or restricting educational offerings as the impetus for advancing faculty senate resolutions, but specific conflicts over CRT often came on the heels of previous political efforts to dictate faculty activity. At North Dakota State University (NDSU), faculty members viewed the May 2021 passage of SB 2030, which barred professors from partnering with Planned Parenthood for sex education in secondary schools, as a precursor to the state's anti-CRT legislation. According to Florin Salajan, an education professor at NDSU, the sex education law indicated that legislators were "willing, able, and capable of putting restrictions in place that affect higher education."[4] Both Salajan and Anastassiya Andrianova, an associate professor of English at NDSU, interpreted North Dakota's anti-CRT law as evidence that local politicians were restricting education based on their own moral beliefs about what constituted appropriate discourse. The proximity of the two laws also highlighted the imbrication of restrictions on teaching about gender and sexuality with education around race and racism.

At several universities, administrative leadership's responses to COVID-19 highlighted the deterioration of shared university governance and primed faculty members to join the senate resolution campaign. As COVID swept across the country, administrators at Michigan State University (MSU) pushed the faculty to take salary and benefit cuts due to fears of the pandemic's toll on the university budget. When the university did well financially during the pandemic, professors had to fight to restore their salaries and benefits in the face of a recalcitrant administration. Professors confronted "constant stonewalling," according to Anna Pegler-Gordon, professor of History and Asian American Studies at MSU's James Madison College.[5] To Pegler-Gordon, this lack of fiscal and financial transparency reflected university leadership's myopic vision of shared governance. "They only listen to our advice when it's what they want to do anyway," Pegler-Gordon observed. "They're very, very happy to ignore our advice." COVID-induced challenges were not unique to MSU. For professors at various schools, lackluster policies during the pandemic provoked affective and emotional changes in their workplaces. "I don't have the same sense of loyalty [to the university] because I haven't felt like even my life mattered," explained one professor at a different university.[6] These feelings encouraged faculty to assert their position on anti-CRT legislation as an affirmation that they would not be overlooked again.

Rapid changes within higher education have made university governance into what Heather Pincock described as a "game of whack-a-mole." An associate professor of conflict management at Kennesaw State University in Georgia, Pincock lamented, "I wish this Teach the Truth issue could have been the one thing that we were all mobilized around, but it was just one thing after another."[7] In light of the onslaught of new and recurrent issues, the willingness of faculty members to expend the political capital necessary to pass resolutions testifies to their refusal to allow divisive concepts legislation to go unchallenged.

EDUCATION SCHOOLS AND ROBERT'S RULES

A broad coalition of professors participated in the faculty senate resolution campaign, but their distinct approaches to the issue were influenced by their varying educational and professional backgrounds. Most of the resolution's advocates had histories of active involvement in faculty senates, councils, or the American Association of University Professors (AAUP). Both self-identified activists, including those with union connections, and faculty governance stalwarts spearheaded efforts to pass resolutions. Faculty in education colleges and departments advocated for resolutions in large part because of their fears about the censorial legislation's impact on pre-K–12 teachers. Far from monolithic, faculty members leveraged their diverse fields of study, knowledge of faculty governance, and personal experiences to garner support for the resolution.

Mark James, an associate professor of English at Molloy University on Long Island, New York, received an early version of the African American Policy Forum (AAPF) resolution template due to his seat on AAUP's Committee A on Academic Freedom and Tenure. He initially hesitated to bring it forward due to the conservatism of his university's faculty council and the local community. Molloy is a Catholic university in a conservative-leaning and racially segregated suburb of New York City. The Proud Boys have marched near campus twice. James overcame his hesitancy when the parent of a graduate student started "raising hell" because a professor of color had discussed critical race theory. While the resolution passed unanimously, faculty members held discrepant understandings of its meaning. James viewed the resolution as an affirmation of critical race theory as an arena for knowledge production. Other faculty members interpreted the resolution "purely [based] on the idea of academic freedom" and made subsequent efforts to negate or debunk CRT without understanding its basic tenets.[8]

Contests over the meaning of academic freedom, its relationship to CRT, and the implications behind the resolution also emerged at the University of Minnesota (UMN). Gopalan Nadathur, a professor of computer science and engineering and former chair of the Academic Freedom and Tenure Committee, jumped on the resolution as part of a concerted national action to "express solidarity with people who have less protections, like K–12 teachers." Yet Nadathur and his committee expressed some confusion about the "value judgments" in the template circulated by AAPF and the AAUP. "Academic freedom allows you to express your value judgments rather than being forced to adhere to those of another [party]."[9] UMN's resolution focused on rejecting the restraints imposed by divisive concepts legislation and affirming the benefits of "pursuing a deeper understanding of social issues."[10] The Academic Freedom and Tenure Committee rebuffed efforts to remove "critical race theory" from the resolution's title because members felt that doing so would subvert CRT's specific meaning.

Many faculty members in states with active battles over anti-CRT legislation viewed the resolution as a tool to raise the issue with colleagues and, in Andrea Gore's words, "get ahead of any legislative changes."[11] With anti-CRT legislation already on the books for K–12 schools in Texas, Gore and her colleagues anticipated that higher education would be their state politicians' next target. Gore used the resolution template to raise the issue with colleagues. A different faculty senator at a public university in the South saw the resolution as a tactic to gauge "How like-minded are the faculty? How easily can they be mobilized to symbolically say something about an issue?"[12] In essence, the resolution served as a stress test for faculty support.

Not all faculty senates initially viewed the resolution as a strategic countermeasure. At the University of Tennessee, Knoxville, faculty representatives worried that the resolution might jeopardize their university's standing with local politicians or undermine the Office of Government Relations and Advocacy's lobbying to restrain legislative action. The executive team of UTK's faculty senate and the Diversity and Inclusion Committee discussed the AAPF template in September 2021 but worried that its passage would be "poking a stick in the eye of the legislature." However, the introduction of a bill targeting higher education spurred UTK professors to send letters to each member of the state legislature explaining how limits on diverse thoughts and ideas imperiled Tennessee students' "competitive advantage in a global market."[13] This letter served as the basis for a modified resolution that passed the UTK Faculty Senate in March 2022.[14]

Professors capitalized on union connections to build solidarity with K–12 educators and participate in political protests. United Campus Workers, a wall-to-wall union of staff, faculty, graduate, and undergraduate workers organizing across the South, has helped organize faculty and build coalitions with K–12 teachers around educational censorship.[15] Liz Canfield, an associate professor of Gender, Sexuality and Women's Studies at Virginia Commonwealth University (VCU), noted that the resolution "help[ed] folks coalesce around a common vision."[16] Beyond the university, organized labor's opposition to anti-CRT bills has not always been successful. In some states, local teachers' unions have failed to sway legislators with their arguments that CRT is not taught in K–12.[17] Unions nonetheless served as a crucial space for political action and coalition building.

Faculty members in education schools played an outsized role in articulating the impact of divisive concepts laws on educational institutions at every level. Five of the seventeen professors interviewed held appointments within colleges of education or departments of teaching and learning. They largely framed their resolutions in terms of professional, even ethical, obligations to pre-K–12 teachers and students rather than academic freedom or shared governance. At two universities, education professors drafted resolutions from scratch. Education professors consistently refuted arguments that legislation focused on pre-K–12 did not constitute a problem for higher education. They insisted that university instruction could not be separated from previous schooling.

Donna Ford, Distinguished Professor in the College of Education and Human Ecology at Ohio State University, never saw staying silent as an option. Ford's commitment to ensuring that the nation's predominantly white and female teaching force "grapples with their biases and stereotypes" led to collaboration with colleague and fellow faculty senator Caroline Clark on a resolution supporting educators' rights to teach about racism.[18] Clark's leadership on the resolution was inspired by her former students, now K–12 teachers, who "were texting me saying 'This bill is going to kill us. This *is* killing us.'"[19] Already involved in the National Council of Teachers' efforts to advance similar resolutions, Clark was determined to bring this perspective to her university. "Our resolution was different from other universities," Ford observed, "because we talked about the impact that it will have on [preschool] to 12 if we didn't do this in higher education."

Education professors were keenly aware that anti-CRT bills did not need to become law to have a negative impact on education and educators. Sara McDaniel, a professor at the University of Alabama's College of Education, argued that politicians had "introduced the boogeyman."[20] Conservative legislators' and activists' purposeful misinterpretations and misrepresentations of core concepts led to the doxxing of professors, erroneous reports that educators were teaching CRT, and the suspension of racial equity initiatives in schools. The passage of educational gag laws in North Dakota made teachers "hesitant about what they want to teach . . . and how they're going to teach it," remarked education professor Florin Salajan.[21] Caroline Clark noted that classroom monitoring has felt "very much like the Red Scare." To their credit, education professors have not backed down, even when it cost them professional opportunities. "I'm willing to accept that I am not the darling of the State Department of Education," McDaniel reflected. "If I ever was, I'm definitely not anymore."[22]

POKING THE BEAR

The challenges faced by education faculty members were unique but not exceptional. In states where anti-CRT/divisive concepts bills passed or are poised to return for future deliberation, faculty members in all fields expressed concern about potential repercussions, including retaliatory cuts to public university budgets, targeted harassment on social media, getting passed over for promotions or research opportunities, and even job loss. Resolution advocates repeatedly fielded concerns that passing a strong resolution would be "poking the bear" and might engender political retaliation.[23] Developing strategies to allay their colleagues' concerns proved crucial to the passage of faculty senate resolutions.

In several schools, university leadership entreated professors to sit tight and allow upper administration or government liaisons to handle the issue. At the University of Alabama in Tuscaloosa, administrators urged professors to leave the issue to the university lobbyist. However, education professors dissatisfied with the lobbyist's inaction put forth a resolution calling on the university president and board to oppose pending legislation. As a countermeasure, the faculty senate president advanced a competing resolution limited to affirming academic freedom and freedom of speech. While the education faculty's resolution prevailed, the countermeasure signaled apprehension among administrators and some professors.[24] A similar conflict played out at the University of South Carolina, where the state controls 10 percent of the university budget. According to education professor Meir Muller, university administrators who feared that faculty would "ask for too much and lose everything" pushed "for a quiet campaign" to remove institutions of higher education from pending anti-CRT bills. While faculty senators like Muller recognized that administrators were trying to secure the "best outcome for our universities," they were unsatisfied by the administration's milquetoast response and engaged in a host of actions from passing a faculty resolution to giving public testimony against pending bills.[25]

These conflicts were not limited to states with active legislative battles around anti-CRT bills. Faculty senators at the University of Minnesota faced pushback from colleagues who warned that the resolution would draw the ire of politicians and nearby residents. Professor Nadathur viewed such arguments as a diversion: "My reading is that the fear of what the legislature can do, in most cases, is being used to push a particular viewpoint, because there isn't anything else you can use to argue against a resolution of this sort in the climate that is in play in the country today."[26]

If premonitions of political retaliation served as a smoke screen for faculty members wary of explicitly opposing resolutions, professors also openly expressed their objections to the content of resolutions. Some conservative professors erroneously claimed that resolutions required all faculty to teach critical race theory or complained about being "forced to teach [about] equity."[27] Slippage around academic freedom's definition played into right-wing talking points about silencing conservative students. One professor observed that while administrators consistently affirmed academic freedom, they echoed conservative talking points by casting academic freedom in terms of the "marketplace of ideas" and students' right to not be "shut down" in campus debates.[28]

Such claims ignored how the real burden of speech falls overwhelmingly on marginalized faculty members and those pushing for change. Hierarchies internal to the university and the lack of material and legal support for faculty members made these challenges even more difficult to navigate. Tenure status influenced educators' willingness take a position that might endanger their professional standing. Professors with clinical positions and year-to-year contracts were more susceptible to pressure from higher administration. Untenured instructors were more likely to stay quiet out of fear of losing promotions or their jobs. Employment insecurity, Sara McDaniel opined, "limits how well we can govern."[29]

A further challenge within universities lay in the uneven burden of anti-CRT and divisive concepts legislation across disciplines. Education professors expressed acute concerns about legislation's negative impact on teachers in training. Faculty in the humanities and social sciences feared punishment for using specific texts and restrictions on their research. Though scholars in these fields worried that STEM professors did not fully appreciate the stakes of anti-divisive concepts legislation, the scientists interviewed for this project easily identified areas of their work that could be affected. Science professors Andrea Gore and Louis Gross pointed to teaching about reproduction and evolution as potential subjects of controversy and highlighted the resources that professional associations have provided to educators teaching these subjects.[30]

As the passage of more than fifty resolutions across the country attests, these challenges are not insurmountable, but they must be addressed consciously. A deliberate response may require going back to first principles. Throughout the interviews, questions emerged over the applicability of AAUP's academic freedom guidelines—passed in the 1940s and expanded and affirmed in 1969/1970—to contemporary faculty life. Professors like Sean Meehan, who teaches English at Washington College in Maryland, wanted to know what AAUP's principles from the mid-twentieth century "mean now for the twenty-first century?"[31] Especially today, when academic freedom issues often emerge around campus events, diversity initiatives, or social media—which many academics use to share their scholarship with a wider public audience—the traditional guidelines can be hazy. Perhaps we might ask whether the fight around anti-CRT and divisive concepts legislation is best fought on the grounds of academic freedom or if another framework would provide a stronger foundation.

LESSONS

The successful passage of the recent faculty senate resolutions offers useful lessons about concerted, professional responses to legislative restrictions on education. Heather Pincock observed that resolutions are a "beginning step, not an ending step" in faculty efforts to address pressing educational and governance issues.[32] Several professors indicated that resolutions were most effective when faculty members contemplated follow-up actions and identified ways to harness the energy generated by their resolutions for use in further organizing.

Open communication, consultation, collaboration among stakeholders, and transparency of action foster resolutions that can increase understanding, generate faculty support, and provide a basis for future efforts. They allow faculty representatives to, in Florin Salajan's words, "advocate for policies and interests that expand beyond the faculty."[33] Faculty activists were keenly aware that politicians and conservative activists have deployed educational gag orders to shape interpretations of US history and culture, reassert racial and gender hierarchies challenged by social movements and street protests, and dictate the future of education. Adopting this broader perspective enabled faculty members to connect the defense of their professional right to teach contentious topics to national struggles for equity and justice.

Many of the faculty members interviewed stressed the need to use new tactics in the campaign against educational gag rules. Donna Ford and Caroline Clark emphasized the importance of stories and personal narrative, rather than mere argumentation, in changing people's minds. Personal stories, Ford observed, "tug at the heart" and "increase compassion and empathy."[34] This approach may be counterintuitive for faculty members trained in studied argumentation. And yet, "debate and argument usually doesn't change minds. Listening and storytelling changes minds," Clark explained.[35] These tactics are important because advocates for divisive concepts legislation have relied heavily on emotion and affect. Politicians and parents have argued that learning about slavery, discrimination, and oppression makes students feel bad, sad, or guilty. Educators might find success by flipping this narrative and interrogating the emotional ramifications of censorship. How, for example, is education hampered by a refusal to engage with the complex realities of our lives? What alternative relationships might be fostered by an honest reckoning with our collective histories?

Like all political change, faculty resolutions were collaborative and cumulative efforts. Sara McDaniel noted that fighting educational censorship is "emotionally exhausting work," which can leave activists second-guessing themselves to the point of self-defeat. Collaborators kept the work grounded, provided necessary reassurances, and allowed activists to take turns fielding questions and driving the work forward.[36] All political work involves moments where it is tempting to throw up one's hands and walk away, so tenacity is imperative. Meir Muller cautioned against "mak[ing] assumptions that you won't be successful." While each individual campaign may not generate the desired outcome, the accumulation of efforts ultimately leads to progress.[37]

Professors should also exploit the resources and knowledge available within the university community. Louis Gross encouraged fostering relationships with staff in government relations offices who are knowledgeable about state (and national) politics and willing to discuss issues and strategies. These staffers may be unable to stop unfavorable legislation, but they strive to make the situation "livable," while preserving the political relationships on which institutional funding relies. At the same time, faculty should not shy away from using their institutional memory to pressure administrators who often jump from school to school. Long-term faculty can leverage their deep understanding of the university's history and operations to their benefit.[38]

Despite their accomplishments, the insights gleaned from faculty in deeply conservative states carry a darker shadow. While Alabama's anti-CRT bills failed, professors who publicly opposed the legislation faced targeted harassment. Escalating threats led professors to go into hiding, seek alternate employment, and even leave the state and university.[39] Fear and political pressure have stalled efforts toward faculty senate resolutions at other Alabama universities. McDaniel acknowledged that outside observers may struggle to understand why seemingly straightforward tactics, like faculty resolutions, can be dead ends. She encouraged individuals and institutions with greater margins for action to provide resources or time to help faculty members in states or schools with less leeway. Even "camaraderie and acknowledgement would be good," McDaniel added.[40] Ultimately, the highly uneven nature of US politics and the culture wars in education demand a coordinated national campaign that builds on lessons learned and networks built by faculty members who have mobilized to pass faculty senate resolutions.

CONCLUSION

Faculty senate resolutions offer professors a platform to articulate their positions on key issues, build political alliances, and assert their vision for higher education. Educators across the country have deployed resolutions as political tactics in the contemporary culture war in education. However, as nonbinding statements, their individual impact is limited. The power behind the national campaign lies in its ability to mobilize faculty members for collective action.

Faculty have effectively used resolutions as educational tools to increase awareness and understanding of the anti-CRT/divisive concepts issue. Resolutions can serve as stress tests of institutional support. Passage of a resolution requires faculty members to voice their position (yea, nay, abstain), allowing organizers to evaluate their colleagues' willingness to speak openly on the issue and thus serving as a springboard for future actions. However, using resolutions as a stress test requires candid discussion before and during their passage. A resolution expressing support for academic freedom without specifying attacks on teaching about race or gender may pass faculty bodies with minimal resistance but prove ineffective in building toward further activity. Faculty resolutions are most influential combined with tactics like public testimony before legislators, collaboration with government relations offices, and relationship building with educators from pre-K through high school.

The struggle to defend educators' rights to teach "divisive concepts" reminds us that academic freedom is a tool toward a greater goal, not the goal itself. If this perspective is lost, academic freedom runs the risk of merely maintaining the status quo. As this battle continues, educators in all disciplines and levels will need to stake out a proactive vision for education's contribution to progressive social change. As this volume attests, those frameworks exist, but we need to harness them toward powerful and resilient movements.

For many faculty members, particularly those with histories of activism, the resolution was not a starting point for their work but rather one of the many steps in the fight to build a better university and a fairer educational system. For Liz Canfield, resolutions are outlets where faculty's "myriad and sundry activisms" punch through to the surface.[41] Faculty senate resolutions can communicate to colleagues, students, and K–12 teachers that they are not alone. They can signal to politicians that faculties will not quietly allow external actors to run roughshod over the profession, particularly when the future of students, education, and democracy is at stake. The power of the resolution does not lie in its writing but in the effort expended to make one's corner of the world amenable to passing one.[42]

10

Academic Freedom

It's a Question of Job Security

HELENA WORTHEN AND JOE BERRY

"**C**ONTINGENCY" IS THE broad term that describes the spectrum of conditions of faculty working in higher ed without tenure or the prospect of tenure.[1] Today, over three-fourths of all higher ed faculty in the United States work as contingents. Contingency means one's job is "contingent upon funding, enrollment, or other factors." These "other factors" may include favoritism, discrimination, retaliation, student complaint, the desire for "fresh blood," or no reason at all.[2] At the time of this writing, politics is a significant "other factor" driving the rapid expansion of contingency. The gag laws being passed in Florida are examples of ways that faculty can be threatened with job loss if they include certain topics in their curriculum.[3] In reality, even tenured faculty can become contingent if, as in Kansas, Georgia, and other states, legislative efforts succeed in eliminating tenure.[4] A contingent is effectively an "at-will" worker.[5]

The overall culture of academic freedom in higher education is at risk for everyone. In the American Association of University Professors (AAUP) 1940 Statement of Principles, academic freedom is explicitly linked to the form of job security known as tenure: "The common good depends upon the free search for truth and its free exposition. . . . Academic freedom is essential to these purposes and applies to both teaching and research." The statement explains that tenure [is] "indispensable to the success of an institution in fulfilling its obligations to its students and to society."[6] In other words, without the protections provided to faculty by the security of tenure, they cannot practice academic freedom, and commitments to students and society cannot be reliably fulfilled.

The reality of practicing academic freedom as a contingent varies from state to state and between public, private nonprofit, and for-profit sectors. Modifications to pure contingency—in other words, the introduction of some constraint on total management rights—may take place through the medium of a union contract, which in turn is the product of organizing and bargaining. Very few private for-profit sector colleges or universities have unionized faculties. In the private nonprofit sector, a surge of union organizing has taken place in the last decade and contracts with modest job security provisions for contingents have been signed.[7] It is mainly in the public sector that state-level laws affect organizing and, therefore, the potential for job security for any and all public sector faculty. For example, in Texas, state law *prohibits* colleges and universities from signing collective bargaining contracts with faculty workforces. In Pennsylvania, state law *enables* local unions in state colleges and universities to bargain on behalf of all faculty. In California, state law *limits* the workload of nontenured community college faculty to 67 percent of a full-time faculty load. In New York, the Taylor Law *forbids* strikes in higher ed and imposes severe penalties on unions that strike. In Illinois, state collective bargaining law *was changed* to cover community college faculty who work less than a 50 percent load. All of these various situations address how much, if any, academic freedom a faculty member can hope to exercise. Some of these instances—like the last one, Illinois—may seem like trivial tweaking, but the difference between being included under a collective bargaining law or not probably meant the difference for many faculty between continuing in a teaching career or not. The historic spread of contingency since the 1970s, when it arose as a management strategy for dealing with budget cuts, enrollment fluctuations, the rise of unionization, and the changing demographic of faculty, has effects far beyond the direct individual experience of faculty who are employed on a contingent basis.[8] Contingency impacts entire systems. This is because academic freedom, in the classroom but more obviously in governance, research, and the public sphere, is an outcome of a collective culture. This culture depends on the moral, ethical, and academic activity of peers who are, at least to the extent that they do their work without fear, equals. A collective culture is weak when it depends on people who are very unequal in power. On the other hand, to try to exercise academic freedom alone in a college or university may be courageous but is usually neither practical nor effective.

THREE STORIES ABOUT CONTINGENCY

To describe the range and some of the experiential meaning of contingency, this chapter tells three stories. We will begin with a narrative about a faculty member who is trying to work in one of the states where explicit direct attacks on academic freedom are taking place. This narrative will follow this woman's experience as she suffers the step-by-step dismantling of her work, losing protections at each step: it tells how a good job can become a bad job. We concealed her identity for her protection. The second story, also about a woman, Suzanne Jones in Texas, now well-known because of her fight, covers the attack on her personally and the fight that she engaged in to defend herself and her job. Her experience illuminates the limits of a defense based on freedom of speech, her best option given where she worked. The third story is about the rise of Higher Education Labor United (HELU), a new organization that puts ending contingency high on its agenda. It claims the radical vision of "wall to wall and coast to coast," meaning organizing all the workers in higher education, not just faculty, and coordinated bargaining and organizing, on a national scale, coast to coast. Since there are so many public sector colleges and universities located in states without higher ed collective bargaining enabling laws, HELU's "coast to coast" vision bridges the different extremes of contingency between the Suzanne Jones's story and some of the faculties that have unions and reasonable contract articles covering contingent faculty. We include a description of a contract article from the Pennsylvania State College and University system to show how a union can negotiate a degree of job protection for contingents and consequently make the exercise of a certain level of academic freedom possible.

A final comment before we start the next section: Many readers are familiar with terms other than "contingent." They are numerous. Some in current use are "adjunct" (probably the most common term), "non-regular" (an almost meaningless term that mainly means "not tenure line"), and "part-time" (a term that obscures the fact that many contingent faculty work full-time, teaching a full load at a single institution).[9] William A. Herbert, Jacob Apkarian, and Joseph van der Naald sort faculty employment into four categories based on whether a job is full-time or part-time, tenure/tenure track or not tenure/tenure track. In the case of California, "part-time temporary" is the official term in the community colleges for the 38,000 or more contingent faculty who are often rehired year after year. These and many more (see Joe Berry's list of over thirty in his book *Reclaiming the Ivory Tower*) all refer to contingent faculty status.[10] "Contingent" therefore is a term that covers all of these situations except for tenure/tenure track.

A FACULTY JOB DISMANTLED ONE PIECE AT A TIME

The story that follows depicts contingency as a spectrum of insecurity starting near the top, with someone who is hired to teach full-time and expecting to go up for tenure but who is not yet tenured. As her job is dismantled, we see how she has to become increasingly cautious as she is exposed to increasing contingency. Contingency here is a continuity of losses. This happened to take place during and immediately after the COVID-19 pandemic, which was seized upon as an opportunity by higher ed managers to increase their power over their employees and by many state political leaders to subvert the influence of established higher ed institutions in the public sphere. Together, these authorities weakened the nation's faculties by reducing their job security in a variety of ways, as Colleen Flaherty pointed out in her survey of the impact of COVID on adjunct work.[11] Higher ed managers, of course, were not alone in pursuing this tactic.

This woman was first given a full-time position as a spousal hire (a job offered to one partner to facilitate hiring the other partner into a tenure-track position) in a humanities department at a major state university. Her status at the outset, uncertain and lower than her husband's, is not unusual. She understood this to be a job that led to promotions such as those on the tenure line but like many people, she had accepted her contract as it was offered to her without trying to nail down the details. Then just as her job started, she was told that it had been changed "for COVID-related austerity reasons" into a one-year contract position. It would be renewable for four years, after which it would either roll over to tenure-line or end. If it ended, she was told that she might continue to teach as an adjunct, hired from one semester to the next.

Even the first step down in rank, from a job that is presumed to be leading to tenure to a job that is a one-year contract position, is enormous. It altered not only how she approached her job in the classroom but also how she had to relate to her colleagues, both informally and formally. She was no longer an equal among tenured and tenure-line colleagues on committees that she might be assigned to. Votes in meetings became a choice loaded with political consequences, not a matter of professional judgment. She could no longer expect to stay long-term on research teams she might join or apply for grants that might be long in arriving. Even though this change in rank happened to her individually, awareness of what had happened sent a signal of how vulnerable faculty could be to the rest of her department. However, the couple had a preschool-aged child and her husband was not interested in moving, so she chose to stay in this position.

Then as COVID waned, the governor and the legislature in this state joined with other conservative state legislatures to pass laws to prohibit discussions of "sensitive issues" in education.[12] "Sensitive issues" includes race and gender. Faced with the difficulty of teaching history or any social science or humanities discipline without talking about race and gender, this woman looked for community among her fellow academics to find out what their reaction would be. But because of COVID, most faculty were now working remotely. There was no ongoing opportunity to meet in hallways or department offices and discuss this threat. There was no culture of academic support to rely on. She hoped to hear some senior job-secure tenured professor raise the question of how to deal with these laws in a departmental Zoom meeting, but it did not happen. For someone now on a year-to-year contract, raising the issue in a departmental Zoom meeting without the cover of a more powerful faculty member speaking first would have been risky.

Since the university's full-time faculty had representation through a union, she investigated to see what the union's response to this legislation had been. However, under COVID, the union, like the faculty generally, had no visible presence on campus. Like her department, the union had suffered a loss of collective agency.

The union leadership had already sought legal advice about how faculty members should respond to the new legislation. In various communications, the union told its members that they should base their behavior on their individual sense of exposure to "risk." Those who felt that their normal curriculum would put them at risk of failure to get expected promotions or losing their jobs should manage their teaching to minimize that risk and totally avoid those topics. Those with less risk might proceed cautiously and those who believed that they had little exposure should proceed "as usual." In these communications, the union said it would defend any individual faculty member who was retaliated against. Thus, the burden of choosing to do one's job in the face of these threats was placed on the individual instructor.

This story points out several concrete locations where the power to practice academic freedom could have been exercised if, in fact, it had not already been lost by the woman herself, by her department, by the union, and by the institution itself. But it also tells us something about where that lost power ends up: how carving out a path of diminishing job security for faculty simultaneously constructs a path of increasing managerial control for administrators. Administrators as managers, often lacking tenure themselves, are open to becoming politically captured by local and state-level interests in a way that tenured faculty are not. This, in turn, passes control to political interests outside the college or university.

That leaves those remaining faculty who do have job security as the bulwark against the anti-science, anti-intellectual, anti-internationalist, racist, and sexist attacks of their state's politicians, transmitted through the university's managers. Today the tenured job-secure faculty across the United States is less than a quarter of the entire faculty workforce. They may not be realistically able to play the role of defenders of faculty rights anymore. If a faculty is represented by a union, that union may also be dominated by the tenured few who have not been mobilized to fight for many years. If the union has not gone through a transformation to raise a new generation of leadership from the current contingent majority, it is likely to be at a loss about where to begin.[13] It also may be disproportionately led by department chairs, elected or appointed, who have great power over all contingent faculty.

Although the faculty union in this case is now fighting back, there is no happy ending to this story at the present time. COVID gave higher ed management an undreamed-of opportunity to make changes while avoiding "troubles on campus" such as it experienced in the 1960s and 1970s; the chances of faculty or student organizing to resist political intervention like these gag laws became close to zero when campuses emptied. The legal advice initially offered by the union highlights how an attack on higher education can find a soft spot in the defense of academic freedom even in the ranks of a union. Contingency is a trap that closes slowly over time, often taking incremental steps that one by one may not seem to matter much.

ACADEMIC FREEDOM AND FREEDOM OF SPEECH

"Academic freedom" is a term that sounds as if it applies to something unique to faculty.[14] This is a problem. As Ellen Schrecker said, "It is difficult to explain how academic freedom benefits society, especially to a public already upset about the rising costs of higher education and jealous of the economic security tenured faculty members enjoy."[15] But there are other ways to describe the right that people have to talk freely, especially about their jobs, whether they are at work or not, at home or in public places. One of these is the "freedom of speech," referred to in the First Amendment to the US Constitution. This forms a barrier against government (but not private employers') interference with free expression. How much it actually applies to and protects public sector employees is a matter of active litigation, but overall, "freedom of speech" is a vast category limited only by libel laws. The notorious *Citizens United* Supreme Court case shows how broadly this category can be interpreted when there are no legal limits on how much money can be donated to political campaigns because any limits would be an ongoing unconstitutional and governmental violation of free speech.

The following story describes one such case in which a freedom of speech defense was raised on behalf of Suzanne Jones, an outspoken faculty member at Collin College, a public community college district in Texas. Texas is one of five states where public sector collective bargaining for higher education faculty is illegal. After teaching at the college for twenty years, Jones was fired for signing a petition to remove Confederate memorials from streets in Dallas, for trying to form a chapter of the Texas Faculty Association, and for criticizing the college's COVID reopening plan.

The suit that Jones filed against Collin was handled by the Foundation for Individual Rights and Expression (FIRE), which describes itself as placing "a special emphasis on defending the individual rights of students and faculty members on our nation's campuses, including freedom of speech, freedom of association, due process, legal equality, religious liberty, and sanctity of conscience."[16] The word "individual" is significant when we are comparing the concepts of academic freedom and freedom of speech. A lawsuit based on the right to freedom of speech in the First Amendment sense can and often does apply to unpopular speech of any sort, coming from both ends of the spectrum, left to right. It can be individual speech or an expression of collective speech. The exercise of academic freedom, on the other hand, arises from and depends on a professional culture of academic freedom. This culture is weakened when some individuals are more protected than others.

In November 2022, a settlement with Collin College was announced. The college agreed to a two-year $230,000 teaching contract for Jones and to pay $145,000 in attorneys' fees. While the contract is more than double what Jones would have been paid under her previous contract, she is only allowed to teach remotely on the Collin College online system and will lose her job after two years.[17] Twenty years of continuous employment did not mean "tenure." The value of this agreement to the political forces looking for ways to manage and control the kind of public good that faculty provide exceeds the price of the settlement because it signals, as far and wide as the news of the settlement travels, that the power to decide what gets taught and learned in Texas—and beyond—is ultimately not under the control of the faculty. It is with whatever government is in power at the time. In another district in Texas, where the majority of the student population enroll needing basic skills remediation, faculty were told to find a way to bring two-thirds of them up to a C or risk being laid off for "poor pedagogy."[18] Given that public education funding is partially based on student head count, this suggests a clear link between contingency and the goal of maintaining a funding stream. "Follow the money" applies here too.

WHAT STRATEGY IS RADICAL ENOUGH TO DEAL WITH THESE ATTACKS?

If we think of contingency as the overarching condition that leaves faculty vulnerable to threats of all kinds but especially the current threats of political interference with the faculty's power to exercise academic freedom, what response can be raised? One problem is that degrees of contingency vary by state. In states where legislation encourages higher ed collective bargaining, some unions have been able to negotiate contract articles that establish a floor of job security under contingents. In others, the best hope is lobbying a sympathetic state legislature.[19] There is a human tendency for people who are safe from threats to ignore people who are exposed and at risk. Higher Education Labor United (HELU), which seeks to promote solidarity on campuses, has begun carrying out its national organizing strategy to improve working conditions in higher education through collective bargaining. At an information-sharing Zoom conference on job security, several reports about bargaining to reduce contingency were presented.

One of those reports gives a sense of the nitty-gritty that must be taken into consideration when a contract provision dealing with contingency gets written. It was negotiated in the Pennsylvania State College and University system, where adjuncts are represented by the Association of Pennsylvania State College and University Faculties. Their contract, bargained in 1999, was not put into operation until 2010. It contains a "conversion" article, informally referred to as "*person* conversion" because the actual person holding the position gets the converted position, that is, converted from adjunct to tenure line. This is in contrast to a "*position* conversion" where, for example, if a dozen adjuncts are each teaching one class, those positions would get converted into three tenure-line positions carrying four classes each. In this contract, after adjuncts have put in five years of continuous service at the workload level of twenty-four credit hours per year (the definition of full time), their service automatically triggers a vote by their department's faculty to convert them into tenure-line faculty. The timeline is loosely based on the AAUP concept that anyone who teaches for five or six years should be tenured. In recent years, about 30 percent of adjuncts were teaching at the level of twenty-four credit hours per year. Individuals can turn down this opportunity, but the trigger is automatic. Because the evaluation regimen for all faculty members, both tenure-line and nontenure-line, is very demanding, with an evaluation every year, even for people who teach just one semester, there is a great deal of documentation already in the pipeline for these conversion votes.

Although this contract provision does create a stepwise process for going from contingent to tenure-line, it does not end contingency perfectly. Departments are allowed great latitude for what to base their vote upon: a dossier, teaching evaluations, recommendation letters, CVs, and so on. Each faculty member gets the packet and studies it before voting. It is also possible, due to the vagueness of the contract over the protocol, that a department could just decide to vote no all the time, a situation regarded as an "internal culture problem." The union's position is that the department's decision is not subject to grievance.

This "person conversion" process has resulted in many conversions of adjuncts into tenure-line faculty members. Once someone is in a full-time pathway, if they lose their position, the union will grieve it. For example, if someone in their third year is doing well and suddenly doesn't get hired, the union takes it up. There is also a hiring preference for reappointment in adjunct positions, which clicks in after someone has taught sixty credits, but there is, at the present time, no "upgrading" preference for hiring an inside candidate when a new tenure-line comes available.[20]

HELU: "WALL TO WALL AND COAST TO COAST"

Participants in the 2021 HELU conference came from states all over the country, some with strong collective bargaining laws, others with none, or actual prohibitions. This attempt to cross state lines to find common ground across the whole range of contingency is one of the central tactical goals of HELU. Let us look, therefore, at the background and current prospects of the movement in higher ed to eliminate contingency—and thereby making the exercise of academic freedom possible.

Resistance to interference with academic freedom has been fundamental to organizing among contingent faculty, all the way back to the 1980s, when the share of faculty contingents began to noticeably rise. In most workplaces, the common trigger issue for organizing is "respect." The same is true for contingent faculty. Low wages may be what drives them out of the field, but disrespect is what triggers organizing.[21] Healthcare workers defend "patient safety." K–12 teachers organize around "the schools our students deserve," the slogan of the Chicago Teachers Union in 2012. Academic freedom is a respect issue.

Time and again, efforts to organize and resist have risen, spread, won some battles, faded, and merged but never gone away. We have a history of them in our book *Power Despite Precarity*.[22] Then a new generation of organizers, outraged at student debt, admissions scandals, administrative salaries, and so on, showed up. Many of them came from the grad student movement. They worked with the Bernie Sanders 2016 presidential campaign on the College for All Act (Sanders/Pramila Jayapal, D-Wash.) and expanded it beyond free college tuition and debt relief to labor issues, including working conditions for faculty and all higher ed workers. Although the act failed to pass, activists from many parts of the higher ed labor movement—labor historians, union leaders, Scholars for a New Deal, COCAL (Coalition on Contingent Academic Labor), and others—regrouped and formed Higher Education Labor United in 2020. They put forward a radical vision statement and, by the fall of 2021, had endorsements for it from over 113 local unions and organizations.

A national winter summit in early 2022 led to a commitment to build a sustainable bottom-up organization to do what none of the twelve national unions in the higher ed sector had ever done: unite, take on the neoliberal business model of higher education, and turn it around to provide a desperately needed public good.[23] The twelve national unions include the two big traditional teacher unions, the NEA and the AFT, both of which have a mostly K–12 membership; the AAUP, now affiliated with the AFT; the steelworkers (USW); electrical and machine workers (UE); auto workers (UAW); communication workers (CWA); service employees (SEIU); Union of Needletrades, Industrial and Textile Employees and Hotel Employees and Restaurant Employees (UNITE HERE); International Brotherhood of Teamsters (IBT); National Nurses United/California Nurses Association (NNU/CNA); and the American Federation of State, County and Municipal Employees (AFSCME). At the time of this writing, HELU is staffed and incorporated with an acting executive board, working with local unions and organizations, and social justice organizations and groups from states where there are no local collective bargaining unions, to build financial and human resources to carry the fight forward.

The HELU slogan "Wall to Wall and Coast to Coast" sets a very ambitious target, but it is no more radical than the gag laws and attacks on tenure we can see around the country. "Coast to coast" commits to a national campaign, as compared to state by state, and binds faculties without collective bargaining laws together with faculties in states where fairly advanced union contracts cover contingents. The first strategic level will be coordinated bargaining: information sharing, advising and consulting, and solidarity actions. "Wall to wall" is an even more radical goal: claiming allies across not just contingent and tenure-line workforces but across all the other workforces in higher ed: staff, clerical, custodial, food services, healthcare, and so on. In many colleges and universities all the workforces have union representation, but "wall to wall" implies more than that. It calls for solidarity and cooperation and a topsy-turvy impact on the acutely status conscious faculty, who will need to be open to learning from people without advanced degrees. The language of "free speech on the job" and "just cause discipline and discharge" is the academic freedom vocabulary that cuts across all these workforces. Implicit in this slogan is a question about the purpose of higher ed for our society today.

The higher education crisis is a crisis within the climate crisis, and "wall to wall and coast to coast" is our response, but what kind of higher ed system would that create? Is there any kind of worker included in HELU's wall-to-wall vision who does not need respect for their work, the right to exercise their skills and knowledge to the standards of their community, with appropriate tools and safety protections? Whether it is in the power plant that heats and lights the college or university, the hospital where students learn to care for patients, the research labs and libraries, or the classrooms. Or the public sphere, where people testify, report, entertain, explain, and argue? Are there any kinds of workers whom we can afford to employ as at-will workers, contingents who are exposed to threats of job loss that makes it impossible to exercise academic freedom? The answer to this question will put meat on the bones of HELU's vision.

11

My Battle to Preserve Academic Freedom at the University of Florida

SHARON D. WRIGHT AUSTIN

C URRENTLY, SEVERAL EFFORTS are occurring at universities all over the country to stifle free speech and academic freedom. Many of these involve attempts to control the curriculum. At other times, faculty have been reprimanded for expressing unpopular opinions. A cancel culture that includes reprimands and firings retaliates against individuals who express ideas incongruent to those of the state. In addition, some universities are trying to implement post-tenure reviews as a veiled attempt to silence and intimidate tenured faculty. These efforts are a part of a larger effort to deprive individuals of their civil rights, civil liberties, and political rights. On one hand, universities claim to value diversity, equity, and inclusion yet, on the other hand, they give in to demands from outsiders to dictate how courses should be taught, what should be taught, and what outside activities professors engage in. This cowardice results in unfair, stressful, and discriminatory actions toward university faculty members.

Today, we are witnessing a new version of McCarthyism on college campuses. Professors who refuse to cater to the whims of administrators risk punishment, retaliation, or termination. This is troubling for all university faculty members but especially for untenured academics who lack job security. It also exposes professors, many of whom have given years of service to their universities, to public humiliation in an age when anonymous trolls engage in cyberbullying with mean-spirited comments.

This chapter examines the University of Florida's attempt to stifle the speech and outside activities of its faculty. I chronicle the challenges I endured when attempting to serve as an expert witness in a voting discrimination case. In *League of Women Voters of Florida, Inc. v. Lee*, state political actors were accused of discriminating against Black and Hispanic/Latine voters by enacting the SB 90 law.[1] Several civil and voting rights groups challenged the constitutionality of this law and invited me to serve as an expert witness. In this role, I was responsible for conducting research on racial voting discrimination in Florida, providing a deposition, and testifying. Eventually, I, along with other UF faculty members, had to file a lawsuit to change our university's conflict of interest (COI) policy to remove prohibitions on participating in cases challenging state political actors.

THE ATTACK ON ACADEMIC FREEDOM AND THE IMPORTANCE OF EXPERT WITNESSING

During the summer of 2021, I was asked to serve as an expert witness for the first time. I had previously participated in a workshop, sponsored by civil rights organizations, that was designed to train expert witnesses. Many of the nation's most prominent expert witnesses, who had played key roles in voting rights cases, were approaching retirement. Therefore, individuals, like myself, who had been teaching civil rights, voting rights, history, and politics courses for years were invited to learn about statistically analyzing data, creating maps, and other aspects of expert witnessing.

A couple of weeks later, I received an email invitation to serve as an expert witness for a case challenging the recently enacted SB 90 law in Florida. I argued that SB 90 was a part of a long history of attempts by legislators and governors to discriminate against African American and Hispanic voters. The report emphasized that African American and Hispanic/Latine voters had made political progress, but such progress had usually been followed by a backlash from the legislature and governor. In addition, when African Americans and Latines took advantage of new or expanded voting laws and procedures (such as early in-person, drop box, absentee, and/or mail voting), the legislature enacted laws that made it more difficult for these citizens to benefit from these laws and procedures. I argued that SB 90 was yet another attempt to disenfranchise Black voters.

Individuals and groups immediately challenged SB 90 after its enactment. Florida governor Ron DeSantis referred to SB 90 as an election reform to prevent electoral fraud.[2] However, he acknowledged that no serious voting irregularities had occurred during the November 2020 election.[3] Key provisions of the bill include:

▪ Floridians now must provide a driver's license number, state ID number, or the last four digits of their Social Security number to request a vote by mail ballot.

▪ Instead of requesting a mail ballot through the next two general elections (for the next four years), requests are limited to the next general election (for two years).

▪ Drop boxes can only be used during early voting hours unless they are located at a Supervisor's office, and the boxes must be physically supervised while in use. Relying on remote video surveillance is not allowed. Failure to provide adequate supervision carries a $25,000 fine for leaving drop boxes unattended during early voting hours.

▪ Nonprofit organizations seeking to register voters must now include a mandatory disclaimer "warning" voters that their registrations may not arrive on time and are required—under penalty of severe fines—to deliver completed registrations to the voter's individual county within 14 days. Many of these organizations successfully mobilized black voters, especially during presidential elections.

▪ The bill expands the definition of "solicitation" to include "engaging in any activity with the intent to influence or effect of influencing a voter" and it extends the "no-solicitation zone" to the 150 feet around ballot drop boxes.[4]

My university denied my request to serve as an expert witness on *League of Women Voters of Florida, Inc. v. Lee* in October 2021. A year earlier in 2020, the Florida legislature had passed legislation requiring every state university to implement policies that, "[a]t a minimum, . . . require employees engaged in the design, conduct, or reporting of research to disclose and receive a determination that outside activity or financial interest does not affect the integrity of the state university."[5] In response, UF adopted a conflicts of commitment and conflicts of interest policy to ensure that professors' activities do "not conflict, or appear to conflict, with their professional obligations to the University."[6] The policy governs conflicts of commitment that require professors to devote excessive amounts of time to outside activities, taking their focus away from their university employment. It also covers conflicts of interest that occur "when a University Employee's financial, professional, commercial or personal interests or activities outside of the University affects, or appears to affect, their professional judgement or obligations to the University."[7] To prevent both types of conflict, the policy requires professors to report all outside activities—"any paid or unpaid activity undertaken by an Employee outside of the University which could create an actual or apparent" conflict—through UF's Online Interest Organizer (UFOLIO)."[8] The university established a conflict of interest (COI) program that employed six staff members.[9] Led by Gary Wimsett Jr., JD, the assistant vice president for conflicts of interest, UF COI operated under the supervision of the Offices of the Provost and Senior Vice President for Academic Affairs.[10]

The current version of the university's Conflicts of Commitment and Conflicts of Interest Policy went into effect on July 1, 2020. It requires faculty members to file a request on UFOLIO, the university's online conflicts system, each time they seek to participate in an outside activity. The policy gives the university the right to deny the request if the outside activity conflicts with state interests but does not define what those interests are. Before the new policy went into effect, faculty members had to file a COI report only once a year. According to UF's website, the new COI program was created to serve as "a centralized office dedicated to review of disclosures of outside activities and interests. In an environment of heightened external pressure, the COI Program represents an important step in UF's continued commitment to transparency, accountability, and shared responsibility as stewards of the public trust. The UF COI Program embraces professional ethics as an essential component of institutional integrity and is here to support the growth of UF employees engaged in important teaching, research, and public service activities."[11]

Despite this language, the conflict of interest policy was used to attempt to silence me and two other political science professors by preventing us from serving as expert witnesses in the case. The three of us tried to reason with the administration, to no avail. Two of my political science colleagues had already received their denials when I received mine. More specifically, the assistant vice president for conflicts of interests wrote in response to my

UFOLIO request: "UF will deny its employees' requests to engage in outside activities when it determines the activities are adverse to its interests." Because UF is a state actor, he reasoned, "litigation against the state is adverse to UF's interests."[12] Based on this logic, the decision could be interpreted to mean that the university has an interest in maintaining voting discrimination. My report, as well as those of my colleagues, supported the case of those plaintiffs who, like the NAACP, the ACLU, the League of Women Voters, the Advancement Project, and others, challenged voting discrimination in the case. So, was I being told that I, a Black woman from the South whose parents lived in the Jim Crow society of Mississippi, was prohibited from using my education, intellect, and resources to fight discrimination against minority voters? This was completely unacceptable to me.

My colleagues and I reached out to the American Civil Liberties Union for help. One of their attorneys sent a letter to the administration stating that this action violated my First Amendment right to freedom of speech and violated principles of academic freedom. I had already written the report and was preparing for my deposition when I received the denial. I was not aware that I needed permission to serve as an expert witness. For years, UF professors had served in this vital role for lawsuits with no requirement for permission and no mention of a potential conflict of interest. The ACLU attorney pointed out that the "First Amendment prohibits the government from burdening public-employee speech so long as: (1) the employee is speaking in their capacity as a private citizen; (2) on a matter of public concern; and (3) the employee's interest in speaking, and the public's interest in receiving the employee's speech, outweigh the government's legitimate interests as an employer. *See, e.g., Lane v. Franks*, 573 U.S. 228 (2014); *Garcetti v. Ceballos*, 547 U.S. 410 (2006)."[13] Because I would be speaking in my capacity as a private citizen, not as an employee of the university, and speaking on a matter of public concern, there should not have been a problem. In addition, my interest in sharing my expertise on minority politics and voting discrimination on an issue of importance to the public was more important than any opposing interest UF might have had.

After receiving a letter from an ACLU attorney and the publication of a *New York Times* article about our denials, the university changed its explanation.[14] On October 30, 2021, the university suggested the reason for the disapprovals was not only because the expert witness testimony was adverse to the university's interests, as they had originally stated in our UFOLIO denials, but because the other professors and I would be compensated for our time and expenses. In response to the extensive media coverage and social media debates, President Fuchs and Provost Glover issued a statement claiming falsely that the only problem was our compensation, saying, "if the professors wish to testify pro bono on their own time without using university resources, they are free to do so."[15] In the same statement, Fuchs and Glover announced the creation of a task force to "review the university's conflict of interest policy and examine it for consistency and fidelity."[16] Finally, UF's general counsel emailed our attorneys, explaining that we could serve as expert witnesses if the work was "done on their personal time, in their personal capacity, without the use of any University resources and without compensation."[17]

The compensation argument was false and ridiculous. For decades, professors across the country have received compensation for their expert witness work. This is very intense work that requires them to write reports often in a short time frame while still carrying out their professional duties. Therefore, the idea that my colleagues and I would have to do this kind of work for free made no sense. Other professors, including those at UF, had been getting paid for years and it had never been an issue. At no time were we ever told that we could serve as long as we did not receive pay. The university seemed to be scrambling to find a position to cover itself. Their arguments made no sense because they knew that we would be expressing our own individual opinions in our capacities as witnesses and therefore would not be speaking on behalf of the university. Also, there was no evidence that the time we spent serving as witnesses would interfere with our duties as professors. They were clearly lying.

Each time the university responded with a justification for its action, our attorneys caught them in lies. After President Fuchs's announcement, reports surfaced that the university had denied permission for similar activities to several other faculty members. All of the individuals who were denied had sought permission to participate in lawsuits challenging various discriminatory acts by state actors, including the governor. In July 2020, the dean of UF's law school denied a request by four law professors—Kenneth

Nunn, Mark Fenster, Teresa Jean Reid, and Sarah H. Wolking—to sign an amicus curiae brief in *Jones v. DeSantis*.[18] In that case, civil rights groups challenged a state law that required ex-felons to pay outstanding fines before having their voting rights reinstated.[19] In 2018, 65 percent of Florida voters approved Amendment 4, allowing many ex-felons who had served their sentences to have their voting rights restored.[20] In response, Governor DeSantis signed Senate Bill 7066 in June 2019, which required ex-felons to pay any outstanding fees before their rights could be restored.[21] A trial court ruled that this "pay-to-vote" system was unconstitutional, but it was reversed on appeal.[22] The four UF law professors were later allowed to sign the brief in support of the lawsuit challenging SB 7066 on the condition that they did not list their university affiliations. Professors Nunn, Fenster, Reid, and Wolking received no compensation for signing the amicus curiae brief. Of the ninety-three professors who signed the brief, they were the only ones without university affiliation.[23] At around the same time, the University of Florida denied a request by Dr. Jeffrey L. Goldhagen, a pediatrician and a professor at the University of Florida College of Medicine, to submit a sworn statement in litigation concerning legislation banning mask mandates in schools.[24] He also did not seek or receive compensation for his testimony.[25]

While the state denied permission to me and others who challenged discriminatory behavior on the part of the state, it did not oppose professors who wrote reports in support of the state's positions. Florida International University (FIU), another public university, requires professors to inform the institution of outside activities that may pose a conflict of interest with the "university, the Board of Governors, and/or the State of Florida" schools.[26] However, FIU approved without any opposition Professor Dario Moreno's UFOLIO request to receive compensation for his expert testimony in support of SB 90 on behalf of the Republican National Committee and the National Republican Senatorial Committee, the defendants in the same lawsuit my colleagues and I were challenging.[27]

Ironically, the UF president announced that the university would give the three of us permission to serve as expert witnesses only hours before we filed the *Austin et al. v. University of Florida Board of Trustees* lawsuit. All of these events were covered by the local and national media. Because the conflict of interest policy remained in effect, we had no choice but to file a lawsuit on November 5, 2021, the same day that the university reversed its denials of our UFOLIO applications. If the policy remained in effect, the university could continue to discriminate against professors, in violation of the First Amendment.

We had received permission to serve as expert witnesses for the one case we were working on, but what about future cases? What about other faculty members in situations similar to ours? We received permission because a firestorm took place after our situation was reported in the *New York Times* and other media outlets. Our case also ignited vigorous debates on Twitter. The university wanted the media attention to end but cared nothing about our larger concerns. We and other university faculty members had to file the lawsuit.

TAKING MY UNIVERSITY TO COURT

On November 5, 2021, we filed our lawsuit seeking a preliminary injunction because the revised conflict of policy was still problematic in that it violated our First Amendment rights. In the future, we and other faculty might still be denied opportunities to serve as expert witnesses if we challenged the actions or legislation of state political actors. Under the revised policy, the university still maintained the option of denying us if our speech did not align with the viewpoints of the legislature or the governor. As a result, we sought a preliminary injunction barring UF from continuing to enforce its conflict of interest policy with regard to future requests to serve as expert witnesses. We also challenged UF's policy on the signing of amicus briefs by law professors. We argued that both the COI and amicus briefs policies were prohibited by the First Amendment. The other plaintiffs and I then requested that the preliminary injunction bar UF from applying its policy to future requests to serve as expert witnesses or sign on to amicus briefs.

On January 21, 2022, Judge Mark E. Walker issued a preliminary injunction that prohibited the continued enforcement of UF's conflict of interest policy on providing expert witness testimony or legal consulting in litigation involving the State of Florida, but denied our right to challenge the amicus brief policy. Judge Walker's decision mentioned the fact that the administration denied our UFOLIO requests because of its desire to receive continued support from state political leaders. For several years, UF had aspired to achieve a top-ten and later a top-five ranking among public universities. In 2015, when the university was ranked fourteenth among public universities, then-president Bernie Machen announced a five-year plan (UF Rising) to hire new faculty and pursue other incentives to improve its ranking. I was completely in support of this plan. Eventually, the university achieved both goals. UF is still ranked in the top five.

However, because of the tense political climate in Florida, UF officials knew that they had to maintain a favorable relationship with state governmental actors for continued support. As Judge Walker mentioned in his decision, the chairman of the UF Board of Trustees, Morteza "Mori" Hosseini, once said, "[w]e had fought so hard over the years to get funding so our faculty could have raises, so our students could have good housing, so our employees' families could have daycare."[28] "Think of everything we've been able to accomplish during the past five years," he continued, "all made possible through the support of our state leaders."[29] Later in an address to the board of trustees, Chairman Hosseini stated that UF would not allow its faculty to offend state legislators by "advocat[ing] personal political viewpoints to the exclusion of others. . . . It must stop, and it WILL stop."[30] In December 2021, Hosseini again made UF's intentions clear when he accused us and other professors of "taking second jobs," "using their positions of authority to improperly advocate personal political viewpoints," and "misusing their positions. Let me tell you, our legislators are not going to put up with the wasting of state money and resources, and neither is this board."[31]

In his decision, Judge Walker agreed with our allegation that the conflict of interest policy resulted in a First Amendment violation and stated:

> Plaintiffs have shown a First Amendment injury at the hands of Defendants' policy. Plaintiffs have shown that their speech is being chilled by the policy. That Defendants ultimately granted Plaintiffs' requests does not ameliorate the constitutional injury because Plaintiffs' injury is ongoing. Further, Defendants' cosmetic revisions fail to extinguish the policy's First Amendment infirmities. While the policy now codifies "a strong presumption in favor of permitting faculty members to work as paid experts against the State,"

ECF No. 43 at 8, it does not limit the University's discretion in reviewing requests or set time limits for such reviews. Thus, the revised policy retains the very features that Plaintiffs challenge and continues to chill Plaintiffs' speech just like the original policy before it got its facelift. . . . Accordingly, this Court concludes that Plaintiffs are suffering an irreparable injury.[32]

Judge Walker refused to enjoin the university from enforcing the amicus brief policy, however. He reasoned that the core issues in our case involved the conflict of interest policy. Although we provided evidence that UF professors were denied opportunities to sign amicus briefs, we failed to provide enough evidence about the amicus policy. In addition, UF later amended its policy to allow professors to list their UF affiliations. Therefore, we were not entitled to a preliminary injunction on this issue. Nevertheless, we achieved a substantial victory in the fight to protect academic freedom on our campus and perhaps on others as well.

CONCLUSION

In conclusion, my experiences are indicative of the current attack on higher education. I sometimes ask myself, "Why me?" A dedicated UF employee since 2001, I never would have thought that I would file a lawsuit against my university. Despite this incident, the University of Florida is an excellent school of which I am proud to be a member. However, it is vital that university faculty, staff, and students fight discrimination in all forms.

Although it is difficult to prove discrimination, one must fight it anyway. A trial court found several provisions in the SB 90 law unconstitutional in the *League of Women Voters of Florida, Inc. v. Lee* case. The ruling, overturned on appeal, is still pending. I have served as an expert witness on other voting discrimination cases that have received favorable verdicts. I am proud to say that I am doing my part in fighting efforts to disenfranchise minority voters and prevent them from electing their preferred representatives. I am also continuing to do the work that I love when teaching and mentoring students, doing other university service, and publishing research.

I am now one of six plaintiffs in *Pernell et al. v. Florida Board of Governors*, a lawsuit challenging the HB 7 law (Stop W.O.K.E. Act) that was filed in 2022. A federal judge issued a preliminary injunction to block the enforcement of several provisions of this law.[33] The W.O.K.E. acronym stands for Wrongs to Our Kids and Employees.[34] The Stop WOKE Act promotes censorship and discrimination because it imposes requirements on educators in public higher education institutions when teaching racial issues. When I was a student, professors failed to discuss race at all or sometimes were blatantly biased against Black students. Now I, as a Black professor, must monitor what I say and sugarcoat my discussions of race? This is unacceptable, an academic freedom and constitutional violation. Instead of asking "Why me?" I now ask myself: "Why not me?" Because of my educational training and unique background, I have much to contribute. I have a voice that needs to be heard. I will not stop fighting discrimination, and I hope other educators will join me as I continue to seek justice and fight for academic freedom.

12

Florida Faculty Unions and the Struggle for Public Education

KATIE RAINWATER

U NDER THE GOVERNORSHIP of Ron DeSantis and the supermajority Republican state legislature, academic freedom in Florida's state universities
and colleges is in peril. The political views and course content of Florida
faculty are under scrutiny by the state, and restrictions have been placed
on instruction about race and gender through the (partially enjoined) Stop
WOKE Act.[1] Other threats include the decimation of tenure with a proposed
post-tenure review policy and the promised transformation of the New College of Florida, the state's public liberal arts university, into an institution
modeled on the conservative Christian private institution, Hillsdale College.[2]

While under siege in Florida, educators elsewhere in the country have
asserted their collective power to realize unprecedented victories. Teaching
assistants and researchers in the University of California system waged the
largest strike in US higher education history to combat inadequate compensation.[3] A revitalized teachers' labor movement in Chicago, Los Angeles,
and elsewhere has shown how educators can use collective action to realize
improvements in the public education system including more counselors
and school nurses, restrictions on class sizes, and community schools, all in
service of realizing what the Los Angeles teachers' union called "the schools
our students deserve." These victories occurred after rank-and-file educators
pushed their unions to break with a service model of unionism that resolves
grievances and settles contracts in partnership with the boss, embracing in
its stead a unionism that organizes members to fight the boss to improve
education and to realize a more equitable society.[4]

In this essay, I argue that faculty unions in Florida must organize alongside students, teachers, parents, and working-class Floridians to safeguard not only academic freedom but also the institution of public education. I read the attack on academic freedom as one dimension of a broader attack on fully funded public education and argue that fighting for the former entails fighting for the latter. As with other recent labor wins in the education sector, succeeding in this struggle will require our unions to break from the service model to boldly organize in worksites and communities. I first describe DeSantis's assault on academic freedom in the context of the privatization of education. I then offer a vision of unionism capable of fighting the Right's assault on public education. I write from Florida International University (FIU), a large public research institution where I work as a visiting assistant teaching professor. I am on the chapter council of my local union, UFF-FIU, a chapter of the United Faculty of Florida (UFF), which represents full-time faculty and some graduate students at all of Florida's public universities and some of its colleges.

THE PRIVATIZATION OF EDUCATION AND THE ASSAULT ON ACADEMIC FREEDOM

The contemporary assault on academic freedom in Florida is one front of a decades-long project by business and political elites to privatize public education. Governor Ron DeSantis, elected in 2019, has furthered a privatization project rooted in the education "reform" of former governor Jeb Bush (1999–2007) and advanced under former governor Rick Scott (2011–2019) that seeks to disinvest from public education and eliminate the unions and tenured educators opposing this agenda. In addition to undermining the conditions that facilitate educators' collective action, the Florida state legislature is trying to maintain control by silencing perspectives that question the concentration of power and wealth in the hands of a tiny minority and by creating programs to disseminate its extremist ideology through Florida's public educational institutions. These efforts threaten academic freedom and compromise opportunities for students to develop an informed and critical understanding of their society.

Florida's public schools and universities are among the most poorly funded in the nation. In the 2018–19 school year, on a per student basis, Florida funded K–12 students at $11,003 per student, 71 percent of the national average of $15,487.[5] In higher education, per-student funding (state appropriations plus tuition) is $13,438, just 75 percent of the national average of $18,154.[6] Funding is also inequitably distributed, with less funding allocated to high poverty K–12 districts[7] and to the universities that disproportionately serve working-class and minority students.[8] And not all the inadequate state funding earmarked for public educational institutions even reaches them. For the 2022–23 school year, an estimated 10 percent of state allocations for public K–12 schools is being redirected to private schooling through a voucher program started under Bush and expanded under DeSantis.[9]

Jeb Bush promoted the idea that quality public education is realizable by imposing state standards and fostering market competition. At the K–12 level, districts, schools, and teachers compete for performance funding and bonuses through an intensive standards-based testing regime. Students and parents are encouraged to think of themselves as astute educational consumers and choose from an expansive charter and private school sector when their local public schools underperform.[10] Similarly, Scott instituted a performance-based funding system for universities, which allocates funding according to such criteria as cost of degree, earnings of graduates, and STEM degrees awarded.[11] The State University System of Florida's new MyFloridaFuture dashboard tool encourages students to select majors according to projected earnings[12] as authorities move to "re-tool" or "terminate" "unproductive academic programs."[13]

In Florida, as elsewhere, attacks on educators' unions and tenure are central to the privatization project. Scott signed legislation that requires K–12 unions to undergo recertification if membership drops below 50 percent.[14] DeSantis has proposed raising the membership threshold to 60 percent and barring automatic dues deductions.[15] Scott eliminated tenure for teachers and tied renewal of teacher contracts to test scores.[16] A proposed post-tenure review policy now threatens to undermine faculty tenure by introducing new evaluative criteria (including compliance with state laws and the Stop WOKE Act) and fast-tracking termination.[17]

We're told that the education "reforms" are working, and that Florida has realized a winning combination of "high quality and low cost" education.[18] DeSantis and his cronies point to Florida's high achievement on metrics such as the fourth-grade reading test and the *U.S. News & World Report* ranking. But these metrics don't reliably assess educational quality. Florida's fourth-grade test scores are artificially inflated by a Florida law requiring educators to retain third graders who fail a reading test.[19] At the university level, an increasing reliance on online learning and a contingent workforce improves cost of degree metrics, but it comes at the expense of opportunities for students to forge close relationships with one another and with faculty, which are important for intellectual and personal growth.[20]

The privatization project plants the seeds for its own reproduction by creating generations of students who have never experienced education as a quality public good or had the opportunity to grapple with the status quo, challenging content alongside their classmates and instructors. But amidst signals that Americans are becoming intolerant of inequality—the murder of George Floyd inspired the largest protests in US history, record numbers of youth openly defy the gender binary, and more Americans support unions than ever—the Right has become even more preoccupied with the suppression of ideas it finds threatening and the use of publicly funded institutions for their dissemination. This strategy has been articulated on a national level by the conservative think tank activist Christopher Rufo, and Florida is on the front lines of its implementation.[21]

The state legislature is obsessed with suppressing what it refers to as "woke indoctrination."[22] This is evident in the Stop WOKE Act, which prohibits university and K–12 educators from endorsing certain concepts related to race and biological sex. K–12 teachers are also subject to the "Don't Say Gay" law, which places restrictions on discussion of sexual orientation and gender identity.[23] The Florida Department of Education rejected textbooks informed by social-emotional learning[24] and an AP African American Studies course.[25] Beyond content bans, under the guise of promoting transparency, the state legislature has produced a climate of surveillance, surveying faculty for their ideological viewpoints,[26] requiring inclusion of faculty syllabi in a searchable database,[27] and requiring universities to report spending on diversity, equity, and inclusion initiatives, instruction on critical race theory, and gender-affirming care.[28]

While the Right works to minimize space for teaching about social (in)equality in public schools and universities, it is carving out more space within these institutions for its ideology. And, as Kathryn Joyce has brilliantly documented, the support for these programs no longer comes from right-wing institutes but by "leveraging direct funding from state governments."[29] Examples include a state-funded summer civics initiative that trained K–12 teachers in a sanitized version of history,[30] the establishment of the University of Florida's Hamilton Center for Classical and Civics Education and the Adam Smith Institute at FIU,[31] and the planned transformation of New College of Florida into "Florida's classical college."[32]

FRAMING

Given the severity of threats facing Florida educators, what are unions to do? First, as social movements, unions have a vital role to play in "framing"— providing a perspective that names the problem, proposes a solution, and makes an appeal to become involved in the movement. The union should structure its vision around two principles: first, in the words of a slogan developed by educators at the University of Central Florida in response to the Stop WOKE Act, "we educate to liberate not indoctrinate," and second, no matter how far from it we are now, fully funded public higher education is necessary and possible.

Political parties engage in framing. But the messaging of the Florida Democratic Party does not provide the incisive analysis that the moment requires. Charlie Christ used a "Freedom to Learn" slogan in his failed campaign for governor against DeSantis in 2022. His platform included the following plank:

Getting politics out of our schools.

- Parents send their children to school to learn. Injecting politics into our schools hurts students and disrupts their education.
- This is the real indoctrination happening in schools—not Critical Race Theory and Don't Say Gay. Those are not and never have been taught in our public schools.
- Classrooms should be above politics, and as Governor, Charlie will hold this principle sacrosanct.[33]

Good educators don't tell their students what to think, and they strive to create classrooms where students feel comfortable sharing their interpretations. But curriculum and pedagogy choices are inherently political. Educators either try to create a more equal and democratic society or they are proponents of the status quo. Instead of retreating to the myth of teacher neutrality, we need to be explicit about the content of the politics in question. The Right is trying to suppress discussion of social inequality to maintain control of its wealth and power. We are teaching about social inequality as part of a project to realize a more democratic and equal society.

This means we must not only defend teaching about social (in)justice but also use the moment to highlight the gross inadequacy of public good provision in Florida. In response to the Florida Department of Education's rejection of textbooks that promote social and emotional learning (SEL), we need to explain that this pedagogy recognizes that academic success is contingent upon meeting students' broader needs. And that while teaching emotional awareness and responsible decision-making through SEL is important,[34] with 17 percent of Florida children in poverty,[35] many of our students need support beyond SEL instruction. We need a community school model that would offer school-based health and social services, such as in-school health clinics and full-time school social workers, as well as expanded and enriched learning time, and family and community engagement.[36]

Our response to "Don't Say Gay" should reiterate how important it is for queer youth to see themselves in picture books and history lessons. We should explain that expectations for students to conform to the gender binary—conveyed with vitriol in policies on bathrooms and sports—and lack of access to gender-affirming care is killing our children, as evident in the higher suicide rate for trans youth. We also need to talk about why the Right is so invested in the gender binary. The binary presupposes the pairing of a masculine breadwinner in the workplace with a feminine caregiver at home. This construct suggests that a social need—the production of future generations—is the responsibility of the family, not the state. Floridians pushed back against this assumption in 2002 when they voted for a ballot initiative establishing voluntary pre-kindergarten. Yet instead of a quality program of childcare and education, Floridians received a program of very poor quality underwritten with "utterly insufficient funding."[37]

We should respond to the directive that universities detail their spending on diversity, equity, and inclusion (DEI) by explaining that, as access to higher education has expanded, the experience has become more stratified. People of color and women are disproportionately represented in contingent faculty positions[38] in which their compensation and voice in shared governance falls dramatically short of that of tenure-track faculty. Working-class students and students of color are disproportionately concentrated in the universities with the least resources and funding.[39] Equity requires dramatically more funding to fully support all faculty and students.

Of course, inclusion also means responding to the non-white, non-masculine-identifying students and faculty that have entered universities in increasing numbers since World War II. Students in the 1960s had a vision for how to do this when they demanded the creation of centers—Black Studies, Ethnic Studies, Women Studies—that would provide intellectual homes and spaces of support for them on campus and would make university research and outreach responsive to the needs of historically marginalized groups. Where, we should ask, is the funding for centers of community engagement, such as FIU's African and African Diaspora Studies Program, the Center for Labor Research and Studies, and the Center for Women's and Gender Studies?

Finally, we need to make it clear to people why we can't have nice things: the Right refuses to pay for them. This is another respect in which Crist's campaign messaging fell short. Crist called for increased funding for education. But he didn't explain how he'd pay. He complained that sales taxes were too high and promised "you'll never have a state income tax."[40] But this framing obscures the class-specific nature of the tax burden. Despite its low-tax reputation, Florida is "a high-tax state for low- and moderate-income residents," who pay eight to five times more in the consumption taxes as a share of their income than do Florida's wealthy residents.[41] Nor are the elite paying at work; because of tax loopholes, one-fifth of all corporations earning more than $250 million pay nothing in corporate taxes.[42] Messaging about fully funding public education must include messaging about progressive taxation.

ORGANIZING THE WORKPLACE

Our aim is not merely to put forward a compelling analysis of what is wrong but to organize our membership. As the leadership of the United Teachers of Los Angeles (UTLA) write, "A union is [not] primarily a vehicle designed to allow a small number of activists to pass progressive positions and work on specific issues without engaging the larger membership. . . . A union's most important purpose is to democratically organize a supermajority of members to act collectively . . . and force those in power to give us what we need."[43] The following discussion of two attempts to organize around academic freedom at FIU shows how complicated organizing can be.

THE FREEDOM TO TEACH, FREEDOM TO LEARN CAMPAIGN

When the Stop WOKE Act (HB 7) went into effect, our statewide union distributed classroom guidance. All members of the United Faculty of Florida were encouraged to insert a disclaimer into their syllabi: "No lesson is intended to espouse, promote, advance, inculcate, or compel a particular feeling, perception, viewpoint, or belief."[44] Each member was encouraged to choose a teaching strategy according to their individual comfort level with risk. Instructors who wished to work in a "low risk" environment were instructed not to "teach or address any of the topics prohibited in HB 7" and to remove "all posters and art in your office that 'endorse' positions prohibited by HB 7." Faculty pursuing a "reasonable risk" pathway were to add disclaimers to the presentation of content about race and gender. To avoid prohibitions on concepts that suggest students bear personal responsibility for actions committed in the past, for example, faculty were to preface content with the statement, "I am not suggesting anyone bears individual responsibility . . . about [X]." Finally, faculty comfortable with a "higher risk" were told to change nothing.

As stated in our union's constitution, one of our objectives is "to achieve and safeguard . . . academic freedom."[45] Were we to abandon this principle as soon as it was challenged? What about our students, who deserve to learn about race and gender? Appalled by the statewide union's timid classroom guidance and frustrated by our own local's inaction, a small group of union members began discussing an alternative approach. We agreed that in the short term it would be impossible for faculty to build enough power to get the law revoked, but we could organize to minimize the impact of the law on campus by getting faculty to commit to not changing their teaching.

We got our local union to send an email to our bargaining unit calling upon faculty to include the collective bargaining agreement language, recognizing the academic freedom of faculty in their syllabi in place of the disclaimer promoted by the statewide union and a similar one promoted by the administration. We invited faculty to attend union meetings to develop a campaign to fight HB 7. The campaign had three objectives: safeguarding academic freedom at the university, raising awareness about the harms of political interference, and building coalitions to preserve and strengthen public education. We made three asks of our members: raise visibility—by posting on social media, wearing a button, and teaching students about academic freedom—attend a teach-in on academic freedom on campus, and sign a pledge. The teach-in, organized in collaboration with student groups, was lively. It included music and speeches from students followed by an educational seminar featuring talks from academics, a labor organizer, and a student representative.[46] In the pledge, faculty members promised to uphold academic freedom in the classroom and demonstrate if anyone in the state university system was disciplined. The pledge was signed by about one hundred faculty members in a bargaining unit fourteen times larger.

CUBAN PRIVILEGE

Less than two months after the teach-in, we were confronted with a violation of academic freedom. FIU's Cuban Research Institute (CRI) had invited Boston University sociologist Susan Eckstein to give a talk on her book *Cuban Privilege: The Making of Immigrant Inequality in America*. A newly elected Trump-endorsed Miami-Dade County commissioner, Kevin Cabrera, criticized the event in a statement: "It is shocking that FIU's Cuban Research Institute would welcome such hate-filled, inflammatory, anti-Cuban rhetoric to Miami-Dade County."[47] News of the event circulated on social media after a Cuban American influencer encouraged his viewers to protest.[48] On December 2, the president of FIU released a statement to the university community explaining:

> After learning of the event several days ago, it became clear to me that we had an opportunity to enhance it by including other points of view so that we could have a balanced and objective discussion. The event now ensures that we meet the academic rigor and standards of debate and preserve everyone's right to express their point of view while remaining mindful and sensitive to the experiences of our community. Dr. Orlando Gutiérrez-Boronat, spokesperson for the Cuban Democratic Directorate and author of "Cuba: The Doctrine of the Line," will participate as the discussant.[49]

Gutiérrez-Boronat was not an expert in Eckstein's field nor were his scholarly credentials on par with hers. But, as an avowed anti-socialist whose book was prefaced by a *Breitbart News* editor, Gutiérrez-Boronat would undoubtably provide a discussion pleasing to Cabrera.

Faculty involved in the Freedom to Teach campaign devised a plan for the union's chapter council. Beginning with faculty affiliates of the CRI, we would call on union members to a sign a letter demanding that Eckstein be welcomed to campus without the proposed discussant. If the administration could not be moved, we considered inviting Eckstein to give her talk sans discussant at the union hall. When the chapter council convened, some argued that the revised format of Eckstein's talk did not violate academic freedom because Eckstein and the CRI director agreed to it. Others found the administration's statement problematic but argued that the union would not succeed in removing the discussant so we shouldn't try. After our proposal to organize against the format change was defeated, the chapter council decided to write an open letter observing the violation of academic freedom. Union leadership produced a draft that glossed over the academic freedom violation; it was discarded for a more critical draft, but ultimately, union leadership failed to send any letter.

As Eckstein related in a *Miami Herald* op-ed after the talk, Gutiérrez-Boronat "used the opportunity to spend 90 percent of his time not addressing the topic of my book. Instead, he talked about human-rights abuses in Cuba."[50] The media characterized the event as "a lively debate involving a range of voices and viewpoints"[51] and the presentation and discussion as "a thoughtful point-counterpoint."[52] With the union leadership declining to frame it otherwise, it was all too easy for the public to accept the administration's perspective that the event was exemplary of "academic freedom and civil discourse."[53] We needed to explain that academics don't have an obligation to give class, seminar, or public lecture time to an "opposing viewpoint" even though this is what the Right wants us to believe as they decry a lack of "viewpoint diversity" to subvert the university for their own ends. We needed to explain that a speech denouncing the Castro regime would only distract from a book talk about US immigration policy. Most importantly, we needed to show our members that we could collectively reject a vision of our university in which the administration invites the Right to codetermine content and programming.

REFLECTION

If judged by the criteria of "democratically organiz[ing] a supermajority of members to act collectively," then these interventions were a failure. Only a minority of members participated in the campaign and plans to organize around Eckstein's talk never advanced beyond the chapter council. Nevertheless, academic freedom is a deeply felt issue. When FIU's faculty senate convened following the event, they passed a resolution objecting to the administration's intervention. Although the outcome of our organizing efforts was disappointing, the strategy of organizing union members in potentially winnable struggles on campus is sound. Success will require persistent effort to overcome the atomization of faculty and organizing as a caucus of the union rather than as an official union committee.

Our campaign was premised on the understanding: first, "our academic freedom in this current climate is a freedom that exists *only to the extent that we exercise it* and that it is, conversely, *ours to give away* if we decide to accede to the terms [of the Stop WOKE Act]" and, second, "unity is our best defense."[54] We wanted to normalize the rejection of unjust laws and to build a collective that had the power to reinstate anyone terminated. Given the weak state of the local union, it was understandably difficult for faculty to feel protected by it.[55] In recent years, union leadership has narrowly conceived of its role as bargaining for salaries and benefits within the context of contract negotiations, to the exclusion of most other issues. When faculty members have concerns, they seek to resolve these concerns by asking department heads to appeal to administrators. Unsurprisingly, the faculty looked to administration for resolution to the issues raised by HB 7. Unlike the statewide union, our administration insisted that faculty *not* remove course content; nevertheless, in courses offered by the teaching center on campus, they instructed faculty members how to present content in conformity with the law.

We sought to have organizing conversations with members to invite them to participate in our campaign. There was no representative structure in the union (such as a stewards council) to facilitate these conversations, so we set out to create this structure by recruiting representatives from each department to talk to their colleagues. Many potential representatives told us that they were not in regular communication with their colleagues. With the shift to online and hybrid teaching and the dramatic reduction in real salaries, many faculty members have moved far from campus and even out of state. It will require tremendous effort to overcome this atomization and recreate a sense of community and collective purpose.

A second issue we faced is that of a union leadership opposed to our vision of unionism. UFF-FIU pursues "win-win" bargaining where it seeks to collaborate with administrators to negotiate contracts that are "wins" for both parties. Pursuit of this strategy has left leadership reluctant to criticize the administration lest "the good relationship" be disrupted. We launched the campaign from within the union after passing a proposal through chapter council following the initial objection of union leadership. Running the campaign as part of the union had the advantages of access to the union email list and to union funds. Nevertheless, rooting our organizing in a body headed by leaders who did not share our vision came with serious limitations. Little officer time was dedicated to the campaign, and our campaign communications were subject to scrutiny by leadership. When those leaders declined to organize around the CRI event, we were left without an organization to organize an action. Responding to similar constraints in other unions, union reformers have avoided these setbacks by forming caucuses, or groups of union members who organize their colleagues around a shared vision. Caucuses provide a way of "being the union" when the union itself fails to perform its role.[56]

ORGANIZING THE COMMUNITY

But even if we begin to win campus battles, we would still be losing the war. The Right is not only winning but is locking in its wins in a way that makes them hard to reverse. Redistricting, repressive, scarcely legal "voter fraud" crackdown, and the gutting of voting rights restoration make realizing a change in the legislature extremely difficult. The board of governors, the boards of trustees, and the judiciary have been stacked over the past two decades with proponents of privatization.

What should we do? In November, our statewide union told us that we could make everything better with a Get Out the Vote (GOTV) campaign. We watched as our union dues returned to us in the form of hand sanitizers with GOTV logos and GOTV signs for our front yards. We were encouraged to hold GOTV rallies on our campuses—not discussing candidates, in compliance with state law, but assuming students would vote for the Democratic Party. And then, when DeSantis won reelection and the Right assumed a supermajority in the state legislature, it was clear we had achieved nothing. Our union dues had not been expended to expand the ranks of organized academic workers or to organize the public around a vision or to build lasting coalitions.

The union could continue narrowly pursuing its decades-long strategy of legislative advocacy. Or it could experiment with another strategy modeled with great success by the United Teachers of Los Angeles (UTLA). As UTLA leaders observed, "public education is a social good in which parents, youth, and community deserve and want to be involved. To build the leverage to win the schools our students deserve . . . we need a broad labor/community movement."[57] UTLA is building this labor/community movement by building an alliance of existing community groups and a new "parent/community organizing arm" of their union. They invite alliance members to help them develop their "common good" demands for the bargaining table. Through this process, they build the power to win their demands by building community support for the union and its strikes and school board candidates.[58]

Strikes are illegal for public sector workers in the state and our adversaries are the unelected boards of trustees and a board of governors handpicked by the far-right governor. Nevertheless, by forging relationships with students and with other academic and campus workers, we would be in a better position to realize the changes that we need to see. Alongside the cost-of-living adjustment that we need, we could consider bringing issues to the bargaining table such as graduate student stipends or undergraduate housing insecurity or other issues as co-determined by our students and coworkers. These groups could attend our negotiating sessions in accordance with Florida's open bargaining laws thereby creating a larger coalition and heightened pressure.

Following a sweep of candidates supported by DeSantis in local school board races throughout Florida,[59] we may consider getting involved in school board elections. Many of us are parents and all of us have a personal stake in the quality of the state's K–12 public schools from which we receive most of our students. Although victories in these local, potentially winnable races wouldn't translate into increased leverage at the bargaining table or in the state legislature, the campaigns would offer a platform to communicate our vision of education as a public good and would be one step toward creating the coalitions that we need to contest state-level races, the outcome of which determine higher education policy and the composition of the board of governors and boards of trustees.

Another potential pathway is revealed by the Massachusetts Teachers Association (MTA)'s November 2022 victory on the Fair Share Amendment, a ballot initiative that amended the state constitution to add a 4 percent surcharge to personal income tax above $1 million and earmarked the revenue for public education.[60] Ballot initiatives fostering redistribution have proven popular in states of all political persuasion[61] and Florida voters have a track record of supporting progressive ballot measures, including voter rights restoration, a $15 minimum wage, and taxes to fund education at the county level.[62] Of course, the electorate's propensity to approve progressive ballot initiatives is matched by the zeal of the Right to find ways to subvert them.[63] But part of the beauty of a ballot initiative campaign is that winning it would require organizing tens of thousands of people around a shared vision of public education. If we organized deeply enough, we could ensure not only that the measure passed but also that we had built the power to defend it.

CONCLUSION

That the union could be a political force—that it could determine conditions of learning in our universities or appropriations from the state legislature—can feel like a distant possibility. Building power will no doubt take time and require experimentation with strategy. Animated by a commitment to teaching to liberate and to fully fund public education, we must organize our campuses and communities one conversation and meeting at a time. Academic freedom as well as the future of public education depend upon it.[64]

13

Schools of Education Under Fire

MARVIN LYNN, MICHAEL E. DANTLEY,
AND LYNN M. GANGONE

THE DEMONIZATION OF CRITICAL RACE THEORY (CRT) is a red herring designed to rally voters to support right-wing politicians in the 2022 and 2024 elections. But its current impact on colleges of education and teacher preparation programs is real and enormously destructive, further contributing to the decline in interest in teaching as a profession at a time when the shortage of qualified educators is acute. The authors of this chapter serve key leadership roles with the American Association of Colleges for Teacher Education (AACTE), the leading voice for educator preparation in the nation. Together, they assessed the specific ways in which the hysteria surrounding CRT impacted schools and colleges of education is manifesting, and they developed a racial and social justice task force that took specific actions focused on better preparing education deans, associate deans, and other leaders in educator preparation with the necessary tools to effectively combat disinformation.

The lead author of this chapter (Marvin Lynn) has been working as a critical race theory scholar since the late 1990s. Introduced to the concept by his professor, Dr. Daniel Solórzano at UCLA, in 1998, he also had the opportunity to learn directly from scholars in the law such as Kimberlé Crenshaw, Cheryl Harris, and Devon Carbado—all professors at the UCLA School of Law—who were, and continue to be, at the vanguard of the movement. Critical race theory specialists—both in the law and in education—were part of a small community of scholars of color who had a vested interest in transforming the nature of scholarship in law and education. Legal scholars like Derrick Bell, often referred to as the "father of critical race theory," sought to reshape how we understood America, its laws, and its policies.[1] Through allegorical texts written during the Reagan era of the late 1980s, Bell illustrated how the law was, in fact, deeply steeped in white supremacist thought and practice.[2] His work spawned a whole new generation of scholars concerned about the imprint of race in the law. Students of Bell, such as Kimberlé Crenshaw, coined the phrase "critical race theory" at a legal conference in 1989. Since that time, critical race theory scholarship in the law flourished while continuing to be marginalized within mainstream legal scholarship. For example, few law schools offer subfields or courses in the area. The presence of law school courses on CRT is still heavily dependent upon whether critical race theory legal scholars hold positions in those universities. Suffice to say, CRT is not universally taught in law schools.

Despite current myths propagated by those on the conservative right, CRT is not widely used in the field of education either—at any level. However, education has been one of the few disciplines where scholars could choose to explore how critical race theory could be used and applied. Most of us would credit William F. Tate and Gloria Ladson-Billings with introducing the field to this area of study.[3] In a recent discussion with the NAACP, however, Ladson-Billings suggests that Derrick Bell was the first person to apply the concept of critical race theory to the field of education.[4] Bell has been widely known for calling attention to the way the *Brown v. Board of Education* decision was not an instance of altruism or an expression of this nation's commitment to social justice but a matter of "interest convergence." The nation's interests in putting forward a cleaner image of itself was aligned with African Americans' need to receive a quality education. Built on the work of Bell and others, there is a rich history of critical race scholarship in education. Chapters in the second edition of the *Handbook of Critical Race Theory in Education*, for example, address a range of topics including music education, the overrepresentation of Black and Brown students in special education, charter schools, hip-hop education, teacher education, critical mixed method approaches, and women of color scholars.[5] The thirty-two substantive chapters that constitute this compendium are divided into four key areas that are reflective of the way critical race scholarship in the field of education is understood: the foundations, intersectional frameworks, research methods, and policy analyses.

While the field has blossomed in some ways, it is also true that critical race theory—as a concept—both in the law and in education has remained obscure over the last three decades. While a few scholars are well recognized for their work in the field, the field itself had not significantly expanded beyond the scope identified by scholars in both fields more than three decades ago. As a person deeply embedded in this area of study for the last twenty-five years, the lead author finds it utterly shocking that critical race theory has somehow become a household term. Today, a Google search on the concept produces over 244,000 results! One can easily find explanations of the theoretical concept in mainstream news outlets like PBS, the *New York Times*, and *Education Week* due to the political right's demonization of CRT as an idea. The right's attack on CRT was part of a well-coordinated assault on the freedom of speech, academic freedom, and democracy that began with the Trump administration's executive order banning CRT, which coalesced with an attack on the Capitol, and has resulted in legislation across the nation that has attempted to ban the teaching of race in K–12 and higher education classrooms across the nation.[6] According to PEN America, there have been 193 educational gag order bills introduced in 41 state legislatures since January 2021.[7] Nineteen such gag orders have become law in fifteen different states, and four other states have passed either policy or executive orders restricting the teaching of race. Seven of those states (Idaho, Iowa, Florida, South Dakota, Mississippi, Oklahoma, and Tennessee) have higher-education gag orders in place.

The gag orders restrict the teaching of race in the classroom. While most of the national attention has gone to K–12 educators and leaders who have been dismissed from jobs because of their insistence on addressing issues of race, the University of Florida has been in the spotlight because of its refusal to approve an academic program designed by Dr. Chris Busey, a professor of teacher education. The academic program was said to have a focus on racism. Professor Busey filed a grievance against the university as a result. He has also been featured in the national news media regarding the issue.

In early 2023, the presidents of the Florida College System published a letter disavowing critical race theory. While the letter does not state that the topic will be banned, it does equate the teaching of race with forms of indoctrination and harassment. This is consistent with the conservative discourse about "woke studies"—a pseudonym for "politically and socially progressive thought" in general. Florida's governor, Ron DeSantis, has also demanded that officials at public universities share information with him about the ways they may have used public dollars to develop programs that emphasize diversity, equity, and inclusion.

Oklahoma's gag order also extends to higher education. As a result, the University of Oklahoma was forced to limit its course offerings in areas such as African American studies. Higher education faculty at the university joined forces with local educators and the NAACP to file a lawsuit against the state for infringement on academic freedom and freedom of speech. The lead author wrote a brief for that lawsuit that defined and argued for why "resource pedagogies" are important and must be maintained in pre-K–12 schools, as well as in higher education. Resource pedagogies, according to Alexandra Reyes and Taylor Norman, view students' culture and language as assets on which teachers can build a rich foundation to construct curriculum and teaching practices that are deeply connected to children's lives.[8] Django Paris notes that resource pedagogies "repositioned the linguistic, cultural, and literate practices of poor communities—particularly poor communities of color—as resources."[9] Culturally responsive teaching, culturally relevant teaching, and culturally sustaining pedagogy are defined as resource pedagogies. In Oklahoma, these practices, which have been shown to positively impact the learning and development of students of color, are outlawed. Teacher education programs are also restricted from using these strategies to prepare teachers to teach all children well.

Faculty in ethnic studies at the University of Oklahoma argued that restrictive state policy that did not allow them to openly address issues of race and gender in the classroom would not only severely limit opportunities for students to learn from a diverse set of authors, such as Toni Morrison, it would also create an unwelcoming environment for students of color in the classroom. Former president Trump's original executive order focused on the eradication of teaching perceived to engender white guilt about racism in the United States. State gag orders have followed a similar path. In doing so, they have constructed law and policy at the state level that upholds the rights of one community (white students) to feel safe in the classroom by denying others (Black, Brown, and Indigenous students) the opportunity to share their full stories and learn about their history in the classroom.

The coauthors of this chapter live in states where anti-CRT laws have not been passed. As a result, our higher education faculty do not have to navigate potential legal challenges should they pursue the topic of race in their courses. However, conversations in the Ohio state legislature are being held, suggesting that a ban on CRT in state-supported schools may be imminent. In Colorado, there has been tension over state laws that require schools to integrate ethnic studies and LGBTQ+ history into the K–12 social studies curriculum. The State Board of Education, which was perhaps more conservative leaning at the time, attempted to sanitize certain aspects of the standards by limiting the presence of LGBTQ+ history in the curriculum. The presence of laws that restrict the teaching of race in some states impacts the lives of teachers everywhere. The public sanctioning and, in some cases, dismissal of K–12 teachers because of their commitment to teaching race has had a chilling effect on educators at all levels.

THE IMPACT ON TEACHER EDUCATION

Recently, Ashley White, in collaboration with AACTE and its president and CEO, Lynn Gangone, produced a report titled *The State of Education Censorship in Institutions of Higher Ed and Implications for the Field.* According to Gangone, the report "outlines the state of current educational censorship to date through an examination of themes relevant to proposed and enacted legislation."[10] As the report makes clear, teacher education has historically struggled to offer a curriculum that adequately prepares teachers to teach all children well. Many preservice teachers—who are mostly white, middle-class, cisgender women—enter their teacher preparation programs with limited knowledge of, understanding of, or experience with students who differ from them in terms of race, ethnicity, linguistic background, and social class. Because teacher education programs often lack the capacity to help preservice teachers gain the requisite skills to be successful teachers of students of color, they often leave these programs with limited knowledge about how to effectively teach all children well. As a result, education disparities between students of color and white students continue to widen.

To be clear, this problem was not the result of the current political climate in our nation. The recent spate of legislation calling on schools and some universities to restrict conversations about race, gender, and/or human sexuality in higher education further limits the ability of teacher preparation programs to train educators how to teach all children well. In other words, restrictive laws on the teaching of race only further exacerbate a problem that was already a major challenge for the profession.

Legislation that is being proposed in some states, or law in other states, is designed to restrict and severely limit book choice, curriculums, and what can and cannot be said in K–12 and higher education classrooms. The chilling effect of such legislation is profound. The number of individuals seeking to become teachers, working in the classroom, or leading schools has steadily diminished over the years, as noted in AACTE's *Colleges of Education: A National Portrait*.[11] During the COVID-19 pandemic, teachers were demonized and blamed for everything from learning loss to the inability of some schools to quickly pivot to online learning. These teachers were never expected to know or engage in these activities prior to the pandemic. And now, with the introduction of legislation that seeks to "chill" the classroom environment and ban books, the teacher and education leaders' pipeline has come to an excruciating halt. Both the pandemic and the recent legislation are likely to have a deleterious impact on the availability and preparation of teachers for years to come.

AACTE'S STANCE IN PROTECTING ACADEMIC FREEDOM

AACTE has taken a strong stance against educational censorship in education. In 2021, in response to members' concerns about emerging gag orders at the state level, teacher educators called upon our leadership to develop a set of tools and resources to support them in their efforts to combat educational censorship. We took several steps to address member concerns. The organization had already begun to develop a set of online racial justice tools that are available to all members. This work began with our strategic planning effort that centered issues of diversity, equity, and inclusion. It continued with the development of online resources in our racial and social justice hub. Next, we formed a racial and social justice task force designed to coordinate our efforts and develop a pathway for continuing this work at multiple levels.

In the fall of 2021, the Executive Leadership Team of the AACTE Board of Directors formed a Board Task Force on Racial and Social Justice. It included board members Marvin Lynn (chair), Monika Williams Shealey, Michael Dantley, John Henning, and Gaëtane Jean-Marie. Michael was AACTE board chair-elect at the time, and Monika was secretary-elect. Marvin became secretary-elect and now serves as secretary. Michael is serving as outgoing chair and Monika is chair-elect. Those within the highest rungs of leadership served on AACTE's Racial and Social Justice Task Force. It was a clear demonstration of the organization's commitment to this important issue.

The purpose of this task force was to provide the AACTE board of directors and executive leadership team with recommendations for steps to promote racial and social justice in educator preparation and, by extension, in the broader fields of K–12 and higher education. Committee members were responding to the following questions, which had organically emerged from our member institutions during conferences and professional development meetings:

1. What role can AACTE members play in promoting racial and social justice, and what can AACTE do as an association to support that work?
2. How can AACTE's existing and planned work in diversity, equity, and inclusion (e.g., anti-racist pedagogy webinar series, special education, and Black and Latino male teacher networked improved communities (NICs), and the AACTE Holmes Program) be strengthened to promote racial and social justice more assertively?
3. What role should AACTE play in countering attempts to impede the promotion of racial and social justice in educator preparation?

The task force met twice to discuss its specific purpose, and it developed a plan for approaching the targeted outcomes-related questions. AACTE staff leaders Jacqueline Rodriguez and Nicole Dunn, who oversaw many of the current AACTE initiatives, were invited to participate as key members of the team. The committee developed the following set of recommendations, which were later adopted by the executive committee of the board.

1. AACTE should focus on providing professional development opportunities for its members and for interested nonmembers. AACTE, under the leadership of Jacqueline Rodriguez and Nicole Dunn, has already initiated two important initiatives including:

   - The Educating for Democracy Pilot, an initiative to provide focused professional development to AACTE members. The initiative could be targeted at leaders and teacher educators.
   - The Racial and Social Justice Hub, a website that houses key online resources on combating racism, heterosexism, and censorship. Additional materials regarding democracy and democratic education could be provided.

These efforts must be continued and supported at the highest level by the organization. Task force members will work closely with staff to help facilitate and plan these activities, as needed.

2. AACTE should partner with other organizations such as the National Educational Association (NEA), American Federation of Teachers (AFT), American Educational Research Association (AERA), Carnegie Project on the Education Doctorate (CPED), Council of Academic Deans from Research Education Institutions (CADREI), Teacher Education Council of State Colleges and Universities (TESCU), Association of Independent Liberal Arts Colleges for Teacher Education (AILACTE), and Historically Black Colleges and Universities (HBCUs) to organize public dialogues about educational censorship and the importance of focusing on racial and social justice in schools and universities.

   a. AACTE staff has already established the Annual Meeting Deeper Dive Session as part of a four-part collaboration with AERA on education censorship, attacks against anti-racist teaching, and racial and social justice.

b. In addition, the task force could meet with leaders from these organizations to discuss how we might partner to continue these important conversations.

c. Collaborative efforts could lead to the development of joint policy briefs or analyses that examine the impact of legislation on teacher education.

  ▪ AACTE might also pursue grant opportunities aimed at supporting further exploration of these issues at multiple levels. Federal grant opportunities, as well as small grants, should be explored. AACTE could partner with AERA to explore the impact of anti-CRT legislation on students, teachers, and scholars of color.

3. AACTE could convene teacher education leaders to discuss strategies for addressing race in teacher education. In doing so, the organization could more easily respond to the following questions:

a. What concerns do teacher education leaders have about the teaching of race at their institutions?

b. What supports, in addition to those already established, could be put into place to support their efforts?

  ▪ This could perhaps occur through a preconference meeting at AACTE of the Diversified Teacher Workforce Targeted Action Group (DTW TAG) or in conjunction with the Holmes Program.

4. AACTE should develop a plan for communicating its actions in this area broadly to the membership but also the wider community. AACTE members can support the writing of opinion pieces and other tools designed to communicate AACTE's deep engagement with this issue.

As a result of the work of the task force, AACTE developed an online Racial and Social Justice Hub, which captures our activities in this area and contains a set of resources that can be used by members to address concerns about how to navigate in environments where educational gag orders are in place. In collaboration with several partners listed previously, AACTE also developed a series of dialogues on educational censorship and democracy. Most of these discussions involved teacher educators, education deans, pre-K–12 school leaders, and community leaders and activists. Those recorded discussions can be found on AACTE's Racial and Social Justice Hub. The hub also includes information about current legislative efforts and provides resources for teacher educators who may be experiencing professional challenges related to educational gag orders.

CONCLUSION

AACTE will continue to lead the effort to protect academic freedom, free speech, and, ultimately, democracy in education. We will be particularly focused on continuing to provide strong support to teacher educators, deans, and our community and school partners who are struggling with the chilling effects of the legislative efforts described previously. Through the hub and our continued partnerships with a variety of organizations, think tanks, and universities, we will continue to provide resources in this area. We believe that we must continue to work together to advance our field in ways that also advance democracy in the United States.

APPENDIX

THE COEDITORS HAVE COMPILED A LIST of essential documents on the culture war on education that have been referenced in this volume. Please scan the QR code at the end of the appendix to access the documents online.

The documents are divided into three sections, including key statements and reports from organizations engaged in the battle to preserve academic freedom from legislative encroachment; sample faculty senate resolutions, including the original template that faculty senates have used as a guide to passing resolutions that reaffirm their institutional commitment to academic freedom; and sample education gag orders, including Donald Trump's Executive Order 13950, which served as a catalyst for state legislative efforts to suppress teaching on issues pertaining to race and ethnicity, gender, and sexual identity.

Key Statements and Reports

1. American Association of University Professors (AAUP), American Historical Association (AHA), Association of American Colleges and Universities (AAC&U), and PEN America, Joint Statement on Legislative Efforts to Restrict Education About Racism and American History
2. AAUP, Legislative Threats to Academic Freedom: Redefinitions of Antisemitism and Racism
3. United Faculty of Florida supports the rights of all Floridians to learn without authoritarian control and to exercise their constitutional freedoms as Americans.

Sample Faculty Senate Resolutions

1. Sample Template
2. Jackson State University Resolution
3. Ohio State University Resolution
4. University of Texas, Austin, Resolution
5. University of California Academic Council Statement on CRT and Academic Freedom
6. University of Alabama Resolution

Legislative Gag Orders

1. Trump Executive Order
2. Florida's "Don't Say Gay" Legislation
3. Florida's HB 7 (Stop WOKE Act)
4. PEN America Index of Educational Gag Orders

LIST OF CONTRIBUTORS

SHARON D. WRIGHT AUSTIN is a professor of political science at the University of Florida. Her research focuses on African American and urban political behavior. She is the author of *Race, Power, and Political Emergence in Memphis*; *The Transformation of Plantation Politics: Black Politics, Concentrated Poverty, and Social Capital in the Mississippi Delta*; and *The Caribbeanization of Black Politics: Race, Group Consciousness, and Political Participation in America*. She has also published several articles and book chapters. Her most recent books include *Political Black Girl Magic: The Elections and Governance of Black Female Mayors* and, coedited with Caroline Shenaz Hossein and Kevin Edmonds, *Beyond Racial Capitalism: Cooperatives in the African Diaspora*.

MICHAEL E. DANTLEY is the recently retired dean of the College of Education, Health, and Society and professor emeritus of educational leadership at Miami University, Oxford, Ohio. Before his last higher education position, Dr. Dantley served as dean and professor of educational leadership of the School of Education at Loyola University in Chicago, Illinois, and associate provost and associate vice president for Academic Affairs at Miami University. His research focuses on leadership, critical spirituality, and social justice especially leadership in urban school contexts. He currently serves as the chair of the Board of the American Association of Colleges of Teacher Education, on the steering committee of Education Deans for Justice and Equity, and on the steering committee of the Coalition of Black Education Deans. He also is the CEO of MED Consulting, LLC, in Cincinnati, Ohio.

SONNET GABBARD teaches in the departments of Race, Gender, and Sexuality Studies and Women's and Gender Studies at Butler University and DePaul University. She has BA in political science from Butler University, an MA in women's, gender, and sexuality studies (WGSS) from the University of Cincinnati, and a PhD in WGSS from Ohio State University. Dr. Gabbard's work engages with transnational queer studies and feminisms, critical development and human rights discourses, and nationalism and post-conflict studies. Her research critically examines the relationships between development agencies/organizations and feminist and LGBTQ grassroots activist movements. She is also interested in queer BIPOC representation in popular culture and thinking and writing about feminist pedagogy and research methodologies.

JONATHAN FRIEDMAN, PhD, is the director of free expression and education programs at the literary and human rights nonprofit PEN America, where he oversees research, advocacy, and education related to free speech on campus, academic freedom, educational gag orders, book bans, and general free expression issues in schools, colleges, and universities. An interdisciplinary scholar by training, he served as lead author on the PEN America reports *Banned in the USA: Rising School Book Bans Threaten Free Expression and Students' First Amendment Rights* (2022), *Educational Gag Orders: Legislative Restrictions on the Freedom to Read, Learn, and Teach* (2021), and *Chasm in the Classroom: Campus Free Speech in a Divided America* (2019). He also led the production of the *Campus Free Speech Guide* (2020).

LYNN M. GANGONE, EdD, has served as AACTE's president and CEO since 2017, her fourth higher education association leadership role. Her experience includes work at the New York State and New Jersey State Education Departments, Centenary University (New Jersey), the Maryland Independent College and University Association, University of Denver, and the American Council on Education. She has held faculty appointments at two Colleges of Education, George Washington University Graduate School of Education and Human Development as a visiting professor, and a full professor (clinical) at University of Denver's Morgridge College of Education. Dr. Gangone, a sought-after TEDx speaker and commentator, has been featured in national publications such as the *New York Times, Time, USA Today*, and the *Washington Post.*

HEATHER MONTES IRELAND (she/ella) is an assistant professor in the Women's and Gender Studies Department and affiliated faculty in the Latin American and Latino Studies Department, the Critical Ethnic Studies Program, and the LGBTQ Studies Program at DePaul University. Her research and teaching specializations include women of color studies, Latina/Chicana/Boricua feminisms, queer of color critique, economic violence, and the gender and sexual politics of racial capitalism.

VALERIE C. JOHNSON is the associate provost of DEI, an associate professor of political science, and an endowed professor of urban diplomacy at DePaul University, Chicago, Illinois. Dr. Johnson's research and teaching explore the intersections of race and class. Her publications include *Black Power in the Suburbs: The Myth or Reality of African American Suburban Political Incorporation* and *Power in the City: Clarence Stone and the Politics of Inequality.* Dr. Johnson is the former national education spokesperson for Reverend Jesse L. Jackson Sr. and the Rainbow PUSH Coalition and has served as a consultant for numerous elected officials and community organizations.

ISAAC KAMOLA is an associate professor of political science at Trinity College, Hartford, Connecticut. He is the author of *Free Speech and Koch Money: Manufacturing a Campus Culture War* (with Ralph Wilson, 2021) and *Making the World Global: US Universities and the Production of the Global Imaginary* (2019). He is the creator of Faculty First Responders, a program that monitors right-wing attacks on academics and provides resources to help faculty members and administrators respond to manufactured outrage.

MARVIN LYNN is a nationally recognized and highly cited scholar whose research critically examines race in schools, the practices of Black male educators, and best practices for advancing teacher diversity in the United States. He has been quoted or featured in national and international news outlets, including the *New York Times*, the *Christian Science Monitor*, BBC News, and Fox

News. His research has also been recognized by the *American Educational Research Association*, the *Critical Race Studies in Education Association*, and the University of the Free State in South Africa. Dr. Lynn is the lead editor of the recently released second edition of *The Handbook of Critical Race Theory in Education*, which features the scholarship of the most prolific scholars in the fields of education and the law. He currently serves as dean of and professor in the School of Education and Human Development at the University of Colorado Denver.

KEVIN MCGRUDER is an associate professor of history at Antioch College. He is the author of *Race and Real Estate: Conflict and Cooperation in Harlem, 1890–1920* and *Philip Payton: The Father of Black Harlem*. Before entering academia, he was director of real estate development of the Abyssinian Development Corporation (Harlem) and executive director of Gay Men of African Descent (New York City).

ANNE MITCHELL is the director of the Critical Ethnic Studies program and teaches at DePaul University in the departments of Women's and Gender Studies and African Black Diaspora Studies. She has an undergraduate degree from Grambling State University, a master's from the University of Minnesota, and a doctorate from Ohio State University. Dr. Mitchell's work primarily focuses on examining Black women, queer people, and Black immigrants to the US through the narrative of the African American civil rights movement with feminist and queer theoretical lenses. Her interests also include critically examining popular culture, including Beyoncé and the WNBA.

IRENE MULVEY is the president of the American Association of University Professors (AAUP). She was elected to that office in 2020, having served multiple terms on the AAUP's governing Council, Committee A on Academic Freedom and Tenure, and Committee T on College and University Governance. She has been a faculty activist and active in the AAUP at the campus, state, and national level for her entire career. She is a professor emerita of mathematics at Fairfield University, where she taught for thirty-seven years.

DENNIS PARKER is director of the National Center for Law and Economic Justice, founded in 1965 to further racial and economic justice. Earlier, he served as the director of the ACLU's Racial Justice Program, leading its efforts in issues which adversely affect communities of color. He was chief of the Civil Rights Bureau in the New York Attorney General's office and, for fourteen years, worked on and directed the educational work of the NAACP Legal Defense and Educational Fund. Parker began his legal career at the New York Legal Aid Society. He writes and lectures extensively on civil rights and is an adjunct professor at Teachers College of Columbia University and New York University Law School. He is a graduate of Middlebury College and Harvard Law School.

KATIE RAINWATER is a visiting assistant teaching professor at Florida International University, where she teaches sociology. Her research on guestworker programs in Asia has appeared in *Work, Employment & Society, International Migration Review*, and *Critical Asian Studies*. Her current research project examines the experiences of farmers and workers in the export-driven shrimp aquaculture industries of Thailand and Bangladesh. She is a member of the United Faculty of Florida and Labor Notes' Public Higher Education Workers Group.

JENNIFER RUTH is an associate dean of the College of the Arts and professor in the School of Film at Portland State University. She writes extensively about academic freedom and higher education in outlets such as the *New Republic, Truthout, Academe Blog, Chronicle of Higher Education, Inside Higher Ed*, and *Ms.* She has authored and coauthored three books, most recently *It's Not Free Speech: Race, Democracy, and the Future of Academic Freedom* (2022) with Michael Bérubé. She served two years as the faculty editor of *The Journal of Academic Freedom* and three years as Portland State-AAUP's vice president of Academic Freedom and Grievances. She holds a PhD from Brown University.

ELLEN SCHRECKER is an American historian who has written extensively about McCarthyism, political repression, and American higher education. Her latest book, *The Lost Promise: American Universities in the 1960s* (2021), provides the first comprehensive analysis of that turbulent decade. Among her previous books are *No Ivory Tower: McCarthyism and the Universities* (1986), *The Age of McCarthyism: A Brief History with Documents* (1994, 3rd ed., 2017), *Many Are the Crimes: McCarthyism in America* (1998), and *The Lost Soul of Higher Education: Corporatization, the Assault on Academic Freedom, and the End of the University* (2010). A retired professor of history at Yeshiva University, she holds a PhD from and taught at Harvard as well as at New York University and Princeton University.

SARAH SKLAW is a research associate with Historians for Peace and Democracy. She received her PhD in history from NYU for her dissertation on US relations with Nicaragua in the late Cold War. Her writing has appeared in NACLA, the *Washington Post*, and the *Fellow Travelers* blog. She works for a community board in Brooklyn.

JAMES TAGER is the research director at PEN America. Tager previously worked with the International Commission of Jurists—Asia & Pacific Program, first as a Satter Human Rights Fellow and subsequently as an International Associate Legal Advisor. Before that, he was a 2013–2014 Frederick Sheldon Traveling Fellow, researching civil society responses to the developing human rights framework within ASEAN (Association of Southeast Asian Nations). He has lived and worked in Thailand, Myanmar, and Cambodia. Tager holds a BA from Duke University and a JD from Harvard Law School.

HELENA WORTHEN and **JOE BERRY** met in the late 1980s at a California Federation of Teachers meeting. She was serving as union rep for her community college contingent colleagues, and he was organizing contingents up and down the state while working as a staffer for another community college union. Since then, the two have been writing, studying, speaking, and agitating on behalf of higher ed faculty, contingent and otherwise. Worthen's book, *What Did You Learn at Work Today: Forbidden Lessons of Labor Education* (2014), won the UALE (United Association of Labor Education) Best Book Award. Berry's 2005 book, *Reclaiming the Ivory Tower: Organizing Adjuncts to Change Higher Education*, is still in print from Monthly Review Press. They have retired from the University of Illinois School of Labor and

Employment Relations, where they worked as labor educators. Together they wrote *Power Despite Precarity: Strategies for the Contingent Faculty Movement in Higher Education* (2021). They are both delegates to Higher Education Labor United (HELU), Worthen from the National Writers Union and Berry from the Coalition on Contingent Academic Labor (COCAL) and from AFT 2121 at City College of San Francisco.

JEREMY C. YOUNG is the senior manager of free expression and education at PEN America, where he advances PEN America's advocacy for academic freedom in higher education and against educational censorship in colleges, universities, and K–12 schools. A former history professor and director of the Institute of Politics and Public Affairs at Utah Tech University, Young holds a PhD in US history from Indiana University and is the author of *The Age of Charisma: Leaders, Followers, and Emotions in American Society, 1870–1940* (2017). He was a 2021 New Leaders Council Fellow and a recipient of the Roger D. Bridges Distinguished Service Award from the Society for Historians of the Gilded Age and Progressive Era.

NOTES

INTRODUCTION: A TIME FOR FACULTY TO ACT

1. Robert C. Post, *Democracy, Expertise, and Academic Freedom: A First Amendment Jurisprudence for the Modern State* (New Haven, CT: Yale University Press, 2012).
2. Ralph Wilson and Isaac Kamola, *Free Speech and Koch Money: Manufacturing a Campus Culture War* (London: Pluto Press, 2021).
3. "Florida College System Censorship Cannot Stand," AAUP, January 20, 2023, https://www.aaup.org/news/florida-college-system-censorship-can-not-stand#.
4. Christopher F. Rufo, "Laying Siege to the Institutions," Hillsdale College, April 5, 2022, YouTube video, https://www.youtube.com/watch?v=W8Hh0GqoJcE.

CHAPTER 1: ACADEMIC FREEDOM AND POLITICAL REPRESSION FROM MCCARTHYISM TO TRUMP

1. Mark James, "Guess Who's Coming to the Lecture?" *Inside Higher Ed*, May 21, 2021, https://www.insidehighered.com/views/2021/05/21/online-education-can-have -negative-impact-academics-doing-antiracist-work-opinion.
2. Jennifer Ruth and Ellen Schrecker, "Faculty, You Have Power! Use It!" *Academe Blog*, February 14, 2022, https://academeblog.org/2022/02/14/faculty-you-have-power -use-it.
3. "Timeline: Remembering the Scopes Monkey Trial," *Consider This*, NPR, July 5, 2005, https://www.npr.org/2005/07/05/4723956/timeline-remembering-the-scopes -monkey-trial, accessed November 11, 2022. For a thoughtful discussion of the at- tacks on academic freedom at the turn of the twentieth century, see Mary O. Furner, *Advocacy and Objectivity: A Crisis in the Professionalization of American Social Science, 1865–1905* (Lexington: University Press of Kentucky, 1975).
4. For an overview of the impact of McCarthyism on the academic community, see Ellen W. Schrecker, *No Ivory Tower: McCarthyism and the Universities* (New York: Oxford University Press, 1986).
5. Richard M. Freeland, *Academia's Golden Age: Universities in Massachusetts, 1945–1970* (New York: Oxford University Press, 1992).
6. For an excellent overview of the decline of public higher education, see Michael Fab- ricant and Stephen Brier, *Austerity Blues: Fighting for the Soul of Public Higher Educa- tion* (Baltimore: Johns Hopkins University Press, 2016).

7. On speaker bans, see Gary Murrell, *The Most Dangerous Communist in the United States: A Biography of Herbert Aptheker* (Amherst: University of Massachusetts Press, 2015); Marjorie Heins, *Priests of Our Democracy: The Supreme Court, Academic Freedom, and the Anti-Communist Purge* (New York: New York University Press, 2013), deals with loyalty oaths and more during the 1960s.

8. Beth Bailey, *Sex in the Heartland* (Cambridge, MA: Harvard University Press, 1999), 45–104.

9. For a fuller discussion of the decline of American higher education, see Ellen Schrecker, *The Lost Promise: American Universities in the 1960s* (Chicago: University of Chicago Press, 2021).

10. On the media and the student movement, see Todd Gitlin, *The Whole World Is Watching: Mass Media in the Making and Unmaking of the New Left* (Berkeley: University of California Press, 2003).

11. For samples of these public intellectuals' critique of the Berkeley unrest, see *The Berkeley Student Revolt: Facts and Interpretations*, eds. Seymour Martin Lipset and Sheldon S. Wolin (Garden City, NY: Doubleday, 1965).

12. Matthew Dallek, *The Right Moment: Ronald Reagan's First Victory and the Decisive Turning Point in American Politics* (New York: The Free Press, 2000), 190.

13. Seth Rosenfeld, *Subversives: The FBI's War on Student Radicals, and Reagan's Rise to Power* (New York: Farrar, Straus and Giroux, 2012), 428; Fabricant and Brier, *Austerity Blues*, 79.

14. Tom Wells, *The War Within: America's Battle over Vietnam* (Berkeley: University of California Press, 1994), 299.

15. "Fact Sheet on Illinois Special Legislative Commission to Investigate Campus Disturbances," New University Conference Papers, box 9, folder 5, Historical Society of Wisconsin, Madison; J. Stanley Marshall, *The Tumultuous Sixties: Campus Unrest and Student Life at a Southern University* (Tallahassee, FL: Sentry Press, 2006), 9.

16. *The Report of the President's Commission on Campus Unrest* (Washington, DC: US Government Printing Office, 1970).

17. William J. Billingsley, *Communists on Campus: Race, Politics, and the Public University in Sixties North Carolina* (Athens: University of Georgia Press, 1999), 225.

18. Richard W. Lyman, *Stanford in Turmoil: Campus Unrest, 1966–1972* (Stanford, CA: Stanford General Books, 2009), 157.

19. Marshall, *The Tumultuous Sixties*, 9.

20. Edward Silva, "Faculty Images of Power and Knowledge," in *Academic Supermarkets: A Critical Case Study of a Multiversity*, ed. Philip G. Altbach, Robert S. Laufer, and Sheila McVey (San Francisco: Jossey-Bass, 1971), 170–77; Earl F. Cheit, *The New Depression in Higher Education: A Study of Financial Conditions at 41 Colleges and Universities* (New York: McGraw-Hill, 1971), 17.

21. Mary Ann Wynkoop, *Dissent in the Heartland: The Sixties at Indiana University* (Bloomington: Indiana University Press, 2002), 77.

22. Patricia J. Gumport, "Graduate Education and Research: Interdependence and Strain," *American Higher Education in the Twenty-First Century: Social, Political, and Economic Challenges*, ed. Philip G. Altbach, Patricia J. Gumport, and Robert O. Berdahl (Baltimore: Johns Hopkins University Press, 1999), 396–426.

23. Roger L. Geiger, *Knowledge and Money: Research Universities and the Paradox of the Marketplace* (Stanford, CA: Stanford University Press, 2004), 59.

24. Nancy MacLean, *Democracy in Chains: The Deep History of the Radical Right's Stealth Plan for America* (New York: Viking, 2017).

25. Lewis F. Powell Jr., "Powell Memorandum: Attack on American Free Enterprise System," Washington and Lee University School of Law, August 23, 1971, https://scholarlycommons.law.wlu.edu/powellmemo, accessed November 12, 2022.

26. John J. Miller, *A Gift of Freedom: How the John M. Olin Foundation Changed America* (San Francisco: Encounter Books, 2006), 105.

27. Matthew Johnson, *Undermining Racial Justice: How One University Embraced Inclusion and Inequality* (Ithaca, NY: Cornell University Press, 2020).

28. Ami Zusman, "Challenges Facing Higher Education in the Twenty-First Century," in Altbach, Gumport, and Berdahl, *American Higher Education in the Twenty-First Century*, 133.

29. Allan Bloom, *The Closing of the American Mind: How Higher Education Has Failed Democracy and Impoverished the Souls of Today's Students* (New York: Simon & Schuster, 1987), 96.

30. George H. W. Bush, "Commencement Address at the University of Michigan," May 4, 1991, YouTube video, https://www.youtube.com/watch?v=01kX1WGdJWc, accessed November 13, 2022.

CHAPTER 2: A KOCH-FUNDED RACIAL BACKLASH

1. For an overview how Koch dark money influences American politics, see Jane Mayer, *Dark Money: The Hidden History of the Billionaires Behind the Rise of the Radical Right* (New York: Anchor Books, 2017); Theda Skocpol and Alexander Hertel-Fernandez, "The Koch Network and Republican Party Extremism," *Perspectives on Politics* 14, no. 3 (2016); Alexander Hertel-Fernandez, Theda Skocpol, and Jason Sclar, "When Political Mega-Donors Join Forces: How the Koch Network and the Democracy Alliance Influence Organized US Politics on the Right and Left," *Studies in American Political Development* 32, no. 2 (2018); Alexander Hertel-Fernandez, *State Capture: How Conservative Activists, Big Business, and Wealthy Donors Reshaped the American States—and the Nation* (New York: Oxford University Press, 2019); Anne Nelson, *Shadow Network: Media, Money, and the Secret Hub of the Radical Right* (New York: Bloomsbury, 2019); Ralph Wilson and Isaac Kamola, *Free Speech and Koch Money: Manufacturing a Campus Culture War* (London: Pluto Press, 2021).

2. Nancy MacLean, *Democracy in Chains: The Deep History of the Radical Right's Stealth Plan for America* (New York: Viking, 2017), 10.

3. Clayton A. Coppin, *Stealth: The History of Charles Koch's Political Activities* (2003), archived at https://ia600705.us.archive.org/3/items/Stealth2003Excerpt/Stealth%202003%20Excerpt.pdf, accessed July 2020; see also Mayer, *Dark Money*, 53.

4. Richard H. Fink, "From Ideas to Action: The Role of Universities, Think Tanks, and Activist Groups," *Philanthropy* x, no. 1 (Winter 1996): 11; Wilson and Kamola, *Free Speech and Koch Money*, 21–28.

5. Lateshia Beachum, "Kochs Key Among Small Group Quietly Funding Legal Assault on Campaign Finance Regulation," Center for Public Integrity, November 15, 2017.

6. Christopher Leonard, *Kochland: The Secret History of Koch Industries and Corporate Power in America* (New York: Simon & Schuster, 2020), 642.

7. Benjamin Wallace-Wells, "How a Conservative Activist Invented the Conflict over Critical Race Theory," *New Yorker*, June 18, 2021; Sarah Jones, "How to Manufacture a Moral Panic: Christopher Rufo Helped Incite an Uproar over Racism Education with Dramatic, Dodgy Reporting," *New York Magazine*, July 11, 2021; Laura Meckler and Josh Dawsey, "Republicans, Spurred by an Unlikely Figure, See Political Promise in Targeting Critical Race Theory," *Washington Post*, June 21, 2021; Sam Adler-Bell, "Behind the Critical Race Theory Crackdown," *The Forum*, African-American Policy Forum, January 13, 2022; Matthew Sitman and Sam Adler-Bell, "How (Not) to Talk About Racism," *Know Your Enemy*, podcast, June 30, 2021.

8. Christopher F. Rufo, "City of Seattle Holds Racially Segregated Civil Rights Training—In the Name of Social Justice," *Separate But Equal*, Substack, July 29, 2020.

9. Christopher Rufo (@realchrisrufo), "We have successfully frozen their brand," Twitter, March 15, 2021, 3:14 p.m., https://twitter.com/realchrisrufo/status/1371540368 714428416?lang=en, accessed December 2, 2022.

10. Manhattan Institute for Policy Research, "Christopher F. Rufo," https://www.city -journal.org/contributor/christopher-f-rufo_1334, accessed June 1, 2022.

11. DeSmog, "Manhattan Institute for Policy Research," https://www.desmog.com /manhattan-institute-policy-research/, accessed July 6, 2022.

12. The Heritage Foundation, "Critical Race Theory Has Infiltrated the Federal Government, Christopher Rufo on Fox News," September 2, 2020, YouTube video, https:// www.youtube.com/watch?v=rBXRdWflV7M.

13. Matt Gertz, "Fox's Anti-'Critical Race Theory' Parents Are Also GOP Activists," Media Matters for America, June 17, 2021.

14. Chloe Simon, "A Former Trump Appointee Is Linked to 'Critical Race Theory' Legislation in over 20 States," Media Matters for America, June 25, 2021.

15. White House, "Executive Order on Establishing the President's Advisory 1776 Commission," November 2, 2020.

16. Nikole Hannah-Jones, "Our Democracy's Founding Ideals Were False When They Were Written. Black Americans Have Fought to Make Them True," *New York Times Magazine*, August 14, 2019.

17. Gillian Brockell, "'A Hack Job,' 'Outright Lies': Trump Commission's '1776 Report' Outrages Historians," *Washington Post*, January 20, 2021.

18. Anne Nelson, *Shadow Network: Media, Money, and the Secret Hub of the Radical Right* (New York: Bloomsbury, 2019), 104–5.

19. Stephanie Saul, "College Fights 'Leftist Academics' by Expanding into Charter Schools," *New York Times*, April 10, 2022.

20. DeSmog, "Texas Public Policy Foundation," https://www.desmog.com/texas-public -policy-foundation/, accessed July 6, 2022.

21. Michael S. Schmidt and Maggie Haberman, "The Lawyer Behind the Memo on How Trump Could Stay in Office," *New York Times*, October 2, 2021; Jean Guerrero, "Donald Trump's Politics of White Fear Have Roots in Southern California," *Los Angeles Magazine*, September 10, 2020.

22. Andy Kroll, "The Dark-Money ATM of the Conservative Movement," *Mother Jones*, February 5, 2013.

23. Conservative Transparency, "The Claremont Institute," http://conservative transparency.org/org/the-claremont-institute/, accessed July 6, 2022.

24. SourceWatch, "Heritage Foundation," Center for Media and Democracy, https://www.sourcewatch.org/index.php/Heritage_Foundation, accessed July 6, 2022.

25. SourceWatch, "Gay Hart Gaines," Center for Media and Democracy, https://www.sourcewatch.org/index.php/Gay_Hart_Gaines, accessed July 6, 2022.

26. SourceWatch, "American Majority," Center for Media and Democracy, https://www.sourcewatch.org/index.php/American_Majority, accessed June 26, 2023.

27. President's Advisory 1776 Commission, *The 1776 Report*, White House, January 2021, 18.

28. For reporting UNC's denial of tenure for Hannah-Jones, see Special Committee, "Governance, Academic Freedom, and Institutional Racism in the University of North Carolina System," American Association of University Professors, 2022; Joe Killian and Kyle Ingram, "After Conservative Criticism, UNC Backs Down from Offering Acclaimed Journalist Tenured Position," *NC Policy Watch*, May 19, 2021.

29. Killian and Ingram, "After Conservative Criticism, UNC Backs Down."

30. Quoted in AAUP, *Report of a Special Committee: Governance, Academic Freedom, and Institutional Racism in the University of North Carolina System*, April 2022, https://www.aaup.org/report/governance-academic-freedom-and-institutional-racism-university-north-carolina-system.

31. Shannon Watkins, "UNC's 1619 Project Hire: A Case Study of Failed University Governance," James G. Martin Center for Academic Renewal, May 10, 2021, https://www.jamesgmartin.center/2021/05/uncs-1619-project-hire-a-case-study-of-failed-university-governance/, accessed October 28, 2022.

32. Killian and Ingram, "After Conservative Criticism, UNC Backs Down."

33. James G. Martin Center for Academic Renewal, "The Pope Center Transition," https://www.jamesgmartin.center/popecenter/, accessed October 23, 2022.

34. According to the 990 filings for the James G. Martin Center for Academic Renewal, the center received $732,339 from contributions (and total revenue of $797,090). According to 990 tax filings from the John Pope Foundation the same year, the foundation gave twelve installments of $45,233 to the Martin Center for a total of $542,808, or 74.1 percent of its total contributions (and 68 percent of the center's total revenue).

35. Matea Gold, "In N.C., Conservative Donor Art Pope Sits at Heart of Government He Helped Transform," *Washington Post*, July 19, 2014.

36. Gold, "In N.C., Conservative Donor Art Pope Sits at Heart of Government He Helped Transform."

37. Gold, "In N.C., Conservative Donor Art Pope Sits at Heart of Government He Helped Transform."

38. Sturgis, "How Art Pope's Money Shaped UNC's Toxic Debate." See also Special Committee, "Governance, Academic Freedom, and Institutional Racism in the University of North Carolina System," 3–4.

39. Note that in North Carolina, a board of governors oversees the UNC state system, while each campus has its own board of trustees. There is no evidence that Pope, in his role on the board of governors, intervened in the UNC-Chapel Hill Board of Trustees' decisions regarding Hannah-Jones's tenure.

40. Special Committee, "Governance, Academic Freedom, and Institutional Racism in the University of North Carolina System," 3.

41. Sturgis, "How Art Pope's Money Shaped UNC's Toxic Debate"; Joe Killian, "Groups with Close Ties to Two UNC Board of Governors Members Issue Blistering Attacks on Nikole Hannah-Jones," *Indy Week*, May 13, 2021.

42. Many libertarian think tanks devote whole sections of their websites to critical race theory. See, for example, the American Enterprise Institute, the Manhattan Institute, the Heritage Foundation, and the Goldwater Institute.

43. Jonathan Friedman and James Tager, *Educational Gag Orders: Legislative Restrictions on the Freedom to Read, Learn, and Teach*, PEN America, 2021, p. 4, https://pen.org /report/educational-gag-orders, accessed October 28, 2022.

44. A live link to the "PEN America Index of Educational Gag Orders" is available at Friedman and Tager, "Educational Gag Orders," PEN America.

45. Don Wiener and Alex Kotch, "ALEC Inspires Lawmakers to File Anti-Critical Race Theory Bills," Center for Media and Democracy, July 27, 2021, https://www.exposed bycmd.org/2021/07/27/alec-inspires-lawmakers-to-file-anti-critical-race-theory-bills/, accessed November 27, 2021.

46. ALEC, "American Civil and History Act," https://alec.org/model-policy/american -civics-and-history-act, accessed November 23, 2022.

47. ALEC, "Honesty in Teaching Act," https://alec.org/model-policy/honesty-in-teaching-act, accessed November 23, 2022.

48. For example, Representative Bell has been an ALEC member since 2019, when he attended the annual meeting; Representative Byrd has been a member since 2020 and sits on the International Relations and Federalism as well as the Criminal Justice task forces; Representative Fine was an ALEC member (2017–19) and attended the 2019 annual meeting; Representative Fischer was the ALEC state chair (2018–20) and attended the 2019 and 2021 annual meetings; SourceWatch, "Florida ALEC Politicians," Center for Media and Democracy, https://www.sourcewatch.org/index.php /Florida_ALEC_Politicians, accessed December 1, 2022.

49. DeSmog, "American Legislative Exchange Council (ALEC)," https://www.desmog.com /american-legislative-exchange-council/, accessed November 27, 2022.

50. Goldwater Institute, "Stop Critical Race Theory and Racial Discrimination in Public Schools Act," https://www.goldwaterinstitute.org/wp-content/uploads/2022/04/CRT -Racial-Discrimination-Model-Policy.pdf, accessed November 27, 2022.

51. State of Arizona, "HCR 2001," House of Representatives, 2022, https://www.azleg .gov/legtext/55leg/2R/bills/HCR2001P.pdf, accessed November 27, 2022.

52. Wilson and Kamola, *Free Speech and Koch Money*, 167.

53. Heritage Foundation, "States Use Heritage's Model Legislation to Reject Critical Race Theory in Classrooms," March 18, 2022, https://www.heritage.org/education/impact /states-use-heritages-model-legislation-reject-critical-race-theory-classrooms, accessed November 27, 2022.

54. James Copland, "How to Regulate Critical Race Theory in Schools: A Primer and Model Legislation," Issue Brief, Manhattan Institute, August 2021, 12–13, https://media4.manhattan-institute.org/sites/default/files/copland-crt-legislation.pdf, accessed November 27, 2022.

55. Eric Kleefeld, "Group's IRS Filing Reveals Nexus of Right-Wing Dark Money and 'Critical Race Theory' Media Hysteria," Media Matters for America, December 7, 2021.

56. Sergio Munoz, "The White Nationalist Ties of the Next Big Civil Rights Case," Media Matters for America, December 21, 2020; Robert Barnes, "How One Man Brought Affirmative Action to the Supreme Court. Again and Again," *Washington Post*, October 24, 2022.

57. Tim Craig, "Moms for Liberty Has Turned 'Parental Rights' into a Rallying Cry for Conservative Parents," *Washington Post*, October 15, 2021; Elizabeth Shockman, "How National Politics Are Changing Minnesota's 2022 School Board Elections," Minnesota Public Radio, November 2, 2022, https://www.mprnews.org/story/2022/11/02/how-national-politics-are-changing-minnesotas-2022-school-board-elections, accessed December 1, 2022.

58. Olivia Little, "Unmasking Moms for Liberty," Media Matters for America, November 12, 2021.

59. Independent Women's Forum (IWF) is the parent organization. Independent Women's Voice (IWV) is its 501(c)4 affiliate. I use IWF here for consistency.

60. SourceWatch, "Independent Women's Forum," Center for Media and Democracy, https://www.sourcewatch.org/index.php/Independent_Women's_Forum, accessed December 1, 2022.

61. Isaac Stanley-Becker, "Koch-Backed Group Fuels Opposition to School Mask Mandates, Leaked Letter Shows," *Washington Post*, October 1, 2021.

62. Independent Women's Voice, "How to Talk About: Critical Race Theory and Anti-Racism," 2022, https://www.iwv.org/wp-content/uploads/2022/02/How-To-Talk-About-Critical-Race-Theory-and-Anti-Racism_IWV.pdf, accessed December 1, 2022.

63. Lisa Graves, "The Independent 'Women's' Voice? Most Known Donors Are Men," PRWatch, Center for Media and Democracy, August 24, 2016; DeSmog, "Independent Women's Voice," https://www.desmog.com/independent-womens-voice/, accessed December 1, 2022; Lisa Graves, Alyssa Bowen, and Evan Vorpahl, "Who Is Behind the 'Toxic Schools' Attack Website? Backgrounder on the So-Called Independent Women's Voice," *True North*, October 27, 2021.

64. Fink is a career Koch network insider, having founded the Mercatus Center (George Mason University), served in leadership roles for Koch Industries, the Koch Foundation, and Freedom Partners, and developed the political strategy ("the structure of social change") that guides Koch's broader political strategy. See Wilson and Kamola, *Free Speech and Koch Money*, 20–28.

65. DeSmog, "FreedomWorks," https://www.desmog.com/freedomworks/, accessed December 2, 2022.

66. Theda Skocpol and Vanessa Williamson, *The Tea Party and the Remaking of Republican Conservatism* (Oxford: Oxford University Press, 2016), 84; Lois Beckett, "Tea

Party-Linked Activists Protest Against 'Election Fraud' in US Cities," *The Guardian*, November 6, 2020.

67. Building Education for Students Together, "School Board Candidate Toolkit," FreedomWorks, 4, August 24, 2022, https://parentsknowbest.com/wp-content/uploads /2022/08/School-Board-Candidate-Preview-82422.pdf, accessed December 2, 2022.

68. Staff, "Governor DeSantis Announces Legislative Proposal to Stop W.O.K.E. Activism and Critical Race Theory in Schools and Corporations," Office of the Governor, Florida, December 15, 2021, https://www.flgov.com/2021/12/15/governor-desantis -announces-legislative-proposal-to-stop-w-o-k-e-activism-and-critical-race-theory-in -schools-and-corporations/, accessed December 2, 2022.

69. Sommer Brugal, "DeSantis Signs 'Stop Woke' Act, Disney Bills Next to a Stage Full of Supporters," *Tampa Bay Times*, April 22, 2022.

CHAPTER 3: THE RISE OF EDUCATIONAL GAG ORDERS

1. PEN America Index of Educational Gag Orders, https://docs.google.com/spreadsheets /d/1Tj5WQVBmB6SQg-zP_M8uZsQQGH09TxmBY73v23zpyr0/edit?usp=sharing, accessed November 15, 2022.

2. For a contemporary look at how Americans respond differently over questions of historical consideration in education, see "History, The Past, and Public Culture: Results from a National Survey," American Historical Association and Fairleigh Dickinson University, August 2021, https://historians.org/history-culture-survey, accessed November 15, 2022.

3. Executive Order on Combating Race and Sex Stereotyping, September 22, 2020, trumpwhitehouse.archives.gov/presidential-actions/executive-order-combating-race -sex-stereotyping, accessed November 15, 2022.

4. Arkansas SB 627, https://www.arkleg.state.ar.us/Acts/FTPDocument?path=%2FACTS %2F2021R%2FPublic%2F&file=1100.pdf&ddBienniumSession=2021%2F2021R, accessed November 15, 2022.

5. PEN America, "Failed Bill Brought by Arizona Democrats Would Have Restricted What Teachers Can Teach," July 5, 2022, https://pen.org/press-release/failed-bill -brought-by-arizona-democrats-would-have-restricted-what-teachers-can-teach, accessed November 15, 2022.

6. Missouri SB 775, https://www.senate.mo.gov/22info/pdf-bill/intro/SB775.pdf, accessed December 20, 2022; letter from PEN America to Missouri School Boards and State Legislatures, November 16, 2022, https://pen.org/press-release/call-for-missouri -school-districts-to-end-book-bans, accessed December 20, 2022.

7. Rosenberger v. Rectors and Visitors of the University of Virginia, 515 U.S. 819, 829 (1995).

8. Melinda D. Anderson, "'These Are the Facts': Black Educators Silenced from Teaching America's Racist Past," *The Guardian*, September 14, 2021, theguardian.com/education /2021/sep/14/black-us-teachers-critical-race-theory-silenced, accessed November 15, 2022.

9. Frank Askin, "Chilling Effect," The First Amendment Encyclopedia, 2009, mtsu.edu /first-amendment/article/897/chilling-effect, accessed November 15, 2022.

10. Previous PEN America reports discussing the chilling effect include: "Cracking Down on Creative Voices: Turkey's Silencing of Writers, Intellectuals, and Artists Five Years After

the Failed Coup," PEN America, June 2021, pen.org/wp-content/uploads/2021/06 /cracking-down-creative-voices-turkey-FINAL.pdf, accessed November 15, 2022; "Arresting Dissent: Legislative Restrictions on the Right to Protest," PEN America, May 2020, pen.org/wp-content/uploads/2020/05/Arresting-Dissent-FINAL.pdf, accessed November 15, 2022; and "Chasm in the Classroom; Campus Free Speech in a Divided America," PEN America, April 2, 2019, pen.org/wp-content/uploads/2019/04/2019 -PEN-Chasm-in-the-Classroom-04.25.pdf, accessed November 15, 2022.

11. See Younger v. Harris, 401 U.S. 37 (1971) (holding that "a chilling effect even in the area of First Amendment rights has never been considered a sufficient basis, in and of itself, for prohibiting state action"); Laird v. Tatum, 408 U.S. 1 (1972); Clapper v. Amnesty International USA, 568 US 398 (2013). But see Baggett v. Bullitt, 377 U.S. 360, (1964); Bantam Books v. Sullivan, 372 U.S. 58 (1963); Americans for Prosperity Foundation v. Bonta, 594 U.S. ___ (2021).

12. See, e.g., *United States v. Stevens* (2010), *United States v. Alvarez* (2012).

13. Grayned v. City of Rockford, 408 U.S. at 109, 92 S. Ct. at 2299 (internal ellipses and quotation marks omitted). See also Kramer v. Price, 712 F.2d (1983) at 177.

14. Hannah Knowles, "Critical Race Theory Ban Leads Oklahoma College to Cancel Class That Taught 'White Privilege,'" *Washington Post*, May 29, 2021, www .washingtonpost.com/education/2021/05/29/oklahoma-critical-race-theory-ban, accessed November 15, 2022.

15. Iowa State University—Frequently Asked Questions—Iowa House File 802— Requirements Related to Racism and Sexism Trainings at Public Postsecondary Institutions, August 5, 2021, https://www.provost.iastate.edu/policies/iowa-house -file-802—requirements-related-to-racism-and-sexism-trainings, accessed November 15, 2022; Daniel C. Vock, "GOP Furor over 'Critical Race Theory' Hits College Campuses," *Iowa Capital Dispatch*, July 3, 2021, iowacapitaldispatch.com/2021 /07/03/gop-furor-over-critical-race-theory-hits-college-campuses, accessed November 15, 2022.

16. Wayne Stafford, "Two Oklahoma School Districts Punished for Violating CRT Ban," KOKH, July 28, 2022, https://okcfox.com/news/local/2-ok-school-district-punished -for-violating-crt-ban-tulsa-public-schools-and-mustang-public-schools-accreditation -with-warning-house-bill-1775-accreditation-with-warning-accreditation-with -deficiencies, accessed November 15, 2022.

17. Lenzy Krehbiel-Burton, "Audio from TPS Implicit Bias Training Was a Voice Reading Presentation Slides Verbatim," *Tulsa World*, August 6, 2022, https://tulsaworld.com /news/local/education/audio-from-tps-implicit-bias-training-was-a-voice-reading -presentation-slides-verbatim/article_140cabde-1524–11ed-b809–1f6eb7ac6c64.html, accessed November 15, 2022.

18. Mica Pollock and John Rogers, *The Conflict Campaign: Exploring Local Experiences of the Campaign to Ban "Critical Race Theory" in Public K–12 Education in the US, 2021–2022*, UCLA/IDEA Publications, January 2022, https://idea.gseis.ucla.edu /publications/the-conflict-campaign/publications/files/the-conflict-campaign-report, accessed November 15, 2022.

19. Ashley Woo et al., *Walking a Fine Line—Educators' Views on Politicized Topics in Schooling*, RAND Corporation, August 10, 2022, https://www.rand.org/content

/dam/rand/pubs/research_reports/RRA1100/RRA1108–5/RAND_RRA1108–5.pdf, accessed November 15, 2022.

20. Nikoel Hytrek, "Why More Students Are Walking Out at Iowa Schools," Iowa Starting Line, April 17, 2022, https://iowastartingline.com/2022/04/17/why-more -students-are-walking-out-at-iowa-schools, accessed November 15, 2022.

21. Hannah Natanson, "'Never Seen It This Bad': America Faces Catastrophic Teacher Shortage," *Washington Post*, August 3, 2022, https://www.washingtonpost.com/educa-tion/2022/08/03/school-teacher-shortage, accessed November 15, 2022.

22. PEN America, "Open Letter to the School Board of the Placentia-Yorba Linda Unified School District," January 11, 2022, https://pen.org/open-letter-school-board -placentia-yorba-linda-unified-school-district, accessed November 15, 2022.

23. CRT Forward Tracking Project, https://crtforward.law.ucla.edu, accessed November 15, 2022.

24. Falls v. DeSantis, 4:22cv166 (2022), https://aboutblaw.com/2G4, accessed November 15, 2022; Honeyfund.com v. DeSantis, 4:22cv227 (2022), https://www.document cloud.org/documents/22065949–1-complaint-honeyfund-v-desantis, accessed November 15, 2022; Pernell v. Florida Board of Governors, 4:22cv304 (2022), https:// www.aclu.org/legal-document/pernell-v-florida-board-governors-complaint, accessed November 15, 2022; Novoa v. Diaz, 4:22cv324 (2022), https://www.thefire.org /research-learn/novoa-et-al-v-diaz-et-al-complaint, accessed November 15, 2022; Equality Florida v. DeSantis, 4:22cv134 (2022), https://www.documentcloud.org /documents/21564702-equality-florida-et-al-v-desantis-et-al-complaint, accessed November 15, 2022; Cousins v. the School Board of Orange County, 6:22cv1312 (2022), https://www.lambdalegal.org/sites/default/files/legal-docs/downloads/cousins _fl_20220726_complaint.pdf, accessed November 15, 2022; BERT v. O'Connor, 5:21cv1022-G (2021), https://www.aclu.org/legal-document/bert-v-o-connor -complaint, accessed November 15, 2022; Mejia v. Edelblut, 1:21cv1077 (2021), https://www.aclu.org/legal-document/complaint-challenging-nh-divisive-concepts -bill-hb2, accessed November 15, 2022.

25. Craig W. Trainor to Mickolyn Clapper, June 14, 2022, https://americafirstpolicy.com /assets/uploads/files/AFPI_Demand_Letter_to_Baxter_Community_School_District _re_HF_802.pdf, accessed November 15, 2022; Jeremy C. Young, "Educational Gag Orders Hit Iowa Schools," *Gazette*, July 27, 2022, https://www.thegazette.com/guest -columnists/education-gag-orders-hit-iowa-schools, accessed November 15, 2022.

26. Anika Exum, "Why Williamson County Parents Are Suing School District, State Education Commissioner," *Tennessean*, July 12, 2022, https://www.tennessean.com /story/news/local/williamson/2022/07/12/williamson-county-parents-wit-wisdom -teaches-critical-race-theory/10029032002, accessed November 15, 2022.

27. Rachel Tucker, "Father Sues Florida School District over LGBTQ Pride Flags in Classroom," October 26, 2022, https://www.wfla.com/news/florida/father-sues-florida -school-district-over-lgbtq-pride-flags-in-classroom, accessed November 15, 2022.

28. Molly Minta, "College Presidents Now Have Final Say on Tenure After IHL Quietly Revises Policy," *Mississippi Today*, April 21, 2022, https://mississippitoday.org/2022 /04/21/tenure-ihl-revises-policy, accessed November 15, 2022; Divya Kumar, "Florida Legislature Passes Bill Allowing More Scrutiny of Tenured Faculty," *Tampa Bay*

Times, March 10, 2022, https://www.tampabay.com/news/education/2022/03/10
/florida-legislature-passes-bill-allowing-more-scrutiny-of-tenured-faculty, accessed
November 15, 2022; Dan Patrick, Statement on Plans for Higher Education and
Tenure, Office of the Lieutenant Governor, February 18, 2022, https://www.ltgov
.texas.gov/2022/02/18/lt-gov-dan-patrick-statement-on-plans-for-higher-education
-and-tenure, accessed November 15, 2022; Piper Hutchinson, "Louisiana Legislature
Approves Task Force to Study Tenure," *Reveille*, May 23, 2022, https://www.lsureveille
.com/news/louisiana-legislature-approves-task-force-to-study-tenure/article_5383fe44
-daea-11ec-8d83–33854e609d64.html, accessed November 15, 2022; Rebecca Kelli-
her, "Wyoming Senate Votes to Stop Funding University of Wyoming's Gender Studies Program," Diverse: Issues in Higher Education, March 1, 2022, https://www
.diverseeducation.com/news-roundup/article/15289113/wyoming-senate-votes-to
-stop-funding-university-of-wyomings-gender-studies-program, accessed November
15, 2022; PEN America, "These 4 Florida Bills Censor Classroom Subjects and
Ideas," March 17, 2022, https://pen.org/these-4-florida-bills-censor-classroom
-subjects-and-ideas, accessed November 15, 2022.

CHAPTER 4: THE EPISTEMOLOGY OF IGNORANCE AND ITS IMPACT ON DEMOCRACY AND HIGHER EDUCATION

1. Charles Mills, *The Racial Contract* (Ithaca, NY: Cornell University Press, 1997), 20.
2. Frederick Douglass (1855), *My Bondage and My Freedom* (New York: Dover, 2012).
3. Paul A. Shackel, "Public Memory and the Search for Power in American Historical
   Archeology," *American Anthropologist* 103, no. 3 (September 2001): 655–70.
4. Nikole Hannah-Jones, "Preface," *The 1619 Project: A New Origin Story*, ed. Nikole
   Hannah-Jones, Caitlin Roper, Ilena Silverman, and Jake Silverman (New York: Random House, 2021), xvii.
5. Carol Anderson, *White Rage: The Unspoken Truth of Our Racial Divide* (London:
   Bloomsbury, 2016), 100.
6. Soraya Nadia McDonald, "The Dangerous Magical Thinking of 'This Is Not Who
   We Are,'" *Andscape* (blog), https://andscape.com/features/capitol-attack-trump-the
   -dangerous-magical-thinking-of-this-is-not-who-we-are.
7. Karen Yourish, Danielle Ivory, Weiyi Cai, and Ashley Wu, "See Which 2020 Election
   Deniers and Skeptics Won and Lost in the Midterm Elections," *New York Times*, last
   modified November 10, 2022, https://www.nytimes.com/interactive/2022/11/09/us
   /politics/election-misinformation-midterms-results.html.
8. Jack Schwartz, "'That's Not Who We Are' Has Never Felt So Inadequate," *The Daily
   Beast*, Last modified 2020, https://www.thedailybeast.com/thats-not-who-we-are-has
   -never-felt-so-inadequate.
9. Paulo Freire, *Pedagogy of the Oppressed* (New York: Continuum, 1970).
10. Heather McGhee, *The Sum of Us: What Racism Costs Everyone and How We Can Pros-
    per Together* (New York: Penguin Random House, 2021), 10.
11. Thomas Jefferson to Charles Yancey, January 6, 1816, manuscript/mixed material,
    https://www.loc.gov/item/mtjbib022264.
12. Michael F. Bennet, "Why Education Is Essential to Our Democracy," *Medium*, Feb-
    ruary 6, 2017, https://senatorbennet.medium.com/why-education-is-essential-to
    -our-democracy-931cfb7a1e1.

13. John Dewey, "Chapter 7: The Democratic Conception in Education," in *Democracy and Education* (New York: Macmillan, 1916), available at https://www.gutenberg.org /files/852/852-h/852-h.htm.

14. National Commission on Excellence in Education, *A Nation at Risk: The Imperative for Educational* Reform (Washington, DC: National Commission on Excellence in Education, 1983), available at https://web.archive.org/web/20201030104244/https:// www2.ed.gov/pubs/NatAtRisk/risk.html, 10.

15. National Commission on Excellence in Education, *A Nation At Risk*.

16. Jaroslav Pelikan, "General Introduction: The Public Schools as an Institution of American Constitutional Democracy," in *The Public Schools*, ed. Susan Fuhrman and Marvin Lazerson (Oxford: Oxford University Press, 2005), xiv.

17. Thurgood Marshall, "Justice Thurgood Marshall Dissents from *San Antonio Independent School District v. Rodriguez* (March 21, 1973)," 1973, available at Ballotpedia, https://ballotpedia.org/San_Antonio_Independent_School_District_v._Rodriguez; https://www.google.com/url?sa=t&rct=j&q=&esrc=s&source=web&cd=&cad=rja &uact=8&ved=2ahUKEwj63q2c0qb8AhUKnGoFHRNvB0sQFnoECDEQAQ &url=https%3A%2F%2Fd1lexza0zk46za.cloudfront.net%2Fhistory%2Fam-docs %2Fmarshall-dissent.pdf&usg=AOvVaw1z0RD8Z1WN-wnnamqojn19.

18. *The Role of the Public Schools in a Democracy*, Bloomington, IN: Phi Delta Kappa, n.d.

19. Steven Shulman, "Contingency in Higher Education: Evidence and Explanation," *Academic Labor: Research and Artistry* 1 (2017): 2, http://digitalcommons.humboldt .edu/alra/vol1/iss1/3.

20. Richard Shaull, "Foreword," in Paolo Friere, *Pedagogy of the Oppressed* (New York: Continuum, 1997), 16.

CHAPTER 5: KNOWLEDGE AND GOOD COMMUNITY ORGANIZING CAN COUNTER THE "DIVISIVE CONCEPTS" CAMPAIGN

1. Benjamin Wallace-Wells, "How a Conservative Activist Invented the Conflict over Critical Race Theory," *New Yorker*, June 18, 2021, https://www.newyorker.com/news /annals-of-inquiry/how-a-conservative-activist-invented-the-conflict-over-critical -race-theory, accessed November 13, 2022.

2. Richard Delgado and Jean Stefancic, *Critical Race Theory: An Introduction*, 3rd ed. (New York: New York University Press, 2017), xv-xvi, 2–9.

3. Christopher F. Rufo, "Cult Programming in Seattle," *City Journal*, July 8, 2020, accessed November 13, 2022, https://www.city-journal.org/article/cult-programming -in-seattle; Christopher F. Rufo, "White Fragility Comes to Washington," *City Journal*, July 18, 2010, www.city-journal.org/white-fragility-comes-to-washington, accessed November 13, 2022.

4. Workshop: Against Critical Race Theory's Onslaught, Reclaiming Education and the American Dream, December 7, 2020, https://www.youtube.com/watch?v=yxz LohOPEr8&t=18s, accessed November 13, 2022.

5. Christopher F. Rufo (@realchrisrufo), "The goal is to have the public read something crazy," Twitter, March 15, 2021, https://twitter.com/realchrisrufo/status/13715410 44592996352?lang=en.

6. Josh Hafner, "How Michael Brown's Death, Two Years Ago, Pushed #BlackLivesMatter into a Movement, *USA Today*, August 8, 2016, accessed November 13, 2022.

7. Ibram X. Kendi, *How to Be an Antiracist* (New York: One World/Random House, 2019), 13–23.

8. Katie Robertson, "Nikole Hannah-Jones Denied Tenure at the University of North Carolina," *New York Times*, May 19, 2022, updated July 15, 2022, accessed November 13, 2022.

9. Sarah J. Purcell, *The Early National Period* (New York: Facts on File, 2009), 39–40; Lorraine McDonnell, Roger W. Benjamin, and P. Michael Timpane, eds., *Rediscovering the Democratic Purposes of Education* (Lawrence: University Press of Kansas, 2008), 47–55; Joseph Kelly, *Marooned: Jamestown, Shipwreck, and a New History of America's Origin* (London: Bloomsbury Publishing, 2018); Adam Serwer, "The Fight over the 1619 Project Is Not About the Facts," *The Atlantic*, December 23, 2019, https://www.theatlantic.com/ideas/archive/2019/12/historians-clash-1619-project/604093, accessed November 13, 2022; "We Respond to the Historians Who Critiqued the 1619 Project," *New York Times*, December 20, 2019, https://www.nytimes.com/2019/12/20/magazine/we-respond-to-the-historians-who-critiqued-the-1619-project.html, accessed November 13, 2022; Eve LaPlante, *American Jezebel: The Uncommon Life of Anne Hutchison, the Woman Who Defied the Puritans* (New York: HarperCollins, 2004).

10. Carol Anderson, *White Rage: The Unspoken Truth of Our Racial Divide* (London: Bloomsbury Publishing, 2020), 3.

11. David A. Bateman, *Disfranchising Democracy: Constructing the Electorate in the United States, the United Kingdom, and France* (Cambridge: Cambridge University Press, 2018); Alexander Keyssar, *The Right to Vote: The Contested History of Democracy in the United States*, rev. ed. (New York: Basic Books, 2000), 23–33.

12. Eric Foner, *Reconstruction: America's Unfinished Revolution, 1863–1877* (New York: Perennial Classics/Harper Collins, 2002), 281–333, 564–601; W. E. B. Du Bois, *Black Reconstruction in America, 1860–1880* (New York: Atheneum/Macmillan, 1992), 580–636, 670–730.

13. Angie Maxwell, Todd Shields, *The Long Southern Strategy: How Chasing White Voters in the South Changed American Politics* (New York: Oxford University Press, 2019), 4–6; Richard C. Fording, Sanford F. Schram, *Hard White: The Mainstreaming of Racism in American Politics* (New York: Oxford University Press, 2020), 65–72; "Rates of Drug Use and Sales, by Race; Rates of Drug Related Criminal Justice Measures, By Race," Hamilton Project, October 21, 2016, https://www.hamiltonproject.org/data/rates-of-drug-use-and-sales-by-race-rates-of-drug-related-criminal-justice-measures-by-race/, accessed December 23, 2022.

14. Tom Mould, *Overthrowing the Queen: Telling Stories of Welfare in America* (Bloomington: Indiana University Press, 2020).

15. German Lopez, "Charlottesville Protests," *Vox*, August 14, 2017, https://www.vox.com/identities/2017/8/14/16143168/charlottesville-va-protests, accessed November 13, 2022; Adam Serwer, "Birtherism of a Nation," *The Atlantic*, May 13, 2020, https://www.theatlantic.com/ideas/archive/2020/05/birtherism-and-trump/610978, accessed December 23, 2022.

16. Stephen Fowler, "Why Do Georgia's Non-White Voters Have to Stand in Line for Hours? Too Few Polling Places," NPR, October 17, 2020, accessed November 13, 2020; Adam Schiff, *Midnight in Washington: How We Almost Lost Our Democracy and Still Could* (New York: Random House, 2021).

17. Eesha Pendharkar, "Legal Challenges to 'Divisive Concepts' Laws: An Update," *Education Week*, October 17, 2022, https://www.edweek.org/policy-politics/legal-challenges-to-divisive-concepts-laws-an-update/2022/10, accessed December 22, 2022.

18. Pendharkar, "Legal Challenges to 'Divisive Concepts' Laws"; Leah Watson, "Lessons Learned from Our Classroom Censorship Win Against Florida's Stop W.O.K.E. Act," ACLU, November 9, 2022, https://www.aclu.org/news/free-speech/lessons-learned-from-our-classroom-censorship-win-against-floridas-stop-w-o-k-e-act?, accessed December 22, 2022.

19. Sara Weissman, "Reauthorization of Higher Education Act," *Diverse Issues in Higher Education*, February 10, 2021, https://www.diverseeducation.com/home/article/15108639/campaign-pushes-for-reauthorization-of-higher-education-act, accessed December 22, 2022; Scholars for a New Deal in Higher Education website: https://scholarsforanewdealforhighered.org/our-work, accessed December 22, 2022; Colleen Flaherty, "An Affront to Public Discourse," *Inside Higher Ed*, June 9, 2022, https://www.insidehighered.com/news/2022/06/09/aacu-and-pen-america-oppose-divisive-concepts-bans, accessed December 22, 2022; PEN America website: https://pen.org/focus-issues, accessed December 22, 2022; Susan Gross Sholinsky, Robert J. O'Hara, Peter M. Stein, Dean R. Singewald II, Kathleen M. Williams, and Constance A. Wilkinson, "NAACP Lays Down First Challenge to Executive Order 13950 Prohibiting Inclusion of 'Divisive' Concepts in Workplace Training Programs," *Workforce Bulletin*, November 3, 2020, https://www.workforcebulletin.com/2020/11/03/naacp-lays-down-first-challenge-to-executive-order-13950-prohibiting-inclusion-of-divisive-concepts-in-workplace-training-programs, accessed December 22, 2022; "National Urban League vs. Trump: Important Facts About LDF's Case Challenging the Trump Truth Ban," NAACP Legal Defense Fund, https://www.naacpldf.org/important-facts-about-ldfs-case-against-the-trump-truth-ban/#:~:text=On%20October%2029%2C%202020%2C%20the,diversity%2C%20equity%2C%20and%20inclusion, accessed December 22, 2022.

20. Asia Ashley, "Teachers, Students, Parents Rally Against Bills Limiting Race Curriculum," *Cullman Times*, June 13, 2022, https://www.cullmantimes.com/news/teachers-students-parents-rally-against-bills-limiting-race-curriculum/article_78c34f18-eb50-11ec-bd21-63c7c7e9f030.html, accessed December 22, 2022.

21. Zinn Education Project, posted March 31, 2010, https://www.zinnedproject.org/whats-new/zinn-education-project-in-mendo-island-jounrnal-ukiah-blog.

22. "About Us," Rethinking Schools, https://rethinkingschools.org, accessed December 22, 2022.

23. "What We Do," Teaching for Change, https://teachingforchange.org, accessed December 22, 2022.

24. "Who We Are," BLM at School, www.blacklivesmatteratschool.com, accessed December 22, 2022.

25. "Our Mission," African American Policy Forum (AAPF), https://aapf.org, accessed December 22, 2022.
26. Historical Newspapers from 1700s–2000s, www.newspapers.com, accessed December 23, 2022.
27. Sarah Schulman, *Let the Record Show: A Political History of ACT UP New York, 1987–1993* (New York: Farrar, Straus and Giroux, 2021).
28. "The Movable Middle," Coursera, https://www.coursera.org/lecture/removing-barriers -to-change/the-movable-middle-suyEl, accessed December 23, 2022; State Innovation Exchange, https://stateinnovation.org/about, accessed December 23, 2022.
29. "From Thomas Jefferson to Littleton W. Tazewell, 5 January, 1805," National Archives, https://founders.archives.gov/documents/Jefferson/99–01–02–0958, accessed November 13, 2022; James Terry White, ed., "Tazewell, Littleton Waller," in *National Cyclopedia of American Biography* (New York: J. T. White Co., 1894), 448.

CHAPTER 6: SUBVERTING THE INTENT OF THE FOURTEENTH AMENDMENT

1. Jonathan Friedman and James Tager, "Educational Gag Orders: Legislative Restrictions on the Freedom to Read, Learn and Teach," November 30, 2021, pen.org /report/Americas-censored-classrooms.
2. Jelani Cobb (@jelani9), "An attempt to discredit the literature millions of people sought out," Twitter, June 11, 2021, 5:21 p.m.
3. "Attorney General Knudsen Issues Binding Opinion on Critical Race Theory," Montana Department of Justice, May 27, 2021, dojmt.gov/attorney-general-knudsen -issues-binding-opinion-on-critical-race-theory.
4. Brown v. Bd. of Educ. of Topeka, 347 U.S. 483, at 494 (1954).
5. See Slaughterhouse Cases, 83 U.S. 36, 71 (1866).
6. Mark Joseph Stern, "Hear Ketanji Brown Jackson Use Progressive Originalism to Refute Alabama's Attack on the Voting Rights Act," *Slate*, October 4, 2022, slate.com /news-and-politics/2022/10/ketanji-brown-jackson-voting-rights-originalism.html.
7. Jacobus tenBroek, "Equal Under Law," 201 (rev. ed. 1974).
8. Regents of the University of California v. Bakke, 438 U.S. 265 at 391 (1978).
9. Plessy v. Ferguson, 163 U.S. 537 (1896).
10. *Plessy* at 552.
11. Sweatt v. Painter, 399 U.S. 629 (1950), McLaurin v. Oklahoma State Regents, 339 U.S. 637 (1950).
12. *Brown* 347 U.S. at 490 n.5.
13. For an overview of affirmative action, see Joseph Lamour, "History of Affirmative Action in Higher Education," Best Universities, best-universities.net/features/history -affirmative0action-higher-education, accessed May 17, 2023.
14. Grutter v. Bollinger 539 U.S. 306 at 332 (2003).
15. Allen v. Cooper, 140 S. Ct. 994 at 1003 (2020).
16. Kimble v. Marvel Entertainment, 576 U.S. 3–7 (2015).
17. Nicholas A. Bowman, "College Diversity Experiences and Cognitive Development: A Meta Analysis," *Review of Educational Research* 4, no. 20 (2010): 80.
18. Adam Harris, "Justice Jackson's Crucial Argument About Affirmative Action," *The Atlantic*, November 1, 2023.

CHAPTER 7: "DON'T SAY GAY" AND CAN'T BE TRANS

1. In this chapter, we use the acronym LGBTQ, which stands for lesbian, gay, bisexual, transgender, and queer. The acronym is used as a catchall for nonheterosexual, sexuality minorities, and/or non-cisgender individuals—anyone who falls under the expansive and diverse non-straight and/or non-cisgender communities, including, but not limited to: lesbian, gay, bisexual, pansexual, intersex, asexual, questioning, Indigenous gender variant communities, transgender, and nonbinary identities. We also use anti-gay, anti-trans, and anti-LGBTQ to refer to homophobic, transphobic, and/or cissexist initiatives and groups.

2. Equality Texas, "Protecting LGBTQ Youth," https://www.equalitytexas.org/protecting -lgbtq-youth, accessed on December 19, 2022.

3. Scholarship produced over several decades explains that sexual dimorphism among the human species is very low. Though biology is often construed to explain sex and gender differences, the reality is our bodies are shaped by culture.

4. Jaclyn Diaz, "Florida's Governor Signs Controversial Law Opponents Dubbed 'Don't Say Gay,'" NPR, March 28, 2022.

5. We use the term "queer" here to designate any young person or child who engages their gender in ways that challenge binary notions of masculinity and femininity, whose physical presentation does not adhere to conservative notions of proper heteronormativity.

6. Laura Briggs, *How All Politics Became Reproductive Politics: From Welfare Reform to Foreclosure to Trump* (Oakland: University of California Press, 2017), 149.

7. According to Briggs, campaigns such as this "imagined queer people who had no children of their own (and so threatened straight people's)." Briggs, *How All Politics Became Reproductive Politics*, 149. It had the opposite effect, as well, of drawing a great deal of attention to LGBTQ issues, motivating many in the gay community to organize in response.

8. Briggs, *How All Politics Became Reproductive Politics*, 149.

9. US Department of Education, "Statement from U.S. Secretary of Education Miguel Cardona on "Don't Say Gay" Law Going into Effect Today," press release, July 1, 2022, https://www.ed.gov/news/press-releases/statement-us-secretary-education -miguel-cardona-dont-say-gay-law-going-effect-today.

10. E. di Giacomo et al., "Estimating the Risk of Attempted Suicide Among Sexual Minority Youths: A Systematic Review and Meta-Analysis," *JAMA Pediatrics* 1, no. 172 (December 2018): 1145–52, doi: 10.1001/jamapediatrics.2018.2731.

11. Matthew Rivas-Koehl et al., "Understanding Protective Factors for Suicidality and Depression Among US Sexual and Gender Minority Adolescents: Implications for School Psychologists," *School Psychology Review* 51, no. 3 (2022): 290–303; B. A. Feinstein et al., "Sexual Orientation and Mental Health Disparities in US Pre-Teens: A Longitudinal Mediation Study," *European Journal of Public Health* 32, Iss. Sup. 3 (October 5, 2022); 15th European Public Health Conference 2022, Berlin, https:// ephconference.eu/Berlin-2022-290.

12. The Trevor Project, *LGBTQ Youth Suicide Prevention in Schools*, August 19, 2021, 2, https://www.thetrevorproject.org/research-briefs/lgbtq-youth-suicide-prevention-in -schools.

13. *LGBTQ Youth Suicide Prevention in Schools*, 2.
14. Gay, Lesbian, and Straight Education Network (GLSEN), 2021 National School Climate Survey, https://www.glsen.org/research/2021-national-school-climate-survey.
15. Southern Poverty Law Center, https://www.splcenter.org/fighting-hate/extremist-files/ideology/anti-lgbtq.
16. Valerie Strauss, "Florida Law Limiting LGBTQ Discussions Takes Effect—and Rocks Schools," *Washington Post*, July 1, 2022.
17. Jeanette Centeno, "We're Still Waiting for Justice for Andreas Garcia," PowWows.com, April 6, 2022, https://www.powwows.com/were-still-waiting-for-justice-for-andreas-garcia, accessed December 20, 2022.
18. In addition to opening opportunities for US citizens to get married, the decision also created new opportunities for immigrants seeking spousal visas, green cards, and other avenues to citizenship for LGBTQ immigrants. Same-sex marriage also created avenues to dual-parental adoption, hospital visitation, benefits coverage, and other privileges afforded to married couples. See Mary Bernstein, Nancy A. Naples, and Brenna Harvey, "The Meaning of Marriage to Same-Sex Families: Formal Partnership, Parenthood, Gender, and the Welfare State in International Perspective," *Social Politics: International Studies in Gender, State & Society* 23, no. 1 (Spring 2016): 3–39, https://doi.org/10.1093/sp/jxv002.
19. Mark Joseph Stern and J. Bryan Lowder, "LGBT Comes to the SOTU," *Slate*, January 20, 2015, https://slate.com/human-interest/2015/01/state-of-the-union-obama-includes-transgender-and-bisexual-in-the-2015-address-for-the-first-time-ever.html.
20. NBC News reported that in 2016–2020 anti-gay organizations saw a 25 percent increase in total donations. Stuart Richardson, "Groups Opposed to Gay Rights Rake in Millions as States Debate Anti-LGBTQ Bills," NBC News, March 23, 2022, https://www.nbcnews.com/nbc-out/out-news/groups-opposed-gay-rights-rake-millions-states-debate-anti-lgbtq-bills-rcna21016.
21. It is not a coincidence that these years—2015 and 2021—bookmarked the election and presidency of ultra-right-wing nationalist Donald Trump.
22. Wyatt Ronan, May 7, 2021, "2021 Officially Becomes Worst Year in Recent History for LGBTQ State Legislative Attacks as Unprecedented Number of States," Human Rights Campaign, https://www.hrc.org/press-releases/2021-officially-becomes-worst-year-in-recent-history-for-lgbtq-state-legislative-attacks-as-unprecedented-number-of-states-enact-record-shattering-number-of-anti-lgbtq-measures-into-law.
23. Civil Rights Act of 1965, https://www.archives.gov/milestone-documents/voting-rights-act, accessed December 21, 2022. This act was proposed in 1964 and ratified in 1965 under Lyndon B. Johnson.
24. Groups working together include, but are not limited to, parental rights groups like Moms for Liberty, the Christian nationalists, and white supremacist groups such as the Proud Boys and the Oath Keepers.
25. Brian Lopez and Emily Hernandez, "Lt. Gov. Dan Patrick Wants Texas Version of Florida Law That Critics Dubbed 'Don't Say Gay,'" *Texas Tribune*, April 4, 2022, https://www.texastribune.org/2022/04/04/texas-dont-say-gay-dan-patrick, accessed December 10, 2022.

26. Heteronormative constructions of the ideal American nuclear family proliferate and combine homophobia and nationalism. One can look at the anti-gay rhetoric deployed by right-wing political figures and nationalists to see how trans and queer communities threaten the proliferation of a (white) nation. See, for example, Siobhan Somerville, *Queering the Color Line: Race and the Invention of Homosexuality in American Culture* (Durham, NC: Duke University Press, 2001), and Roderick Ferguson, *Aberrations in Black: Toward a Queer of Color Critique* (Minneapolis: University of Minnesota, 2003).

27. Anne McClintock, *Imperial Leather: Race, Gender, and Sexuality in the Colonial Conquest* (New York: Routledge, 1995).

28. There is a direct line connecting America's gruesome history of subverting and exploiting the reproductive freedom of Black and Brown communities to contemporary efforts to suppress and obliterate reproductive self-determination. As the state attempts to control reproductive freedom, it seeks to contain, admonish, and destroy trans and LGBTQ rights. Both are sides of the same coin and serve nationalist interests by "protecting" heteronormative family values, alienating those who fall outside of the symbolic national nuclear family.

29. Imara Jones, "An Anti-Trans Hate Machine Threatens Americans' Civil Liberties," *Newsweek*, June 24, 2021, https://www.newsweek.com/anti-trans-hate-machine -threatens-americans-civil-liberties-opinion-1603085.

30. Jo Yurcaba, "'Keeps Me Up at Night': Doctors Who Care for Transgender Minors Brace for Bans," NBC News, May 27, 2021, https://www.nbcnews.com/nbc-out /out-politics-and-policy/keeps-night-doctors-care-transgender-minors-brace-bans -rcna1048.

31. Jo Yurcaba, "Texas Initiated Investigations into Trans Kids Families," NBC News, https://www.nbcnews.com/nbc-out/out-politics-and-policy/texas-initiated -investigations-trans-kids-families-lawsuit-says-rcna18191, accessed December 20, 2022.

32. North Carolina House Bill 2: The Public Facilities and Security Act https://www .ncleg.gov/Sessions/2015E2/Bills/House/PDF/H2v3.pdf, accessed December 21, 2022; the law was later repealed, but it started the wave of anti-LGBT legislation in various states in 2022.

33. Maria Lugones, "Toward a Decolonial Feminism," *Hypatia* 25, no. 4 (Fall 2010): 742.

34. Angela Y. Davis, *Women, Race & Class* (New York: Vintage, 1981).

35. Davis, *Women, Race & Class.*

36. Examining the statistics associated with trans life, as this intersects with the American race relations, illustrates that to be a BIPOC queer person in this country is to be multiply marginalized and outside of advocacy because of a lack of wealth.

37. Keeanga-Yamahtta Taylor, *Race for Profit: How Banks and the Real Estate Industry Undermined Black Home Ownership* (Chapel Hill: University of North Carolina Press, 2019).

38. Randall Robinson, *The Debt: What America Owes to Blacks* (New York: Plume Books, 2000).

39. Rakesh Kochhar and Anthony Cilluffo, "How Wealth Inequality Has Changed in the US Since the Great Recession by Race, Ethnicity, and Income," Pew Research Center, https://www.pewresearch.org/fact-tank/2017/11/01/how-wealth-inequality-has

-changed-in-the-u-s-since-the-great-recession-by-race-ethnicity-and-income, accessed December 20, 2022.

40. Moritz Kuhn, Moritz Shularick, and Ulrike L. Steins, "Income and Wealth Inequality 1949–2016," Federal Reserve Bank of Minneapolis, https://www.minneapolisfed.org /research/institute-working-papers/income-and-wealth-inequality-in-america-1949–2016, accessed December 20, 2022.

41. Bostock v. Clayton County and R. G. & G. R. Harris Funeral Homes Inc. v. Equal Opportunity Commission (Supreme Court decision), https://caselaw.findlaw.com /us-supreme-court/17–1618.html, accessed December 20, 2022. These 2020 rulings established workplace protections.

42. C. Riley Snorton, *Black on Both Sides: A Racial History of Trans Identity* (Minneapolis: University of Minnesota Press, 2017).

43. C. Riley Snorton and Jin Haritaworn, "Trans Necropolitics: A Transnational Reflection on Violence, Death, and Trans of Color Afterlife," in *The Transgender Studies Reader 2*, ed. Susan Stryker and Aren Z. Aizura (New York: Routledge Press, 2013), 66–76. Though we, the authors, do not want to advance a necropolitics of transgender lives, it is important that we highlight that lives are at stake when governments attempt to legislate the existence of a marginalized community.

44. Imara Jones, "An Anti-Trans Hate Machine Threatens Americans' Civil Liberties," *Newsweek*, June 24, 2021, https://www.newsweek.com/anti-trans-hate-machine -threatens-americans-civil-liberties-opinion-1603085.

45. We use "unleash power" in reference to the international grassroots direct action group AIDS Coalition to Unleash Power (ACT UP). ACT UP was instrumental in bringing attention to the HIV/AIDS pandemic and lobbying for medical research and access to lifesaving medications.

CHAPTER 8: THE RESOLUTIONS

1. PEN America Index of Educational Gag Orders, https://docs.google.com/spreadsheets /d/1Tj5WQVBmB6SQg-zP_M8uZsQQGH09TxmBY73v23zpyr0/edit?usp=sharing, accessed November 15, 2022.

2. Kimberlé Williams Crenshaw, "The Eternal Fantasy of a Racially Virtuous America," *New Republic*, March 22, 2021, https://newrepublic.com/article/161568/white -supremacy-racism-in-america-kimberle-crenshaw.

3. Robert Post, *Democracy, Expertise, and Academic Freedom: A First Amendment Jurisprudence for the Modern State* (New Haven, CT: Yale University Press, 2012), 34.

4. "1915 Declaration on Principles of Academic Freedom and Academic Tenure," *AAUP Policy Documents and Reports* (Baltimore: Johns Hopkins University Press, 2015), 5–6.

5. "1940 Statement of Principles on Academic Freedom and Tenure," with 1970 Interpretive Comments, AAUP, https://www.aaup.org/report/1940-statement-principles -academic-freedom-and-tenure, accessed February 6, 2023.

6. Jelani Cobb, "The Republican Party, Racial Hypocrisy and the 1619 Project," *New Yorker*, May 29, 2021, https://www.newyorker.com/news/daily-comment/the -republican-party-racial-hypocrisy-and-the-1619-project.

7. Maia Irvin, "UMN Faculty Senate Passes Resolution to Affirm Academic Freedom," *Minnesota Daily*, January 21, 2022, https://mndaily.com/270488/news/umn-faculty-senate-passes-resolution-to-affirm-academic-freedom.

8. "Faculty Senate of the University of Alabama Resolution in Defense of Academic Freedom," Faculty Senate, University of Alabama, December 16, 2021, https://faculty senate.ua.edu/resolution-in-defense-of-academic-freedom-announcement.

9. "BFA Approves Faculty Council Resolution Against External Limits on Academic Discourse," *CU Boulder Today*, November 5, 2021, https://www.colorado.edu/today/2021/11/05/bfa-approves-faculty-council-resolution-against-external-limits-academic-discourse.

10. Colleen Flaherty, "A Template for Academic Freedom," *Inside Higher Ed*, December 15, 2021, https://www.insidehighered.com/news/2021/12/15/professors-promote-resolution-academic-freedom.

11. Nick Anderson and Susan Svrluga, "College Faculty Are Fighting Back Against State Bills on Critical Race Theory," *Washington Post*, February 19, 2022, https://www.washingtonpost.com/education/2022/02/19/colleges-critical-race-theory-bills.

12. Kathryn Joyce, "Fighting Back Against CRT Panic: Educators Organize Around the Threat to Academic Freedom," *Salon*, March 7, 2022, https://www.salon.com/2022/03/07/fighting-back-against-crt-panic-educators-organize-around-the-to-academic-freedom.

13. Jennifer Ruth and Ellen Schrecker, "Faculty, You Have Power! Use It!" *Academe Blog*, February 14, 2022, https://academeblog.org/2022/02/14/faculty-you-have-power-use-it.

14. Ellen Schrecker, "Across the Country, Faculty Fight to Defend Academic Freedom," *The Nation*, March 30, 2022, https://www.thenation.com/article/activism/academic-freedom-faculty-racism.

15. Jennifer Ruth, "Faculty Stand Together: An Update on the Senate Resolutions," AAUP *Academe Blog*, April 12, 2022, https://academeblog.org/2022/04/12/faculty-stand-together-an-update-on-the-senate-resolutions.

16. "Faculty Senate Resolutions," AAPF, Truth Be Told Call to Action, https://docs.google.com/document/d/1gN93avmQQmNKACdnDPU_bIw3ZG02_pxIo3okI0OJXBs/edit, accessed May 18, 2023.

CHAPTER 9: SILENCE GETS US NOWHERE

1. Andrea Gore, author interview, Zoom, August 9, 2022.

2. Heather C. McGhee and Victor Ray, "School Is for Making Citizens," *New York Times*, September 1, 2022.

3. Louis Gross, author interview, Zoom, August 2, 2022.

4. Anastassiya Andrianova and Florin Salajan, author interview, Zoom, August 5, 2022.

5. Anna Pegler-Gordon, author interview, Zoom, August 5, 2022.

6. Anonymized professor, author interview, Zoom, Summer 2022.

7. Heather Pincock, author interview, Zoom, August 18, 2022.

8. Mark James, author interview, Zoom, August 4, 2022.

9. Gopalan Nadathur, author interview, Zoom, August 10, 2022.

10. University of Minnesota University Senate, "Resolution Defending Academic Freedom as It Relates to Teaching About Race, Gender, Sexuality, and Critical Race Theory at the University of Minnesota," December 2, 2021.
11. Gore interview.
12. Anonymized professor interview.
13. Tennessee University Faculty Senates to Legislators, letter, February 21, 2022.
14. Gross interview.
15. Anonymized professor interview.
16. Liz Canfield, author interview, Zoom, August 9, 2022.
17. Andrianova and Salajan interview.
18. Caroline Clark and Donna Ford, author interview, Zoom, August 19, 2022.
19. Clark and Ford interview.
20. Sara McDaniel, author interview, Zoom, August 11, 2022.
21. Andrianova and Salajan interview.
22. McDaniel interview.
23. Nadathur interview.
24. McDaniel interview.
25. Meir Muller, author interview, Zoom, August 15, 2022.
26. Nadathur interview.
27. Anonymized professor interview.
28. Anonymized professor interview.
29. McDaniel interview.
30. Gore interview; Gross interview.
31. Sean Meehan, author interview, Zoom, July 28, 2022.
32. Pincock interview.
33. Andrianova and Salajan interview.
34. Clark and Ford interview.
35. Clark and Ford interview.
36. McDaniel interview.
37. Muller interview.
38. Gross interview.
39. McDaniel interview; Russell Contreras, "A Critical Race Theory Founder Says He's Being Inundated with Threats," *Axios*, December 3, 2021.
40. McDaniel interview.
41. Canfield interview.
42. Canfield interview.

CHAPTER 10: ACADEMIC FREEDOM

1. William A. Herbert, Jacob Apkarian, and Joseph van der Naald, *Supplementary Directory of New Bargaining Agents and Contracts in Institutions of Higher Education, 2013– 2019* (New York: National Center for the Study of Collective Bargaining in Higher Education and the Professions, CUNY, November 2020), https://www.hunter.cuny .edu/ncscbhep/assets/files/SupplementalDirectory-2020-FINAL.pdf.
2. For an example of a faculty member losing a job, see Stephanie Saul, "At NYU, Students Were Failing Organic Chemistry. Who Was to Blame?" *New York Times*,

October 3, 2022, https://www.nytimes.com/2022/10/03/us/nyu-organic-chemistry -petition.html.

3. Andrew Gothard, "What Happens in Florida: Governor DeSantis Is Leading an Assault on the State's Public Higher Education Institutions," *Inside Higher Ed*, February 6, 2023, https://www.insidehighered.com/views/2023/02/07/floridas-public -universities-are-under-assault-opinion.

4. Ellen Schrecker, "The 50-Year War on Higher Education," *Chronicle of Higher Education*, October 14, 2022, https://www.chronicle.com/article/the-50-year-war-on -higher-education.

5. Melanie Kruvelis, "What Is 'At-Will' Employment, and Why Does It Matter? An Interview with William A. Herbert," *Jacobin*, December 22, 2022, https://jacobin.com /2022/12/at-will-employment-just-cause-nyc-caban. The New York City bill to prohibit terminating employees without just cause is here: https://legistar.council.nyc .gov/LegislationDetail.aspx?ID=5958217&GUID=44D72CEC-FE82–4A43-BA31 –4BB15FBC15EB&Options=ID%7CText%7C&Search="just+cause".

6. "1940 Statement of Principles on Academic Freedom and Tenure," with 1970 Interpretive Comments, AAUP, https://www.aaup.org/report/1940-statement-principles -academic-freedom-and-tenure, accessed February 6, 2023.

7. Herbert, Apkarian, and van der Naald, *Supplementary Directory of New Bargaining Agents and Contracts in Institutions of Higher Education*, 2020.

8. In Joe Berry and Helena Worthen, *Power Despite Precarity: Strategies for the Contingent Faculty Movement in Higher Education* (London: Pluto, 2021), we provide a much more detailed explanation of how these intersecting management challenges were resolved by contingency, which then became a strategy that took over other options and could not be reversed by addressing each challenge on its own.

9. For an illustration of this confusion, see Section I-1 of the Common Data Set Initiative, https://commondataset.org, p. 38, where colleges and universities self-report faculty status data in only two categories, full-time and part-time. We thank Jane Gabin for providing this data source. Also see Jane Gabin, "Who Is Doing the Teaching at U.S. Colleges and Universities?" January 11, 2022, document circulated among academic admissions counselors. In possession of authors.

10. Joe T. Berry, *Reclaiming the Ivory Tower: Organizing Adjuncts to Change Higher Education* (New York: Monthly Review Press, 2005).

11. Colleen Flaherty, "Survey of Adjuncts Finds Pandemic Made Their Situation Worse," *Inside Higher Ed*, February 24, 2022, https://www.insidehighered.com/news/2022/02 /24/survey-adjuncts-finds-pandemic-made-their-situation-worse.

12. See Historians for Peace and Democracy, *The Culture Wars Against Education Archive*. Last updated December 27, 2022, https://www.historiansforpeace.org/wp-content /uploads/2022/12/The-Culture-Wars-Against-Education-12–29.pdf.

13. In *Power Despite Precarity*, we offer a case study about the rise to eventual leadership in the California Faculty Association by the contingent faculty called lecturers. The more militant leadership of these younger faculty members led the union into gaining what was until recently the best contract for contingent faculty in the US.

14. Other workforces might call it "free speech on the job," a right to speak up in defense of doing one's job right. Suzanne Gordon, in *Nursing Against the Odds: How Health*

Care Cost Cutting, Media Stereotypes, and Medical Hubris Undermine Nurses and Patient Care (Ithaca, NY: Cornell University Press, 2012), tells what it was like in the days when nurses had to defer to doctors in making medical decisions.

15. Schrecker, "The 50-Year War on Higher Education."

16. The FIRE (Foundation for Individual Rights and Expression) website includes a portal for submitting a case and finding an attorney: https://www.thefire.org/defending -your-rights/legal-support/faculty-legal-defense-fund.

17. FIRE, "VICTORY: Lawsuit Ends with Collin College Professor Reinstated After Being Fired for Union Advocacy, Supporting Removal of Confederate Monuments," November 3, 2022, https://www.thefire.org/news/victory-lawsuit-ends-collin-college -professor-reinstated-after-being-fired-union-advocacy.

18. The situation is such that we cannot name the college without putting the job of our informant at risk.

19. When lobbying a sympathetic state legislature works, it works well. Enrie Marusya at AFT in Washington State, in a personal email to authors, wrote in February 2023, "I'm delighted to report that our bill mandating 85% pay parity for adjuncts has its first hearing this week." Washington State Legislature, SB 5557-2023-24, https://app .leg.wa.gov/billsummary?BillNumber=5557&Initiative=false&Year=2023.

20. This information was provided to us by Seth Kahn, the delegate at the HELU Zoom conference who made the presentation.

21. Note that although a prominent feature of adjunct or contingent work is sub-living wage compensation and lack of benefits, as far as the focus on academic freedom goes, wages are not the key issue. College and university managers are typically much more willing to bargain increases in wages than any condition that gives the contingent more actual power over their work, such as a seniority process for rehire for each semester.

22. Berry and Worthen, *Power Despite Precarity*.

23. Helena Worthen, "Can HELU Ride the Tiger?" *Convergence Magazine*, April 4, 2022, https://convergencemag.com/articles/can-helu-ride-the-tiger.

CHAPTER 11: MY BATTLE TO PRESERVE ACADEMIC FREEDOM AT THE UNIVERSITY OF FLORIDA

1. League of Women Voters of Florida, Inc. v. Lee, 566 F. Supp. 3d 1238 (N.D. Fla. 2021).

2. Lawrence Mower, "Gov. Ron DeSantis Signs Florida Voting Bill in Front of Trump Fan Club," *Tampa Bay Times*, May 6, 2021, https://www.tampabay.com/news/florida -politics/2021/05/06/gov-ron-desantis-signs-florida-voting-bill-in-front-of-trump-fan -club, accessed December 9, 2022.

3. Bobby Caina Calvan, "DeSantis Signs GOP-Drafted Voting Bill, Legal Fight Begins," *PBS NewsHour*, May 6, 2021, https://www.pbs.org/newshour/politics/desantis-signs -gop-drafted-voting-bill-legal-fight-begins, accessed July 26, 2021.

4. Mower, "Gov. Ron DeSantis Signs Florida Voting Bill in Front of Trump Fan Club."

5. Online Sunshine, "The 2022 Florida Statutes," 2022, retrieved from http://www.leg .state.fl.us/Statutes/index.cfm?App_mode=Display_Statute&URL=1000–1099/1012 /Sections/1012.977.html, accessed December 9, 2022.

6. Austin v. University of Florida Board of Trustees, Preliminary Injunction, filed in the US District Court for the Northern District of Florida, Gainesville Division, case

no.: 1:21cv184-MW/GRJ, January 21, 2022, p. 10, retrieved from https://www
.govinfo.gov/content/pkg/USCOURTS-flnd-1_21-cv-00184/pdf/USCOURTS
-flnd-1_21-cv-00184–0.pdf, accessed January 3, 2023.

7. *Austin v. University of Florida Board of Trustees*, Preliminary Injunction.

8. *Austin v. University of Florida Board of Trustees*, Preliminary Injunction.

9. UF Conflict of Interest Program, "Our Mission, Vision, and Values," retrieved from University of Florida, ufl.edu, December 8, 2022.

10. UF at Work, "As UFOLIO Enters Second Year, New Program Introduced to Provide Guidance, Support," retrieved from University of Florida, ufl.edu, December 8, 2022.

11. UF at Work, "As UFOLIO Enters Second Year, New Program Introduced to Provide Guidance, Support."

12. *Austin v. University of Florida Board of Trustees*, Preliminary Injunction, p. 44.

13. *Austin v. University of Florida Board of Trustees*, Preliminary Injunction, p. 39.

14. Michael Wines, "Florida Bars State Professors from Testifying in Voting Rights Case," *New York Times*, October 29, 2021, accessed December 9, 2022.

15. Ana Ceballos and Mary Ellen Klas, "UF's Ban on Professors Testifying Against State to Be Investigated, Accreditor Says," *Miami Herald*, November 1, 2021, https://tinyurl.com/2p83s3mb, accessed December 9, 2022.

16. Ceballos and Klas, "UF's Ban on Professors Testifying Against State to Be Investigated."

17. Ceballos and Klas, "UF's Ban on Professors Testifying Against State to Be Investigated."

18. Ana Ceballos and Mary Ellen Klas, "UF Restricted Five More Professors in Cases Against the State," *Tampa Bay Times*, November 2, 2021, https://tinyurl.com/553uf-kym, accessed December 9, 2022.

19. Jones v. DeSantis, 975 F.3d 1016 (11th Cir. 2020).

20. Florida Division of Elections, "Constitutional Amendment 4/Felon Voting Rights," October 14, 2020, Florida Department of State, https://dos.myflorida.com/elections/for-voters/voter-registration/constitutional-amendment-4felon-voting-rights, accessed December 9, 2022.

21. Brennan Center for Justice, "Voting Rights Restoration Efforts in Florida," 2019, retrieved https://www.brennancenter.org/our-work/research-reports/voting-rights-restoration-efforts-florida, December 9, 2022.

22. Brennan Center for Justice, "Voting Rights Restoration Efforts in Florida."

23. *Austin v. University of Florida Board of Trustees*, Preliminary Injunction, p. 17.

24. *Austin v. University of Florida Board of Trustees*, Preliminary Injunction, p. 16.

25. *Austin v. University of Florida Board of Trustees*, Preliminary Injunction, p. 16.

26. *Austin v. University of Florida Board of Trustees*, filed in the US District Court for the Northern District of Florida, Gainesville Division, November 5, 2021, p. 14.

27. *Austin v. University of Florida Board of Trustees*.

28. *Austin v. University of Florida Board of Trustees*, Preliminary Injunction, p. 9.

29. *Austin v. University of Florida Board of Trustees*, Preliminary Injunction, p. 9.

30. *Austin v. University of Florida Board of Trustees*, Preliminary Injunction, p. 21.

31. *Austin v. University of Florida Board of Trustees*, Preliminary Injunction, p. 31.

32. *Austin v. University of Florida Board of Trustees*, Preliminary Injunction, p. 67.

33. Leroy Pernell et al. v. Florida Board of Governors of the State University System et al., Case No. 22–13992 (August 2022); Leroy Pernell et al. v. Brian Lamb et al., Case No. 22–13992 (December 2022).

34. NAACP Legal Defense Fund, "Judge Blocks Florida's 'Stop W.O.K.E.' Censorship Bill from Taking Effect in Higher Education," 2022, retrieved from https://www .naacpldf.org/press-release/judge-blocks-floridas-stop-w-o-k-e-censorship-bill-from -taking-effect-in-higher-education, accessed December 9, 2022.

CHAPTER 12: FLORIDA FACULTY UNIONS AND THE STRUGGLE FOR PUBLIC EDUCATION

1. Chelsea Long, "Florida's Colleges Must Administer 'Viewpoint Diversity' Survey. Don't Take It, Faculty Union Says," *Chronicle of Higher Education*, April 5, 2022, https://www.chronicle.com/article/floridas-colleges-must-administer-viewpoint -diversity-survey-dont-take-it-faculty-union-says; Sam Sachs, "Federal Judge Puts Florida's 'Stop WOKE Act' on Pause for Universities," WFLA, November 18, 2022, https://www.wfla.com/news/politics/federal-judge-puts-floridas-stop-woke-act-on -pause-for-universities.

2. Christian Casale, "Battle Looms for Faculty Tenure Review Across Florida," *Independent Florida Alligator*, December 5, 2022, https://www.alligator.org/article/2022/12 /tenure; Josh Moody, "DeSantis Aims to Turn Public College into 'Hillsdale of the South,'" *Inside Higher Ed*, January 11, 2023, https://www.insidehighered.com/news /2023/01/11/desantis-seeks-overhaul-small-liberal-arts-college.

3. Nelson Lichtenstein, "A Landmark Wage Increase at the University of California," *Dissent Magazine*, December 24, 2022, https://www.dissentmagazine.org/online _articles/a-landmark-wage-increase-at-the-university-of-california.

4. Cecily Myart-Cruz and Alex Caputo-Pearl, "The LA Strike: Learning Together to Build the National Movement We Need," in *Strike for the Common Good: Fighting for the Future of Public Education*, ed. Rebecca Kolins Givan and Amy Schrager Lang (Ann Arbor: University of Michigan Press, 2020), 148–61.

5. Holly Bullard, "Funding Florida's K–12 Public Schools: Inadequacy Breeds Inequity," Florida Policy Institute, February 28, 2022, https://www.floridapolicy.org/posts /funding-floridas-k-12-public-schools-inadequacy-breeds-inequity.

6. SHEF State Profile for Florida, State Higher Education Finance, https://shef.sheeo .org/state-profile/florida, accessed January 28, 2023.

7. Bullard, "Funding Florida's K–12 Public Schools."

8. Holly Bullard and Alex Anacki, "Florida's University Performance-Based Funding Program Should Reward Economic Mobility," Florida Policy Institute, January 14, 2022, https://www.floridapolicy.org/posts/floridas-university-performance-based -funding-program-should-reward-economic-mobility.

9. Mary McKillip and Norín Dollard, *Florida's Hidden Voucher Expansion* (Newark, NJ: Education Law Center, September 2022).

10. Sue M. Legg, *Twenty Years Later: The Jeb Bush A+ Plan Fails Florida's Students* (New York: Network for Public Education Action, March 2019).

11. Laura Hoffman, "Performance Based Funding and the Florida State University System: An Exploratory Analysis," PhD diss., University of South Florida, 2020.

12. "MyFloridaFuture Tool," State University System of Florida, https://www.flbog.edu/myfloridafuture/my-florida-future-dashboard, accessed January 28, 2023.

13. State University System of Florida, "2025 System Strategic Plan Amended November 2022," https://www.flbog.edu/wp-content/uploads/2022/11/2025_System_Strategic_Plan_Amended_Nov_2022.pdf.

14. Chris Marr, "Florida Teacher Unions Risk Decertification Under New Law," *Bloomberg Law*, March 12, 2018, https://news.bloomberglaw.com/daily-labor-report/florida-teacher-unions-risk-decertification-under-new-law.

15. Steven Lemongello, "DeSantis Targets Unions, School Boards with 'Teachers Bill of Rights,'" *Orlando Sentinel*, January 23, 2023.

16. Michael Peltier, "Florida Law Backs Merit Pay, Ends Tenure for New Teachers," Reuters, March 24, 2011, https://www.reuters.com/article/us-florida-teachers/florida-law-backs-merit-pay-ends-tenure-for-new-teachers-idUSTRE72N7K320110324.

17. Casale, "Battle Looms for Faculty Tenure Review Across Florida."

18. "MyFloridaFuture Tool."

19. Billy Townsend, "Florida's Education System Is Vastly Underperforming," *Tampa Bay Times*, January 5, 2023, https://www.tampabay.com/opinion/2023/01/05/floridas-education-system-is-vastly-underperforming-column.

20. Herb Childress, *The Adjunct Underclass: How America's Colleges Betrayed Their Faculty, Their Students and Their Mission* (Chicago: University of Chicago Press, 2019).

21. Kathryn Joyce, "Now the Far Right Is Coming for College Too—with Taxpayer-Funded 'Classical Education,'" *Salon*, May 31, 2022, https://www.salon.com/2022/05/31/exclusive-now-the-far-right-is-coming-for-college-too—with-taxpayer-funded-classical-education.

22. Eliza Fawcett and Anemona Hartocollis, "Florida Gives Reasons for Rejecting A.P. African American Studies Class," *New York Times*, January 22, 2023, https://www.nytimes.com/2023/01/21/us/florida-ap-african-american-studies.html.

23. Jaclyn Diaz, "Florida's Governor Signs Controversial Law Opponents Dubbed 'Don't Say Gay,'" NPR, March 28, 2022, https://www.npr.org/2022/03/28/1089221657/dont-say-gay-florida-desantis.

24. Terry Gross, "How Social-Emotional Learning Became a Target for Ron DeSantis and Conservatives," NPR, April 28, 2022, https://www.npr.org/2022/04/28/1095042273/ron-desantis-florida-textbooks-social-emotional-learning.

25. Fawcett and Hartocollis, "Florida Gives Reasons for Rejecting A.P. African American Studies Class."

26. Long, "Florida's Colleges Must Administer 'Viewpoint Diversity' Survey. Don't Take It, Faculty Union Says."

27. "Governor Ron DeSantis Signs Bill to Reform Higher Education in Florida," post, *Ron DeSantis*, April 19, 2022, https://www.flgov.com/2022/04/19/governor-ron-desantis-signs-bill-to-reform-higher-education-in-florida.

28. "DeSantis Seeks Details on University Students' Transgender Treatments," WUSF Public Media, January 19, 2023, https://wusfnews.wusf.usf.edu/health-news-florida/2023-01-19/desantis-seeks-details-university-students-transgender-treatments.

29. Joyce, "Now the Far Right Is Coming for College Too."

30. Travis Gibson, "Florida Teachers Raise Concerns About New Civics Training, Say It Downplays Slavery, Promotes Originalism," WJXT, June 29, 2022, https://www .news4jax.com/news/local/2022/06/29/florida-teachers-raise-concerns-about-new -civics-training-say-it-downplays-slavery-promotes-originalism.
31. Joyce, "Now the Far Right Is Coming for College Too."
32. Moody, "DeSantis Aims to Turn Public College into 'Hillsdale of the South.'"
33. Charlie Crist, "Freedom to Learn," post, *Medium*, July 19, 2022, https://medium .com/@charliecristfl/freedom-to-learn-a4daa58a79b6.
34. Roger P. Weissberg and Jason Cascarino, "Academic Learning + Social-Emotional Learning = National Priority," *Phi Delta Kappan* 95, no. 2 (2013): 8–13.
35. Florida Policy Institute, "2022 Florida Child Well-Being Index," https://www.florida policy.org/posts/2022-florida-child-well-being-index, accessed January 28, 2023.
36. Linda Darling-Hammond, "Establish Community Schools and Wraparound Supports," post, *Restarting and Reinventing School*, 2020, https://restart-reinvent.learning policyinstitute.org/establish-community-schools-and-wraparound-supports.
37. Amy Wilkins, "Half Empty or Half Full? Florida's Voluntary Pre-Kindergarten Standards," *Fwd* 2, no. 1 (2005), https://files.eric.ed.gov/fulltext/ED485527.pdf.
38. Colleen Flaherty, "More Faculty Diversity, Not on Tenure Track," *Inside Higher Ed*, August 22, 2016, https://www.insidehighered.com/news/2016/08/22/study-finds -gains-faculty-diversity-not-tenure-track.
39. Laura T. Hamilton and Kelly Nielsen, *Broke: The Racial Consequences of Underfunding Public Universities* (Chicago: University of Chicago Press, 2021).
40. Kimberly Leonard, "Gov. Ron DeSantis' Democratic Challenger, Charlie Crist, Vows He Won't Impose a State Income Tax in Florida and Says 6% Sales Tax Is 'Too High,'" *Business Insider*, September 9, 2022, https://www.businessinsider.com/democrat -charlie-crist-says-florida-state-income-tax-is-too-high-2022-9.
41. Sadaf Knight, "Florida's State and Local Taxes Rank 48th for Fairness," Florida Policy Institute, October 17, 2018, https://www.floridapolicy.org/posts/floridas-state-and -local-taxes-rank-48th-for-fairness.
42. Esteban Leonardo Santis, "Who Pays Corporate Income Tax in Florida?" Florida Policy Institute, May 2022, https://www.floridapolicy.org/posts/who-pays-corporate -income-tax-in-florida.
43. Cecily Myart-Cruz and Alex Caputo-Pearl, "The LA Strike: Learning Together to Build the National Movement We Need," in *Strike for the Common Good: Fighting for the Future of Public Education*, ed. Rebecca Kolins Givan and Amy Schrager Lang (Ann Arbor: University of Michigan Press, 2020), 151.
44. United Faculty of Florida, "HB 7: What UFF Members Need to Know About the 'Stop WOKE Act,'" July 6, 2022, https://myuff.org/hb-7-what-uff-members-need-to -know-about-the-stop-woke-act.
45. United Faculty of Florida, "Constitution & Bylaws," February 26, 2021, https://myuff .org/wp-content/uploads/2022/02/UFF-Constitution-and-Bylaws-Jan-2022-Final.pdf.
46. Diego Diaz and Christian Miranda, "'A Greater Threat Than McCarthy Ever Was': UFF Teach-in Addresses HB7," *Panther Now*, November 1, 2022, https://panthernow .com/2022/11/01/a-greater-threat-than-mccarthy-ever-was-uff-teach-in-addresses-hb7.

47. Commissioner Kevin Marino Cabrera (@KMCabreraFL), "It is shocking that FIU's Cuban Research Institute," Twitter, November 28, 2022, 8:15 a.m., https://twitter.com/KMCabreraFL/status/1597217596717158401.

48. Katie Coldiron, "Book Talk on Cuban Immigration Gets Heated in Miami," NACLA, January 16, 2023, https://nacla.org/book-talk-cuban-immigration-gets-heated-miami.

49. "FIU Shares Update About Recent Events Related to Book Presentation," *FIU News*, December 2, 2022, https://news.fiu.edu/2022/fiu-shares-update-about-recent-events-related-to-book-presentation.

50. Susan Eckstein, "My Book on 'Cuban Privilege' Has Been Distorted. I'm Setting the Records Straight," *Miami Herald*, December 20, 2022.

51. Coldiron, "Book Talk on Cuban Immigration Gets Heated in Miami."

52. Tim Padgett, "FIU's 'Cuban Privilege' Night Was a Typical—and Yet a Valuable—Miami Moment," WLRN, December 15, 2022, https://www.wlrn.org/commentary/2022–12–15/fius-cuban-privilege-night-was-a-typical-and-yet-valuable-miami-moment.

53. "FIU Shares Update About Recent Events Related to Book Presentation."

54. Unpublished campaign materials.

55. Tenured faculty, however, had the protection of due process enshrined in a collective bargaining agreement that recognizes faculty's right to academic freedom and that was won after struggle in the 1970s following the termination of politically active faculty members.

56. Jesse Sharkey, "Chicago Teachers: Notes from a Fighting Union," *Labor Notes*, November 3, 2022, https://labornotes.org/2022/11/chicago-teachers-notes-fighting-union.

57. Myart-Cruz and Caputo-Pearl, "The LA Strike: Learning Together to Build the National Movement We Need," 150.

58. Kyle Stokes, "Teachers Union Allies Are Back In Control of the LAUSD Board. Here's What That Might Mean," *LAist*, November 23, 2022, https://laist.com/news/education/los-angeles-general-election-lausd-school-board-rocio-rivas-kelly-gonez-united-teachers-utla-charter-schools.

59. News Service of Florida, "DeSantis Committee Gave $2.1M to Florida School Board Candidates," *Tampa Bay Times*, December 20, 2022, https://www.tampabay.com/news/education/2022/12/20/desantis-committee-gave-21m-florida-school-board-candidates.

60. Max Page, "Millionaire Tax Wins in Massachusetts," *Labor Notes*, December 16, 2022, https://www.labornotes.org/2022/12/millionaire-tax-wins-massachusetts.

61. Benjamin S. Case and Michael McQuarrie, *Majority Rules: The Battle for Ballot Initiatives* (Phoenix: Arizona Board of Regents/Arizona State University Center for Work and Democracy, 2022).

62. Zac Anderson, "After String of Victories, Progressives May Not Get Any Amendments on 2022 Florida Ballot," *Sarasota Herald-Tribune*, October 27, 2021, https://www.heraldtribune.com/story/news/politics/2021/10/27/florida-gop-lawmakers-repeatedly-put-hurdles-passing-ballot-measures/8558646002/; Hatzel Vela, "Miami-Dade Public Schools Asking Voters to Renew Funding for Teacher Pay and School

Safety," WPLG, November 2, 2022, https://www.local10.com/news/local/2022/11/02/miami-dade-public-schools-asking-voters-to-renew-funding-for-teacher-pay-and-school-safety.

63. Jennifer Kay, "Florida Citizens Decide Issues, Then Lawmakers Ignore Them," *Bloomberg Law*, July 1, 2021, https://news.bloomberglaw.com/social-justice/florida-1.

64. Thanks to Ron Cox, Robert Cassanello, Martha Schoolman, Ellen Schrecker, Tim Aylsworth, and Barbara Madeloni and the PHEW group for comments and/or conversation related to this essay.

CHAPTER 13: SCHOOLS OF EDUCATION UNDER FIRE

1. Kimberlé Williams Crenshaw, "Twenty Years of Critical Race Theory: Looking Back to Move Forward," *Connecticut Law Review* 43, no. 5 (July 2011): 1253–1354.

2. Derrick Bell, *And We Are Not Saved: The Elusive Quest for Racial Justice* (New York: Basic Books, 1989).

3. William F. Tate, "From Inner City to Ivory Tower: Does My Voice Matter in the Academy?" *Urban Education* 29, no. 3 (1994): 245–69; Gloria Ladson-Billings and William F. Tate, "Toward a Critical Race Theory of Education," *Teachers College Record* 97, no. 1 (1995): 47–68.

4. Gloria Ladson-Billings, "Clearing Anti-CRT Smokescreens: Affirming Diversity, Equity, Inclusion, Belonging and Justice in Schools, Districts, and Institutions of Higher Education," National Association for the Advancement of Colored People's 113th Annual Convention, July 1, 2022, available at https://www.youtube.com/watch?v=k2QSAy_ttEM. Quoted in Ashley White, *The State of Education Censorship in Institutions of Higher Ed and Implications for the Field*, American Association of Colleges for Teacher Education, 2022.

5. Marvin Lynn and Adrienne D. Dixson, eds., *Handbook of Critical Race Theory in Education*, 2nd ed. (New York: Routledge, 2021).

6. Lynn and Dixson, *Handbook of Critical Race Theory in Education*.

7. *Educational Gag Orders: Legislative Restrictions on the Freedom to Read, Learn, and Teach*, PEN America, https://pen.org/report/educational-gag-orders, accessed June 13, 2023.

8. Alexandra J. Reyes and Taylor A. Norman, "Resource Pedagogies and the Evolution of Culturally Relevant, Responsive, and Sustaining Education," in *The Oxford Encyclopedia of Curriculum Studies*, eds., M. F. He and W. Schubert (New York: Oxford University Press, 2021), doi: 10.1093/acrefore/9780190264093.013.1698,https://digitalcommons.georgiasouthern.edu/teach-secondary-facpubs/202.

9. Django Paris, "Culturally Sustaining Pedagogy: A Needed Change in Stance, Terminology, and Practice," *Educational Researcher* 41, no. 3 (2021): 93–97, https://doi.org/10.3102/0013189X12441244.

10. White, *The State of Education Censorship in Institutions of Higher Ed and Implications for the Field*, 4.

11. Jacqueline E. King, *Colleges of Education: A National Portrait*, AACTE, 2018.